save the males

save the males

why men matter
why women should care

Kathleen Parker

RANDOM HOUSE TRADE PAPERBACKS / NEW YORK

2010 Random House Trade Paperback Edition

Published in the United States by Random House Trade Paperbacks,
an imprint of The Random House Publishing Group,
a division of Random House, Inc., New York.

RANDOM HOUSE TRADE PAPERBACKS and colophon are trademarks of Random House, Inc.

Originally published in hardcover in the United States by Random House,
an imprint of The Random House Publishing Group,
a division of Random House, Inc., in 2008.

Grateful acknowledgment is made to Irving Berlin Music for permissions to reprint an excerpt
from "Anything You Can Do" by Irving Berlin, copyright © 1946 by Irving Berlin and copyright renewed. International copyright secured. All rights reserved. Reprinted by permission.

LIBRARY OF CONGRESS CATALOGING-IN-PUBLICATION DATA
Parker, Kathleen.
Save the males: why men matter why women should care/Kathleen Parker.
p.   cm.
ISBN 978-0-8129-7695-3
1. Men.   2. Man-woman relationships.   I. Title.
HQ1090.P367 2008   306.874'2—dc22   2007049637

Printed in the United States of America

www.atrandom.com

4

Book design by Casey Hampton

For Woody, Wood, Henry, John Connor
And, of course,
Popsie

prologue

I know. Saving the males is an unlikely vocation for a twenty-first-century woman. Most men don't know they need saving; most women consider the idea absurd. When I tell my women friends I want to save the males, they look at me as if noticing for the first time that I am insane. And then they say something like "Are you out of your mind? This is still a male-dominated world. It's women who need saving. Screw the men!"

Actually, that's a direct quote.

The reality is that men already have been screwed—and not in the way they prefer. For the past thirty years or so, males have been under siege by a culture that too often embraces the notion that men are to blame for all of life's ills. Males *as a group*—not the random Tom, Paco, or Abdul—are bad by virtue of their DNA. While women have been cast as victims, martyrs, mystics, or saints—rhapsodizing about their vaginas and swooning over their inner goddesses—men have been quietly retreating into their caves, the better to muffle emotions that fluctuate between hilarity (*Are these bitches crazy or what?*) and rage (*Yes, they are, and they've got our kids!*).

In the process of fashioning a more female-friendly world, we've created a culture that is hostile toward males, contemptuous of masculinity, and cynical about the delightful differences that make men irresistible, especially when something goes bump in the night. In popular culture, rare is the man portrayed as wise, strong, and noble. First responders don't count, as it's accepted wisdom post-9/11 that rescue-men are good, but only in a severe pinch and as long as they disappear after the flames are doused. *Nice job, boys, now go home and shut up, and no pinups in the firehouse.* Otherwise, in film and music, men are variously portrayed as dolts, bullies, brutes, deadbeats, rapists, sexual predators, and wife beaters. Even otherwise easygoing family men in sitcoms are invariably cast as, at best, bumbling, dim-witted fools. One would assume from most depictions that the smart, decent man who cares about his family and who pets the neighbor's dog is the exception rather than the rule.

Despite my admiration for the other sex, I confess to occasional ambivalence. As I researched this book, I often thought to myself: What am I doing? I hate men! I told my best male friends this. They laughed. That's because men hate women, too. Sort of. But not really. Every few days, I told my husband and sometimes my sons: "You have to shape up or I can't write this book." As usual, they laughed at me. As usual, I was furious. It may be the particular dilemma of men and women that they are doomed to suffer a love/hate relationship— and why not? It is hard not to despise something that has such a hold on your heart, even if you give that heart freely.

I am frankly an unlikely champion of males and that most hackneyed cliché of our times—"traditional family values." Or rather, I'm an expert on family the same way the captain of the *Titanic* is an expert on maritime navigation. As longtime readers of my column know, my childhood wasn't precisely Rockwellian. Looking back affectionately, I like to think of home as our own little Baghdad. The bunker buster was my mother's death when she was thirty-one and I was three, whereupon my father became a serial husband, launching into the holy state of matrimony four more times throughout my childhood and early adulthood. We were dysfunctional before dysfunctional was cool.

Going against every trend of the day, I was mostly an only child raised by a single father through all but one of my teen years, with mother figures in various cameo roles. I got a close-up glimpse of how the sexes trouble and fail each other and in the process developed great empathy for both, but especially for men. Though my father could be difficult—I wasn't blinded by his considerable charms—I also could see his struggle and the sorrows he suffered, especially after Mother #2 left with his youngest daughter, my little sister. From this broad, experiential education in the ways of men and women, I reached a helpful conclusion that seems to have escaped notice by some of my fellow sisters: Men are human beings, too.

Lest anyone infer that my defense of men is driven by antipathy toward women, let me take a moment to point out that I liked and/or loved all my mothers. In fact, I'm still close to all my father's wives, except the last, who is just a few years older than I am and who is apparently afraid that if we make eye contact, I'll want the silver. (I do.)

My further education in matters male transpired in the course of raising three boys, my own and two stepsons. Who knows? Maybe if I'd been reared by a single mother and had raised three daughters, I'd be lobbing grenades into frat houses instead of trying to save the males. But Fate is a comedian, and Destiny favors a whoopee cushion. As a result of my total immersion in maledom, I've been cursed with guy vision—and it's not looking so good out there.

At the same time that men have been ridiculed in the public square, the importance of fatherhood has been diminished, along with other traditionally male roles of father, protector, and provider, which are increasingly viewed as regressive manifestations of an outmoded patriarchy. The exemplar of the modern male is the hairless, metrosexualized man and decorator boys who turn heterosexual slobs into perfumed ponies. All of which is fine as long as we can dwell happily in the Kingdom of Starbucks, munching our biscotti and debating whether nature or nurture determines gender identity. But in the dangerous world in which we really live, it might be nice to have a few guys around who aren't trying to juggle pedicures and highlights.

Men have been domesticated to within an inch of their lives—attending Lamaze classes, counting contractions, bottling expressed breast milk for HisTurn midnight feedings (I expect men to start lactating before I finish this sentence) yet they are treated most unfairly in the areas of reproduction and parenting. Legally, women hold the cards. If a woman gets pregnant, she can abort—even without her husband's consent. If she chooses to have the child, she gets a baby and the man gets an invoice. Inarguably, a man should support his offspring, but by that same logic, shouldn't he have a say in whether his child is born or aborted?

Granted, many men are all too grateful for women to handle the collateral damage of poorly planned romantic interludes, but that doesn't negate the fact that many men are hurt by the presumption that their vote is irrelevant in childbearing decisions. If a woman does decide to complete a pregnancy—and even if the biological father contributes financially—she is free to move thousands of miles away. Family court judges increasingly approve of virtual visits, aka distance parenting, as a viable alternative to being there. Can virtual dads be far behind as a surrogate parent in a culture where women shop online for designer sperm?

The gradual eradication of men and fathers from children's lives—often in the service of feminist goals that seemed like a good idea at the time—has been our most dubious achievement. Thanks to divorce, unwed motherhood, and policies that unfairly penalize and marginalize fathers, 30 to 40 percent of all American children sleep in a home where their father doesn't. Although most women who marry and have children don't intend to divorce and become single parents, single motherhood by choice is becoming increasingly popular as unmarried celebrities are applauded for accessorizing with designer babies.

The importance of fathers to their children's lives shouldn't require a defense, but statistics are available for those who need convincing. Indeed, growing up without a father is the most reliable predictor of poverty and all the familiar social pathologies affecting children, including drug abuse, truancy, delinquency, and sexual promiscuity. These consequences have been well documented for years, yet some feminists and other progressives still insist that men are nonessential. So pervasive is the unnecessary father meme that a younger generation of women accepts it without much skepticism. "My baby's daddy" is a casual term these days, a bland point of identification rather than a source of pride or an indication of commitment to fatherhood.

Fast-forward to 2005, and someone finally said it out loud. *Are Men Necessary?* was the title of a book by *New York Times* columnist Maureen Dowd, who admits with her opening sentence that she doesn't understand men. Unmarried, Maureen proposed a theory for her own dowdage (new word born right here) and others like her: Men are afraid of smart, powerful, accomplished women. She gathered this from a male friend who said he couldn't ask her out because her job as a *Times* columnist made her too intimidating. Men prefer women who are "malleable and awed," he told her, and predicted that Maureen would never find a mate, "because if there's one thing men fear, it's a woman who uses her critical faculties."

Okay, so maybe some men probably do prefer malleable and awed. After all, what's the alternative—rigid and critical? That sounds like fun. Not that either of those adjectives necessarily describes Maureen, who is probably intimidating to both men and women because she wields words like poison darts. I admire that in a columnist. My own theory is that men haven't turned away from smart, successful women *because* these women are smart and successful. They've turned away because they value their manhood and want to go to their grave intact. (It's a guy thing.) The same feminist movement that encouraged women to use their critical faculties also gave them the green light to be hostile and demeaning toward men.

I'm not suggesting that women have to crown men with acanthus wreaths or spot their shadows by ten paces, but it wouldn't hurt to fix a guy a burger now and then without the woman's acting as though she's just established democracy in the Sunni Triangle. Playing wife and mother to four males the past twenty years or so, I've found that ground beef is the quickest route to male equanimity. There's not much in a healthy boy's world that a burger and a milkshake won't fix. It is helpful if said burger is prepared by a mother who doesn't hate men.

Unfortunately, and sometimes with good reason, many do. Even so, phasing out half the population seems an excessive remedy to a few bad marriages and what otherwise amounts to ennui in our sector of the globe. In less female-friendly countries around the world, men really are to blame for most of the misery—and they'd like to share it with us infidels. What we privileged Westerners refer to as "gender wars" would seem a holiday for women in countries that are incubating the next generation of Islamic jihadists. Yet here in America, we don't seem to get just how great *our* men really are (most of the time).

Consequently, American males baffled by the rage aimed their way have responded in many cases not by being more attentive to women's wishes, but by being far less sympathetic toward the increasingly *un*fair sex.

Who could blame them?

Given the current cultural landscape, women can't pretend to be mystified when men don't volunteer for chivalry after a lifetime of catching grief for opening doors or offering a compliment. Younger women weaned on *Sex and the City* can't expect that what's-his-name is going to feel compelled to call for a second date after a random hookup, or to pick up the tab, or even to remember his "date's" name. Minimized by cultural forces and stripped of the roles that have defined males for centuries, men have been delivered of the expectation that they behave honorably toward the physically more-vulnerable sex and the dependent children she bears. In turn, females hurt by men's lack of attention react in ways that ensure further alienation. It would seem we are locked in a self-perpetuating cycle of mutual enmity.

Thus, to the question of why should we undertake the momentous task of saving the males, I have two answers: The short one is because we love our sons. The longer one is because we love our daughters. Whatever women may think of men, our sons and daughters deserve a fair shot at getting it right, free of their parents' baggage and the recriminations born of the previous generation's struggles with equality. Young men now in their twenties have never experienced a culture in which men were respected or expected to be gentlemen. Male bashing has been treated as humorous retributive justice by women who have been disappointed and hurt by men. Some of that woundedness has been passed on to our daughters, who absorbed the message that men are bad and have turned against their own male peers.

I don't intend to characterize men as victims and women as the enemy. Assigning victimhood and creating special classes of people within the larger American body haven't served us very well, especially as these divisions have pitted women against men. But it is my modest proposition that saving the males will also save women and children inasmuch as they stand to benefit from a society in which men feel respected and thus responsible. This book is not an argument against women's gains, a defense of bad men—and you know who you are—or a paean to the gents running around campfires in loincloths. Just as I keep misplacing my invitation to the Annual Spring Placenta Planting, I can't seem to keep a straight face when men start weeping over hot dogs, Jesus, and beer.

We owe it to the next generation to explain how we got trapped in this gladiatorial arena of sexual hostility and how, with self-awareness (and much good humor), we might extricate ourselves. The losers, if we fail, aren't just men and women, but boys and girls, who, no matter how many ways we redesign the playground, manage to find each other under the jungle gym. Girls want boys' attentions, and boys want girls' approval. Thus it has ever been and, barring pranks in the petri dish, thus it shall remain.

Finally, this won't be a rose-hued defense of the good ol' days or a celebration of Stepford-style, June Cleaver exurbia moms. It is axiomatic in these knee-jerk times that any criticism of feminism means retrofitting women to the kitchen sink or birthing chair. Nonsense. We still live in a free country (for now), and everyone has the option of being sensible. But we've had a few decades of this shtick and have produced a new generation of children tattooed, pierced, angry, depressed, obese, anorexic, drugged, self-mutilating, whoring, pimping, failing. Children who, preferring the hum of a video game to human interaction, occasionally lash out in carnivals of violence, shooting teachers, classmates, and anyone else unlucky enough to intersect with their rage and rifle sights.

Popular wisdom teaches that nature abhors a vacuum. So do children, and so do families. In fatherless, male-bashing America, we might figure something needs tweaking.

contents

Prologue   vii

1. Women Good, Men Bad   3

2. Honk If You Love Daddy   36

3. Faux Pa and the Yadda-Yadda Sisterhood   71

4. Gelding the American Male   91

5. The Vagina Diatribes and the Sacred Clitorati   114

6. Celebrity Sluts and America's Ho-Down   130

7. Sex, Lies, and Bunker Blunders   157

Conclusion   191

Acknowledgments   199

Notes   201

save the males

1

women good, men bad

Males have become the portmanteau cause of evil behavior, and it's acceptable to downgrade males.

—Lionel Tiger, Charles Darwin Professor of Anthropology, Rutgers University

Jackson Marlette was just fourteen when he summed up the anti-male zeitgeist for his father, political cartoonist and author Doug Marlette. They were in a North Carolina chicken joint awaiting their orders when the younger Marlette picked up a tabletop ad boasting boneless chicken and read aloud: "Chicken good, bones bad."

Then, beaming with insight, Jackson made the analogous leap and proclaimed: "Women good, *men* bad!"

Yesssssss! Give that boy a lifetime pass to *The Vagina Monologues.*

———

Fourteen years isn't long to roam the earth, but boys learn early that they belong to the "bad" sex and their female counterparts to the "good." For many, their indoctrination starts the moment they begin school and observe that teachers (who are, for the most part, females)

prefer less rambunctious girl behavior. Boys' programming continues through high school and then into college, where male students are often treated to an orientation primer in sexual harassment and date rape. A friend's son attended one such seminar on his first day at Harvard. "It scared the s—— out of him," his father reported. "He said, 'Dad, I'm never going on a date.'"

Smart lad.

America is a dangerous place for males these days. Look at a girl the wrong way—or the right way, if you're a gal of a certain age (why do you think all those fifty-year-old women are flocking to Italy?)—and you'll get slapped. With an open palm if you're lucky; with a lawsuit if you're not. Or worse, a visit to Human Resources for reprogramming. Misinterpret her body language and you might wind up in prison.

The first hint for Jackson and other boys of the now twentysomething generation that life wasn't going to be precisely fair was when, beginning in 1993, they were told that girls would be getting out of school for "Take Our Daughters to Work Day," a creation of the Ms. Foundation for Women and possibly the daffiest idea ever dreamed up in the powder room. This is ancient history now, but not irrelevant to sexual relations today. The familiar premise was that girls needed to visit the working world in order to visualize themselves in nontraditional roles. If they saw women only in the home, where more-traditional mothers presumably spent their days watching soaps and seducing the gardener, how could they grow up to be firemen, jet pilots, and Harvard scientists?

But there was more to the Ms. mission than role modeling. The subtext was that little girls would absorb the rage of their feminist foremothers and become militant grrrrrls who could, by goddess, kick boy butt—anytime, anywhere. Marie C. Wilson, a former Ms. Foundation president, put it this way: "When girls came into offices, factories, and firehouses, we knew they would see opportunities for their future, but we also anticipated that girls would perceive inequities in the workplace and ask the hard questions that have no easy answers—like why most of the bosses were men and can you have a family and work here, too?"

Such feminist fantasies probably were not the burning agendas of nine- and ten-year-olds—or even teenage daughters—who more likely were tilting toward "Is there a mall near here?" It was assumed, meanwhile, that boys would have no such visionary problems, given that they saw men in professional and other working roles on a daily basis. The feminist narrative, now firmly entrenched in the culture at large, was that boys could afford to stay behind and learn the lesson that would shadow them into adulthood: that they are unfairly privileged by virtue of their maleness, and they will be punished for it.

After a few years of protest from agenda-free parents who had sons as well as daughters, the girls-only day was tweaked in 2003 to include boys under the broader title of "Take Our Daughters and Sons to Work Day"—a nice gesture, if too late for a generation of boys who had obediently absorbed the message that males were guilty for being male and females were entitled to, oh, everything.

Or had they?

More likely, boys had absorbed the message that life isn't fair and that girls are to blame. Girls weren't really to blame, obviously, but kids will be kids. Nobody likes a teacher's pet, and girls were the culture's pets. We browbeat our kids about the importance of sharing and being nice, then one day the gender fairy flits into their lives and sprinkles cootie dust on all things male. Human nature being what it is, boys were unlikely to respond favorably to the news. Getting out of school for a day, after all, is otherwise known as playing hooky—while staying behind with a female teacher, most likely a feminist herself, to have his brain chip tuned must be a little boy's idea of hell. I know it is mine.

That corporate America participated in the go-girl-play-hooky farce merely reflects how effective feminists had been. Men weren't about to protest when daughters began filing in for their state-sanctioned day of privilege. Men have daughters, too, after all. They wanted to do the right thing, even if it was, in fact, the wrong thing for their sons.

If boys weren't perfectly clear on the specialness of girls, female teachers weaned on feminist ideology were poised to fill in the gaps. One of my son's middle school teachers studiously refused to use male pronouns, a curious tic I noticed during an orientation meeting. Every time a pronoun was required, she used *she* or *her,* never *he* or *him,* effectively erasing boys from the classroom. I sympathize with anyone wishing to avoid the awkward his/her construction. I also understand the inclination to alternate between the two—*his* in one sentence, *her* in the next—though such tortured pronoun equity becomes distracting and annoying. I even understand and often resort to the all-encompassing *they* and *their,* which gathers everyone under one gender-neutral third-person umbrella, offending no one and exalting the totality of Gender Oneness.

But Miss Andry, as we affectionately called this teacher en famille, went to the extreme of simply omitting the male sex altogether. Nothing subtle about that. *He* simply didn't exist for her, while *She* was everything a girl-teacher could want. Miss Andry made clear her preference for girls in other ways throughout the year. One memorable day, she brought doughnuts to class just for the girls. When my then eleven-year-old son asked why he couldn't have a doughnut, she said, "Because I don't like boys." Glad we got that straight. To be fair, maybe it was "Girls Day" and Miss Andry was kidding, but little boys that age can be nuance-challenged. We would find it intolerable, certainly, if a male teacher said something similar to an eleven-year-old girl.

Teachers like Miss Andry most likely are products of the pro-girl education reform movement that captured America's imagination in the 1990s. Several books and studies emerged during that time claiming that education reinforced gender stereotypes that were damaging to girls. All those lessons about men drafting the U.S. Constitution and inventing electricity 'n' stuff apparently harmed girls' self-esteem. Where were the mothers of invention?

The Crisis Wars

The girl crisis got rolling in 1989, when Harvard professor Carol Gilligan claimed that her research showed girls suffered from a patriarchal educational system that favored boys and silenced girls. In her words: "As the river of a girl's life flows into the sea of Western culture, she is in danger of drowning or disappearing." As a former girl, I'm thinking: So speak up or swim, sister.

Feminist groups whose existence was predicated on the victimhood of women quickly embraced the girl crisis meme. No crisis, no ism, no research funds. Gilligan's claims were followed by a report from the American Association of University Women called *Shortchanging Girls, Shortchanging America* that spoke of the unacknowledged American tragedy of esteem-bereft girls. Then in 1994, journalist Peggy Orenstein published *Schoolgirls,* about girls' lack of confidence in school owing to the "hidden curriculum" that girls should be quiet and subordinate to boys.

Next came Mary Pipher's 1994 bestseller, *Reviving Ophelia: Saving the Selves of Adolescent Girls,* in which she described America's "girl-destroying" culture. A clinical psychologist, Pipher claimed that girls in early adolescence take a dive, losing the confidence of girlhood and becoming mysteriously sullen and self-absorbed. We used to call this "the teenage years," but suddenly we needed to restructure education to deal with girls who allegedly were lagging behind boys owing to the onset of puberty.

By these descriptions, one would have thought that girls were being shackled to desks (constructed to resemble kitchen stoves) and their mouths duct-taped shut. Congress came to the rescue with the Gender Equity in Education Act, and a new million-dollar industry was born to study gender bias in America's schools. By 1995, the girl crisis was considered so severe that American delegates to the Fourth World Conference on Women in Beijing made girls' low self-esteem a human rights issue.

You can't help admiring the momentum. In just five years, the germ of an idea had become a full-blown movement. Girls had to be saved! No doubt Chinese women, who risk being shot for shouting "Democracy!" in a crowded theater, were amused to hear American women bemoaning the sad girls back home suffering self-esteem issues. Men, meanwhile, have to marvel at the efficiency of their female counterparts. The men's movement has been in gestation for about twenty years and has yet to quicken, much less emerge to alter the gender ecosystem.

It is a wonder that women of my generation, who grew up among smart math-boys—and who somehow survived puberty without a government program—also managed to become doctors, lawyers, journalists, scholars, Supreme Court justices, candidates on presidential tickets, and, yes, even delegates to world conferences. Among those scholars is a national treasure named Christina Hoff Sommers— philosopher and resident scholar at the American Enterprise Institute, author of *The War Against Boys,* and also the mother of a son. Sommers neatly debunked the girl crisis by rudely examining the hard data used in Gilligan's research, which revealed a small sample size of girls at an elite boarding school. Not exactly your average American cross section. I'm not a social scientist, but as a parent I'd venture to guess that Gilligan's girls might be "drowning and disappearing" because they've been coddled and pampered into self-absorption—always a fast track to human misery, though nothing a little yardwork won't cure.

As most of us know, having been children ourselves, girls have problems because growing up is hard to do, and being a girl is biologically unfair. Boys have problems because being a boy is no picnic, either, though they do get to skip the monthly doldrums. What ails most children who are having "issues" is most likely tied to broken families, a confusing, sexually aggressive culture, and gender hostilities created and promoted by academic theorists with time and money to spend.

Inevitably, a boy crisis swiftly followed the girl crisis, and the baby gender wars were off. The boy crisis may also have been overblown, as hysteria tends to be contagious, but in today's culture, where boys take guns to school and kill teachers and classmates, it is easy to assume that boys are, indeed, in trouble. Some are—and statistics show that boys are lagging behind girls in school—but most aren't sitting in their bedrooms plotting mass murders. The upshot and downside of the dueling girl and boy crises produced an egalitarian revolutionary concept: Girls needed to be more like boys, and boys needed to be more like girls.

Sex equity experts—now there's a terrifying thought—put their heads together and began looking for ways to create better little persons. To make girls more assertive like boys, they would make learning more girl-friendly and tweak lessons to balance male and female accomplishments. Making boys more like girls was somewhat more problematic, but never underestimate gender experts. They would start by taming boys' physical natures. At the nineteenth annual conference for the National Coalition for Sex Equity in Education in 1998, participants determined that the American schoolyard is basic training for domestic violence. Playing chase, which you may remember as an innocent form of energy expulsion loosely tied to harmless flirting, was viewed by the sex equitists as a harbinger of future violence. (About five milligrams of Valium should get you through the rest of this paragraph.) A teacher guide called *Quit It!*— a joint production of the Wellesley Centers for Women, the National Education Association, and the Department of Education—offered tips on how to cope with issues such as tag and other games that involve chasing. Here's a sample tip to teachers:

"Before going outside to play, talk about how students feel when playing a game of tag. Do they like to be chased? Do they like to do the chasing? How does it feel to be tagged out? Get their ideas about other ways the game might be played. Then, tell them that they are going to be playing different kinds of tag—'ones where nobody is ever out.' "

Leave it to experts to make work out of play. Once sex equitists get involved in tag, who wants to play anymore? It is little wonder that boys, who are hardwired for chasing—and for whom "being out" is part of mastering disappointment—have to be drugged to sit through classes. The past few years have seen impassioned debate about whether we're overdiagnosing attention deficit/hyperactivity disorder (ADHD), and I don't intend to air those arguments here. If you want to experience the hot winds of Satan, just suggest to a frustrated parent that her child might not need to be taking speed to attend elementary school. Certainly, some children need and benefit from psychotropic drugs, but the explosion of Ritalin and other stimulant medications for ADHD suggests a fad more than an epidemic—or at least a misunderstanding or ignorance of confounding factors. One of those little acknowledged factors is that boys don't hear as well as girls.

In his book *Why Gender Matters,* Maryland psychologist Dr. Leonard Sax reviewed historical findings that suggested that females hear better than males. Every wife in America already knows this, but we seem to find studies more convincing than merely knowing what we know. In the mid-1990s, Sax noticed a stream of elementary school boys coming to his offices for evaluation. The boys' parents invariably arrived clutching notes from school suggesting that Justin and Johnny may have attention deficit disorder. In some cases, Sax found that the boys didn't need medication; they needed a teacher who understood that boys and girls are hardwired differently. Sax remembered earlier research by John Corso at Penn State that found women teachers speak in a tone of voice that Justin barely hears, since boys don't register higher voices as well as girls. Compounding the problem, 98 percent of kindergarten teachers are women, according to 2004 figures from the Bureau of Labor and Statistics. So little Justin stares out the window—or keeps his eye on the fly crawling across the ceiling—and, presto, he's ADD.

"The teacher is absolutely right about Justin showing a deficit of attention," wrote Sax. "But his attention deficit isn't due to 'attention deficit disorder.' It's due to the fact that Justin can barely hear the soft-spoken teacher. The teacher is talking in a tone of voice that is comfortable to her and to the girls in the class, but some of the boys are practically falling asleep. In some cases we might be able to fix the problem by simply putting the boy in the front row."

Other studies have corroborated Corso's findings. Even newborn girls hear better than newborn boys. And surprising no woman on earth, males' hearing of female voices apparently gets worse as they age.

Recognizing and fixing what ails Johnny—such as moving him closer to the front of the room—takes time and trouble. Today's teachers are so stretched by a job that also effectively makes them parents, doctors, psychologists, and disciplinarians that no one can blame them for writing a note home and hoping a pill might fix the problem. But scores of serious medical experts are concerned that we're overdiagnosing and dosing our kids, especially boys. The subtext, meanwhile, seems to be that boy behavior—a precursor to grown-up male behavior—is a disorder that calls for medication. Although the gender gap is closing as girls are increasingly being diagnosed and dosed for ADD, this is one area where boys still lead. Whether girls catch up to boys remains to be seen, but meanwhile, one can't help pondering what anthropologist Lionel Tiger has noted: ADD and ADHD didn't exist until Ritalin did.

Boys Need Men

Something that's hard for many women to admit or understand is that after about age seven, boys prefer the company of men. A woman could know the secret code to Aladdin's cave and it would be less interesting to a boy than a man talking about dirt. That is because a woman is perceived as just another mother, while a man is *Man*. From Mom, boys basically want to hear variations on two phrases, "I love you" and "Do you want those fried or scrambled?" I learned this in no uncertain terms when I was a Cub Scout leader, which mysteriously seems to have prompted my son's decision to abandon Scouting forever.

My co-Akela (Cub Scout for Wolf Leader) was Dr. Judy Sullivan—friend, fellow mother, and clinical psychologist. Imagine the boys' excitement when they learned who would be leading them in guy pursuits: a reporter and a shrink—two intense, overachieving, helicopter mothers of only boys. Shouldn't there be a law against this? We had our boys' best interests at heart, of course, and did our utmost to be good den mothers. But trust me when I say that seven-year-old boys are not interested in making lanterns from coffee tins. They want to shoot bows and arrows, preferably at one another, chop wood with stone-hewn axes, and sink canoes, preferably while in them.

At the end of a school day, during which they have been steeped in estrogen and told how many "bad choices" they've made, boys are ready to make some really bad choices. They do not want to sit quietly and listen to yet more women speak soothingly of important things. Here's how one memorable meeting began: "Boys, thank you for taking your seats and being quiet while we explain our Women's History Month project," said Akela Sullivan in her calmest psychotherapist voice.

The response to Akela Sullivan's entreaty sounded something like the Zulu nation psyching up for the Brits. I tried a different, somewhat more masculine approach: "Boys, get in here, sit down, and shut up! *Now!!*" And lo and behold, they did get in there. And they did sit. And they did shut up. One boy, who shall remain unnamed, stargazed into my face and stage-whispered: "I wish you were my mother."

To adults' continuing surprise, children really do want boundaries. Akela Sullivan and I put our heads together, epiphanized in unison, and decided that we would recruit transients from the homeless shelter if necessary to give these boys what they wanted and needed—men. As luck would have it, a Cub Scout's father was semi-retired or between jobs or something—we didn't ask—and could attend the meetings. He didn't have to do a thing. He just had to be there and respire testosterone vapors into the atmosphere. His presence shifted the tectonic plates and changed the angle of the earth on its axis. Our boys were at his command, ready to disarm land mines, to sink enemy ships—or even to sit quietly for the sake of the unit, if he of the gravelly voice and sandpaper face wished it so. I suspect they would have found coffee tins brilliantly useful as lanterns if he had suggested as much.

Schooling Boys and Girlifying History

This is not quantum physics. Civilizations have known for centuries that boys need men to become men. Yet boys, except those lucky enough to attend all-boys schools, are surrounded by women most of their growing-up years. Just 25 percent of the nation's three million public school teachers are male—the lowest percentage in forty years—according to the National Education Association. Looking at the typical American classroom these days, there's a good chance that boys may be bored witless by classes that are mind-numbingly dull and that favor girl interests. I can't count the number of map-coloring assignments and dioramas my son had to build up through twelfth grade. Can you imagine making a seventeen-year-old male decorate little shoeboxes for a grade that will determine his college options? What kind of sadistic insanity is that?

Not surprisingly, boys report that they don't like school. As we strived to make school curricula more girl-friendly to accommodate Ophelia, we've bored Hamlet to distraction. In every demographic, girls are doing better than boys by nearly every developmental benchmark. Calmly, we notice that girls are more successful students than boys, beginning in kindergarten, where teachers report that girls are more attentive and stick with tasks longer. Such is girl nature. Girls' brains are constructed in such a way that they are excellent at multitasking. Not only that, tasking attentively stimulates the female pleasure centers, hence 42 years of the National Organization for

Women. Girls also earn better grades in high school and are more likely to be straight-A students. More often than boys, girls run for student government and become members of academic clubs, work on the school paper and the yearbook. Girls also score far higher on standardized tests in reading and writing. The only subjects in which boys are still ahead are math and science, but that gap is steadily closing.

Part of girl-powering education has meant that many schools now try to devote as much time to teaching about females as males in history. This is a nice idea, except that women simply haven't accomplished as much as men in the areas that make history. I know this is blasphemy, but there's no way around the facts. Women have done great things, no doubt. *Radium! Madame Curie, you rule!* But when it comes to the kinds of inventions and events that dot history's timeline, men deserve most of the credit. (And blame, too.) Martha Washington was a great woman, to be sure, but she did not, in fact, lead the American Revolution. George did, and it's his face, not hers, on the dollar bill. We have to try to deal with that.

By genuflecting to equity in all matters great and small, we've created a new generation of Americans who may be more sensitive, but they don't know much about history. At Mount Vernon—home of Martha Washington, who was married to what's-his-name—executive director James Rees reels off a series of telling statistics: Only one in ten high school seniors is proficient in American history. A survey of fourth graders found that seven of ten thought the original thirteen colonies included Texas, California, and Illinois. Six in ten couldn't say why the Pilgrims came to America. Only 7 percent of fourth graders could name "an important event" that took place in Philadelphia in 1776. When seniors at the top fifty-five universities in the country were asked to name America's victorious general at the Battle of Yorktown, only 34 percent named George Washington.

Little wonder, given that Washington today receives one-tenth the coverage in textbooks that he received thirty years ago. Rees tells of one textbook that offers fewer than 50 lines of text about Washington but 213 about Marilyn Monroe. Once a constant presence in American classrooms through the Gilbert Stuart portrait that greeted baby boomers each morning, Washington—the ultimate patriarchal figure—has been all but dismissed from school.

This antipatriarchal attitude permeates public education, and boys feel it, even if they don't recognize it. Too often, they simply are not engaged. Their interests aren't valued, and their behavior isn't tolerated. Elementary grade textbooks and literature rarely feature strong, active male roles or tales of valor, high adventure, or, heaven forbid, gallantry, which feminists view as implying that men and women aren't equal. Biographies of presidents and inventors have been replaced by stories of brave and adventurous women. As education scholar Dr. Sandra Stotsky put it: "Students may end up thinking that the West was settled chiefly by females, most often accompanied by their parents." In middle school, the typical fare is young adult literature, short novels in which teens get in touch with their feelings and deal with issues such as drugs, pregnancy, alcoholism, divorce, bullying, and domestic violence.

Avoiding stereotypes is, perhaps, well and good, but the cost of such gender correctness has been that boys no longer read. No one is suggesting that women's accomplishments be excluded from textbooks or that reading lists not include books of primary interest to girls. But the trend toward making all things equal sometimes results in making some things ridiculous. When the first president of the United States gets less space than a dead movie star, something has gone awry on the Potomac.

Today, many boys are dropping out of school, and of those who actually graduate, fewer proceed to college. Thirty years ago, 58 percent of college students were men; today they are a minority at 44 percent. By 2012, women are expected to be awarded 60 percent of bachelor's degrees in this country. No one outside of Misogynists Anonymous would find displeasure in news of girls and women excelling. Who wants less for their daughters? But don't we also want qualified, eligible young men to marry our daughters and father our grandchildren?

The growing gap between young men and women may portend a new dilemma. In 2005, 133 women graduated from college for every 100 men. The gap is expected to grow to 142 females for every 100 males by the end of the decade, according to the Department of Education. Among African Americans, twice as many women as men finish college. It isn't hard to imagine where this achievement gap leads—more single mothers; fewer gainfully employed, responsible fathers; and another cycle in the decline of the American family.

When Harvard professor Harvey C. Mansfield, author of *Manliness,* was asked whom young women would marry, given the paucity of good men, he answered seriously: "They'll have to marry criminals."

Men Not Just Bad; They Stupid

To watch television is to learn that men aren't just bad, they're also morons. A West Coast reader of my syndicated column who described himself as a proud male feminist e-mailed me with an increasingly common lament: "The last few years I have noticed that the plot of seemingly every commercial on TV features a doofus, addled, ten-thumbed idiot of a human called a white male. If the subject is a southern white male, then God help him. . . . Being a white male, I don't think I'm paranoid; I'm certainly not a victim, but why am I a target?"

If you're a male these days, paranoia is not an irrational response. Male bashing is among America's favorite sports and is a popular bonding agent among women. If you Google "male bashing," you get eleven times more hits than for "female bashing"—99,000 vs. 8,930. I signed up for Google to alert me to "male-bashing" news, and I receive at least several notices daily. The reason: Men are easy. And according to the marketplace, it's their turn.

Men—principally white men—enjoyed ten thousand years of club-wielding supremacy, and now women get to play queen of the tar pit. That Sitcom Man has been portrayed mostly as a dolt in recent years is no one's imagination. With few exceptions, the guy is an incompetent fool, while the woman is a hybrid of Heloïse and Hercules with a little Xena on the side. Fathers are routinely shown to be fools and failures, while mothers are successful, competent, and morally superior.

When did men get so stupid?

Actually, men didn't get stupid; women got rich. If you follow the money and household spending, you find that women do most of the buying, including 59 percent of all automotive purchases. Women also watch TV more than men do. Apparently, women—who constitute four out of five sitcom viewers—are attracted to shows and ads that depict men as buffoons. But what do these depictions telegraph to the children who also watch these shows?

Clinical psychologist Dr. Wade Horn, founder of the National Fatherhood Initiative (NFI), observed that twenty-five million American children are more likely to see a father on television than in the home. In 1999, the NFI conducted a study on how fathers were presented in 102 prime-time shows in which the father was a central character. In only four was the father portrayed as present and involved in his children's lives. Otherwise, dear ol' Dad was missing in action. Often when fathers were present, they were characterized as deadbeats, lowlifes, morons, or all of the above. Why is this entertaining? To whom? Surely not to little boys watching to learn how men and daddies act. Or to little girls trying to figure out how men and women interact.

Criticism of today's sitcoms inevitably invites the reminder that television families of the 1950s never existed. Stephanie Coontz, author of *The Way We Never Were: American Families and the Nostalgia Trap,* tells us, for instance, that the lives of married women of the 1950s consisted of "booze, bowling, bridge, and boredom." I don't quite remember it that way, though I'll concede that life wasn't perfect.

While it may be true that the perfect television families of the 1950s and 1960s were rare, there was something reassuring and nurturing in the positive male role models of *Father Knows Best* and *Leave It to Beaver*. Other shows with prominent father figures portrayed men as kind, caring, and competent. In *My Three Sons,* Fred MacMurray was a wise and gentle father to his three boys, aided by the boys' in-house grandfather. Even "Uncle Bill," the confirmed bachelor in *Family Affair,* managed to raise three children he inherited—with the help of his faithful and extremely competent butler. (If you know where to find one of those, I'd like two.) Television fathers generally were both loved and respected, and children saw that message reiterated in their own homes. Importantly, children knew that the grown-ups were in charge and that they were dependable.

What message are they absorbing today when nearly every TV father is either absent or absurd? Or when children are always smarter and wiser than the old man? Not to exaggerate the influence of a single show or episode, but over time, negative stereotyping is absorbed into the culture, and the message is that men are not only bad, they're stupid and unreliable. In *Everybody Loves Raymond,* as just one example, Dad is irresponsible and clueless concerning home and hearth. Others that similarly portray men as bumbling and unreliable include *Malcolm in the Middle, The Simpsons,* and *According to Jim.* Fathers not only don't know best, they hardly know anything at all, while Mom—always the wiser, smarter, and handier—stands ready at the rescue when dear ol' doofus can't figure out the simplest tasks.

All things considered, male bashing is probably not a terrible threat to civilization. Men and women often wage humorous war against each other as a nonviolent way of venting hostilities. It's harmless as long as everybody's having a good time. Less funny, however, is the potential effect of male bashing as it has morphed into boy bashing. We're talking not about a random incident here and there, but about a highly lucrative industry. The apparel company David & Goliath made a bundle selling anti-boy T-shirts with slogans such as "Boys Are Goobers . . . Drop Anvils on Their Heads" and "Stupid

Factory: Where Boys Are Made." When men's advocates, led by Los Angeles–based radio host Glenn Sacks, protested the T-shirts, Todd Goldman, the happy (and very rich) founder and president of David & Goliath argued that kids are cool and appreciate dark humor and that grown-ups should lighten up. Today's children are, indeed, more sophisticated than their parents were at comparable ages, but do they appreciate banal humor concocted by self-interested adults? Goldman also authored a book in 2005, *Boys Are Stupid, Throw Rocks at Them!*, aimed at the teenybopper set, which begins, "Girls are bundles of joy and gifts from heaven. Boys pick their nose in front of 7-Eleven," and ends with, "Just remember. For every stupid, smelly, cootie-ridden boy, there is a rock." Nice.

Boy-bashing T-shirts aren't an isolated phenomenon but are part of a larger picture that may not be harmless. Am I saying that man-hating feminists lead to boy-bashing T-shirts, which then lead to armies of lobotomizing Nurse Ratcheds? Not precisely, but then a zeitgeist isn't made in a day, nor does it flow from a single source.

Over time, kindred cultural and intellectual trends combine to create a certain kind of environment. Today's is decidedly anti-male such that male bashing—followed by boy bashing—permits products and practices that have become not just acceptable but commercially rewarding. The war of the sexes is a moneymaking proposition. Given the spending power of teenagers—an estimated $190 billion in 2006—the market was bound to oblige.

I'm not so worried about boys' self-esteem when confronted with a "Boys Are Stupid" T-shirt stretched across the chest of his heart's desire. I worry more about girls whose hostility toward males is validated by an applauding culture. Let's just say, it sets an approving tone that can't be helpful in our alleged quest for gender equity. In a hopeful sign, magazines aimed at teen girls have begun to take a close look at the bashing trend, as girls are beginning to question whether it's fair to be so mean to boys. We could all take a lesson.

Combine negative stereotyping with a real lack of role models, and we may be creating not-so-funny problems for a generation of

boys. Dr. Jim Macnamara, an Australian professor of public commu-
nication who analyzed two thousand mass media portrayals of men
and male identity, thinks so. His finding that men were depicted
mostly as villains, aggressors, perverts, and philanderers has led him
to wonder how boys will navigate their search for identity.

"Highly negative views of men and male identity provide little by
way of positive role models for boys to find out what it means to be a
man and gives boys little basis for self-esteem," said Macnamara. "In
the current environment where there is an identified lack of positive
male role models in the physical world through absentee fathers in
many families, and a shortage of male teachers, the lack of positive
role models in the media and presence of overwhelmingly negative
images should be of concern. . . . Ultimately such portrayals could
lead to negative social and even financial costs for society in areas
such as male health, rising suicide rates and family disintegration."

The only exception to the negative stereotype is the feminized male,
Macnamara found. "The idealized image of the metrosexual—
largely a creation of the media—only further adds to the confusion
being felt particularly by boys trying to find their identity in the modern world."

Battering Men

Gloria Steinem, Germaine Greer, and other leaders of second-wave
feminism planted the seeds that have now flowered into today's
men/bad template, which paints all men as potential abusers. Steinem
once said: "The patriarchy requires violence or the subliminal threat
of violence in order to maintain itself. . . . The most dangerous situation for a woman is not an unknown man in the street, or even the
enemy in wartime, but a husband or lover in the isolation of their
own home."

Andrea Dworkin used an even broader brush, saying, "Under patriarchy, every woman's son is her betrayer and also the inevitable
rapist or exploiter of another woman."

Inevitable? My boy? Your boy?

While it is statistically true that women are more likely to be hurt or killed by a male family member or acquaintance, it is also true that women instigate "common couple violence" almost as often as men do. I don't mean to minimize the damage men can do. A woman pushing or slapping a man, though not excusable, isn't the same as a man doing the same. Men are stronger and usually bigger, and everybody knows it, so I won't belabor the point. No matter who starts it, in the absence of a weapon, women are going to get hurt more often and more severely. But they're also going to report their injuries more often than men do, which helps explain the skewed impression that only men are violent.

Surprisingly, a 2007 University of Washington study of the connection between teenage violence and domestic violence revealed that women reported *instigating* domestic violence twice as often as men in the previous year. These episodes included women kicking, biting, pushing, shoving, grabbing, and threatening to hit or throw something at their male partner. Researchers also found a strong link between violent behavior during adolescence and later as young adults. If teenage girls are starting fights with their boyfriends, this study suggests that women will instigate violence in their mature relationships as well.

Obviously, family violence is a problem we'd all like to solve, but we're not likely to until we're willing to correctly define the problem. Are men exclusively to blame? No, but you wouldn't know it from the mythology of domestic violence that has evolved the past twenty years or so. That mythology gained traction in 1993 with the Super Bowl legend. Remember that one? The idea, spawned by a coalition of women's groups at a Pasadena, California, news conference and propagated by an eager media, was that the annual football fest caused a 40 percent increase in domestic violence. A reporter for *The New York Times* renamed the annual event "Abuse Bowl" and wrote: "If Super Bowl tradition holds, more women than usual will be battered today in their homes by the men in their lives; it seems an inevitable part of the postgame show. A big football game on television invariably becomes the Abuse Bowl for men conditioned by the sports culture to act out their rage on someone smaller."

A *Boston Globe* writer reported that women's shelters are "flooded with more calls from victims [on Super Bowl Sunday] than on any other day of the year." NBC even ran a public service announcement before the game warning men that domestic violence is a crime.

Within days, everybody in America knew that watching football with a guy was tantamount to stepping into the lion's den. Except it wasn't true. Not any of it. When *Washington Post* reporter Ken Ringle fact-checked the story, he found that the study cited at the news conference and in subsequent stories had been misinterpreted. Ringle contacted one of the study's authors, Janet Katz, a criminal justice and sociology professor at Virginia's Old Dominion University, who said, "That's not what we found at all." What the researchers did find was that increased emergency room visits were not associated with football games in general, or with watching a team lose, but that women admitted to hospitals for gunshot and other wounds increased (though not close to 40 percent) on "win" days. Go figure.

The myth has been so thoroughly debunked that you can now find "Super Bowl Sunday" on the urban-legend-busting website Snopes.com, where a complete history, including the preceding, can be found. How did this story catch hold when so much of it was exaggerated or false? The answer in part is that we tend to believe whatever confirms our preconceptions. Men, see, they're slurping their beer, watching other guys tackle one another while barely clad women vault around on the sidelines. Their testosterone levels build to a tsunami of sexual arousal and repressed brute energy. What else could one expect a bloke to do under such circumstances but cuff the little heifer?

Such are the fantasies that stoke feminist rage and upon which bureaucracies have been built. Silly as it now seems, the Super Bowl story was simply a piece of the larger cultural narrative that men are always inherently violent. This notion played out in bizarre fashion in 2005 when a New Mexico judge issued a restraining order against David Letterman because a woman claimed the host was harassing her through coded behavior during his broadcasts. The woman also thought Regis Philbin and Kelsey Grammer were conspiring against her. The Letterman order was quickly dropped, and the incident became the kind of material for which late-night comedians can only be grateful. But the larger moral of the story is less funny: A man in New York City who doesn't even know the claimant can be considered dangerous and deserving of a restraining order on the basis of . . . *nothing whatsoever.*

If you've been paying attention, you know that men are also dangerous to children. In some places, male phobia has entered the realm of the absurd. Two airlines Down Under, for instance, have policies forbidding a man from sitting next to an unaccompanied child. In 2005, Qantas Airways passenger Mark Worsley, a father of two, was shocked and humiliated when he was asked to remove himself from a seat next to an eight-year-old boy traveling alone.

"I complied straight away and moved seats," said Worsley. "But as I sat on the plane during the flight, I got more and more angry about it. . . . Most males in the world, I'm sure, are perfectly law-abiding, good parents, good fathers, brothers, whatever," he said. "They're basically accusing half the population of the world of being a potential pedophile."

No one's minimizing the horrors that have been inflicted on children by men, or the suffering of those whose names we know too well, from Polly Klaas to Jessica Lunsford, both of whom were abducted and murdered by sexual predators. But neither should we ignore the fact that women abuse and kill children more often than men do. A 1999 federal report found that 70.3 percent of perpetrators of child abuse were women. Of those resulting in death, 31.5 percent were committed by a female parent only, three times the number of those committed by a male parent only. The higher rate of female offenses may be tied to the fact that women typically spend more time with children than men do. Whatever the explanation, these figures show that the sole demonization of men as abusers is inaccurate and unfair.

The repercussions of society's ill will toward men won't long be limited to individual embarrassment. Increasingly, innocent men are afraid to participate fully in society—whether leading Scouts or teaching school—for fear of being scrutinized as possible perverts, kidnappers, and murderers. Eventually, they'll simply stop showing up.

Although men usually prevail in hand-to-hand combat, size and strength are neutralized by guns and knives. In rare cases, they're also neutralized by size, as in the case of Stanley Green, one of the battered male's earliest poster boys. Green, who now travels the world speaking on behalf of battered victims through an organization he helped found, Stop Abuse for Everyone (SAFE), says he was severely beaten by his wife but was ignored by police when he called for help.

A small, reserved fellow, Green is passionate about SAFE's mission to shift thinking away from domestic violence as a women's issue to domestic violence as a people issue that affects men, women, and children of all classes, races, and sexual orientations. The big picture isn't male-on-female violence, he says, but violence in relationships generally. Green also wants to help men who face the same hurdles he did. "Blood streamed down my face," Green says he told police. The officer's response was: "We ain't taking a report from you, buddy."

Most men aren't willing to suffer Green's humiliation and so don't report spousal abuse to police. Advocates for both sides, meanwhile, hurl statistics at each other. Men's groups say radical feminists attempt to cover up wife-on-husband abuse, fearing that funds might be diverted from women's programs to sheltering and counseling for men. Women's groups point to the fact that police reports and hospital records show much higher rates of women being battered. The battle of the sexes has become a battle of the calculators.

If you're not a soldier in the gender wars, it's impossible to imagine all the domestic violence literature, studies, and surveys produced over the past several years—reams of stats, charts, and graphs—all trying to prove who hits more, who hurts the most, and, ultimately, who gets the money and the kids. It is exhausting to contemplate, but the reality is that these numbers can't be ignored. Not only are they used to get billions in federal dollars, they constitute weapons in the cultural battle over how men are defined in society. Believing in man's badness is critical to believing in woman's goodness and, importantly, in her status as victim, which has practical applications. When it comes to child custody disputes, for instance, a charge of domestic violence keeps things simple. Bad men do not get to see their children. Men don't even have to be proven bad to be denied access. Several states have "must arrest" policies, meaning that someone (usually the man) has to be dragged away if a 911 call is made. In California, for instance, officers are encouraged to arrest men rather than women under a "dominant aggressor" doctrine. Even if a woman doesn't want to press charges—and even if there are no signs of violence—police are encouraged to arrest someone.

In other words, an arrest can be made without probable cause. Many jurisdictions also have "no drop" policies, meaning that charges, once filed, can't be dropped. Millions of dollars are channeled to states encouraging "Grants to Encourage Arrest" programs. The intent of these programs is understandable, if sometimes ludicrous. Often people become emotional and dial 911 in a panic—or a gesture of power—without fully contemplating the repercussions to their family.

The result of these reactionary, if well-intentioned, programs has been a steep rise in arrests that may or may not have been warranted. In California alone, a quarter of a million domestic violence restraining orders were active in 2006, according to Glenn Sacks and family law attorney Jeffery Leving, who coauthor columns related to father issues. That meant that about one out of every fifty adult men in California was under a restraining order, which in many cases barred him from his home. Is it possible that one in every fifty men you pass on the street in San Francisco or Los Angeles is a batterer?

Not to belabor the point, but restraining orders are not trivial. First, a man is kicked out of his home. In some cases, he can be jailed if he tries to get in touch with his children. All of this often takes place with little due process, without proof of guilt, necessarily, or even any chance to defend himself. Some of these accused batterers are undoubtedly guilty, but others are victims of a system that operates on a presumption of guilt.

In many cases, a restraining order is issued on a claim of "verbal abuse" or for making a woman feel afraid. Whether the man is guilty or not is irrelevant. What matters is that once an order is issued, it can be considered "a finding of abuse" and used to prevent shared custody of children. In our rush to save those women who desperately need saving, we've criminalized ordinary men who may never have raised a hand against their spouse. One might argue that if even a single person is saved, then these measures are justified. But one can also imagine being denied access to one's own children owing to a baseless accusation by a vindictive spouse—and the anger that also would be justified.

How We Got Here

One of the more curious—and problematic—developments to evolve from the idea that women need special protection from men is "battered woman syndrome"—the excuse that women, because of their own suffering and depression, are unable to defend themselves or their children. This notion gained popular acceptance in 1987 with the appalling case of Joel Steinberg and Hedda Nussbaum. Steinberg, an attorney, was convicted of manslaughter in the death of the couple's adopted child, while Nussbaum was granted immunity after agreeing to testify against Steinberg. Nussbaum was largely viewed not as a culpable co-participant in her daughter's abuse and death, but as a pathetic and ever-suffering victim of the patriarchy. And Steinberg, rather than being recognized as an exceptionally bad man, was characterized more broadly as Man acting as men do.

Fast-forward to 2006 and we see the Nussbaum legacy acted out through Mary Winkler, the thirty-two-year-old mother who fatally shot her minister husband while he lay in bed. Winkler, who confessed to the crime, was convicted of voluntary manslaughter and served just five months, in addition to two months in a mental health treatment facility, and even landed an interview on *The Oprah Winfrey Show.* How did she get off so lightly? Although the couple had argued the night of the shooting, the trial focused on what was characterized as abuse, including "unnatural sex acts" that involved white platform shoes and a wig. In her taped *Oprah* interview in September 2007, Mrs. Winkler revealed that the night of the shooting, her husband had placed his hand over their baby's nose and mouth to quiet her. She took the baby from him and, after getting the child settled, returned to the bedroom to talk to her husband.

And, *boom!* She heard "that awful, awful sound" and ran away, presumably not realizing that she had caused the boom when she took the shotgun from the closet and killed her husband.

Mrs. Winkler's mild punishment for her husband's murder sends a clear message: Women can kill their husbands with relative impunity as long as they can convince a jury that they were in an abusive marriage. This development could be possible only in a world where men have been sufficiently demonized so that anything a woman does, even murder, is considered less offensive than whatever a man does. The operating assumption is that a woman can't say "no" or open the front door and walk out instead of opening the closet where the shotgun is kept. What is also clear is that the definition of "abuse" is highly subjective. I agree that white platform shoes constitute a fashion crime, but are they and a wig—or just certain wigs—cause for lethal revenge?

These days, we've defined down domestic violence so that men who are mere schmucks can be dredged up in the same net that catches men who are truly violent. Under the heading "psychological battery," men are considered abusive if they lie, refuse to help with child care, or withhold information. By that definition, every American marriage is a war zone.

Allstate, one of the corporations that has joined the fight against domestic violence, provides a case in point. Allstate posted profiles of four "abused" women on its website in 2006—a multiculti rainbow coalition of victimhood featuring a white, black, Hispanic, and Asian woman. Two of the women did suffer serious physical abuse, according to their profiles, but the other two, Lisa and Samantha, strike one as victims mostly of inertia.

Samantha's abuse consisted of a controlling husband who liked to pick out her clothes and monitor her spending. He also locked her in the house and took away the phone, she claimed. After ten years, Samantha left. *Ten years?!* Did he lock all the doors from the outside, too? Were there bars on the windows? Nowhere is it mentioned that Brad physically harmed Samantha, but she's a victim of domestic abuse because . . . I have no idea. In a world with so much real violence, is it really necessary to come to the rescue of women who are merely passive?

Next was Lisa, who left her live-in boyfriend after years of "verbal, emotional, and financial abuse." Like Samantha, her fragile psyche was stymied by her live-in boyfriend's demands. What did Boyfriend do? He drove Lisa everywhere to maintain control over her actions. Having a chauffeur isn't all it's cracked up to be, apparently. Lisa saved money to buy a car so she could find a job "and move about freely for the first time in years." The same day she brought home her new car, however, Boyfriend slashed her tires and poured sugar into the gas tank—all before Lisa could secure insurance. Lisa was, of course, devastated. Adding to Lisa's misery, there was no public transportation in her town, and she was fired from her last job for missing so much time from work owing to her lack of transportation. Don't get me wrong: Boyfriend is a first-class creep and one scary dude. While one may feel sorry for Lisa, it is hard to see her as bearing zero responsibility for this dysfunction or this kind of behavior meriting the title of "domestic violence." If men are bad, these women look like nitwits who surely play a part in their own subjugation. And while we may applaud Allstate's efforts on behalf of real domestic violence victims, we nevertheless see that violence is not required for the victimization of women. By including Samantha and Lisa in their lineup of victims, Allstate helps perpetuate the myth of women as helpless, while trivializing the real violence that men and women inflict upon each other.

The Rape of Rape

At the University of Maryland, a feminist group posted pictures of random male students around campus and labeled them "Potential Rapists." Imagine seeing your face—or your son's face—presented that way. No one wishes to make light of rape, but activism aimed at protecting women from predatory men has created a sense that all men are predators.

The redefinition of rape almost to mean sexual intercourse without an affidavit of consent can be traced to well-known second-wave feminists such as Catharine MacKinnon and Andrea Dworkin. Both MacKinnon and Dworkin strongly disavowed ever having said "All sex is rape" or "All men are rapists," phrases variously attributed to both through the years. But it is fair to say that similar-sounding sentiments, if not those precise words, can be found in their writings. The basis for such thinking was that as long as married men were exempt from being charged with marital rape, as was the case until relatively recently, then sex within marriage couldn't be considered voluntary. As Dworkin explained in a 1995 interview with the Dickensian-named British novelist Michael Moorcock, marriage-mandated intercourse made it impossible "to view sexual intercourse in marriage as the free act of a free woman."

Similarly, MacKinnon has written that rape and sex look an awful lot alike. "The major distinction between intercourse (normal) and rape (abnormal) is that the normal happens so often that one cannot get anyone to see anything wrong with it."

These ideas may not represent a precise analogue of rape and sex, but they come pretty close. In any case, as these notions have taken root and flourished within women's studies programs, so has the extrapolation that rape does not require physical force. As another second-wave feminist, *Ms.* magazine editor Robin Morgan, wrote in 1977: "I claim that rape exists any time sexual intercourse occurs when it has not been initiated by the woman, out of her own genuine affection and desire." Morgan also says that man-hating is "an honorable and viable political act, that the oppressed have a right to class-hatred against the class that is oppressing them."

In the context of such sentiments, it's easy to see how the Maryland posters evolved. It's also easy to see how we arrived at such well-known, if fantastical, statistics as that one in four college women is raped. Reality check: If this were true, would any father let his daughter go to college? The figure was derived from a survey by Mary Koss, then professor of psychology at Kent State University, who was commissioned by *Ms.* magazine to conduct a national rape study on campuses. Koss interviewed some three thousand female college students randomly selected and asked them questions.

The problem with Koss's findings is that her questions were framed in such a way that almost any degree of reluctance on the woman's part met the criteria for "rape." One question, for example, asked: "Have you had sexual intercourse when you didn't want to because a man gave you alcohol or drugs?" "Yes" to that question could mean anything from "I drank a bottle of rum and was too drunk to push him off," to "I had a beer and wasn't in the mood, but had sex anyway," to "He drugged my wine cooler and raped me while I was out cold." Another question in the study was more in line with what most of us associate with rape: "Have you had sexual intercourse when you didn't want to because a man threatened or used some degree of physical force (twisting your arm, holding you down, etc.) to make you?"

Whatever the definition of rape, one can easily see that these two questions are not equivalent. Yet, based on such questions, which were given equal weight in the study, Koss determined that 27.5 percent of respondents were either raped or almost raped. Today, more than twenty years later, that one-in-four figure is still part of the official mantra in women's studies programs and campus rape crisis centers, and the perception of males as oppressors and rapists keeps the crisis rolling.

In today's hookup culture, there's so much confusion about what constitutes rape that a new term has emerged—"gray rape"—to describe that hazy area between consent and denial that often becomes blurred in the heat of the night. Did she mean "no" no? Or did she just mean "maybe" no? Does "stop" mean right this very second? Or could it mean, oh, *pleasepleaseplease,* just ten more seconds?

Obviously "no" means "no" and "stop" means "stop" among civilized adults, but those words lose some of their oomph when a person has had a six-pack and half a dozen shots. Inhibitions loosen and judgment is lost. For the female who is too drunk or stoned to communicate her wishes clearly, the result may be an unwanted sex act. But for the male who is too drunk or stoned to clearly understand—or to promptly respond to—a female's wishes, the result may be several years locked up in prison with violent rapists and murderers. Given the level of irresponsibility in both cases, the level of punitive judgment against one seems unfair on its face.

No one's defending men who have *literally forced* women to have sex, but most people would agree that there's a world of difference between "stop" after you've willingly climbed between the sheets with someone you found appealing five minutes earlier, and rape by a stranger at knifepoint. Somewhere between "Oh yeah, baby" and "Um, I've changed my mind" is some sensible ground that shouldn't land a nineteen-year-old guy in prison for several years.

In 1999, a bizarre case at the University of Massachusetts at Amherst brought home how rape hysteria and irrational feminism combine to breed a dangerous anti-male mind-set in our culture. In November, three women said they were assaulted on campus, two claiming to have been raped. Five hundred students convened on November 16 to protest what was being billed as a culture of violence against women. Right in the middle of this passionate show of solidarity, yet another victim materialized ex machina. A thirty-year-old woman, her face streaked with blood, ran up to police and said she had been assaulted at knifepoint. Slow-mo to December 3, and the woman's lawyer issued a statement saying she had made up the attack and had inflicted her own wounds.

What was most interesting about the Amherst case was the reaction of feminist organizations when the knifepoint rape was confirmed false. They said even false rape charges are helpful in advancing a dialogue about violence against women. *Just because it didn't happen doesn't mean it couldn't happen.*

Marta Calas, acting chair of the Women's Studies Department, was generous in extending empathy to the faux victim. In an interview with *Campus Report,* a publication of Accuracy in Academia, a conservative watchdog group that monitors political bias on college campuses, Calas said: "Violence is a discourse that is very present and is given legitimacy in this society. Maybe this person couldn't have another kind of conversation to be heard. . . . [The false claim] should be looked at in the context of how come this course of violence is so available that it becomes one way in which somebody that's already in trouble can have herself be heard."

Well, that's one way to look at it. But by such logic, any lie can be justified as simply exercising one's need to be heard: *No, Officer, he didn't really kill me, but saying he did was the only way I could get anyone to pay attention to me.* One can only be grateful that the woman didn't find it necessary to identify her pretend assailant in her search to have herself heard. Whoever he might have been, he would have been presumed guilty by the sort of mentality that can justify any deceit for the higher purpose of dialogue.

As must be repeated, no one deserves to be raped, nor do guys get a pass for persisting in a sex act after a woman communicates that she wants to stop. But by defining rape down, we've managed to trivialize the serious crime of forcible rape, while making every male a rapist the moment—or ten seconds after—a gal says, "I need to go home."

Timing really is everything.

The Duke Lacrosse Double Cross

It was perhaps inevitable that the "bad men" concept would climax, if you'll pardon the expression, with the 2006 public conviction of three white Duke University lacrosse players for the alleged rape of an African American stripper, Crystal Gail Mangum, at a team party. The Duke saga was a perfect storm of guilt, ambition, righteous outrage, and self-serving sanctimony.

The case is familiar to most sentient Americans, as it became a national exorcism of every ism and phobia known to afflict modern man. White boys, black girls, money, booze, sex, the privileged versus the downtrodden, town versus gown. This yearlong epic of he said/she said began when Mangum alleged that three members of the lacrosse team had forced her into a bathroom during a team party and gang-raped her anally, orally, and vaginally for thirty minutes. America was primed and ready to believe that these young men had done the worst and to convict them without due process.

The assumption of guilt when it comes to males and rape is so entrenched in the American psyche that we ignore our better sense and embrace the righteousness of the mob. The same feminist spirit that successfully fought to eradicate the "she deserved it" attitude toward rape victims inexplicably found acceptable an equally unjust "of course he did it" attitude toward men. As the Duke case played out in the American media, Monika Johnson-Hostler of the North Carolina Coalition Against Sexual Assault was interviewed on *The O'Reilly Factor*. She said that her job was to support any victim claiming to have been raped.

"Even if they weren't?" asked an incredulous Bill O'Reilly.

"I can't say that I've come across one that wasn't," she replied.

Johnson-Hostler apparently has met her first with Ms. Mangum.

On April 11, 2007—almost a year after the alleged rape took place—North Carolina attorney general Roy Cooper announced that he was dropping all charges against the three men and declared them "innocent." Not only was there no credible evidence against the boys, he said, but the evidence gathered by investigators contradicted many of the accuser's claims. In forensic tests, for instance, investigators found no traces of any of the Duke lacrosse players' DNA, but they did find DNA on and in the accuser from at least three other unidentified men. Mangum also changed her story so many times that she ultimately lacked credibility. In but one example, she changed the time of the alleged assault after it became clear that one of those she had selected as an assailant had documented proof that he wasn't at the party when the attack supposedly took place.

As the Duke case makes abundantly clear, we don't hesitate to condemn males no matter the circumstances, no matter the credibility of the accuser or the absence of evidence. As soon as the woman accused the young men, the Duke community, including administrators and faculty and much of the media, began lighting torches and grabbing pitchforks. It didn't matter that the accused hadn't even been officially charged yet, much less had their day in court. Repercussions were swift and excessive. The team's season was canceled; the lacrosse coach was forced to resign; the three young men were arrested and faced a court of public opinion that found them guilty as accused. The state didn't have to prove them guilty as long as District Attorney Mike Nifong called them "hooligans" in the press and made other prejudicial remarks. Nifong persecuted three innocent men in hopes of garnering votes from a largely black electorate and ultimately, lost his job and was disbarred in the process. He also spent one day in jail as a lesson, which can't compare with the year of hell he inflicted on three young men and their families.

In contrast with the accused, the alleged victim was invariably described in the media in dulcet tones as a working mother and honor student. Mangum, alas, was just trying to earn enough money by stripping to pay her college tuition, which Jesse Jackson promised to pay regardless of whether she was guilty.

The salient point here is that throughout the proceedings, the media, townsfolk, and Duke University were ready to accept Mangum's "goodness" without question. Why? Because she's a woman. Perhaps Mangum just made a bad choice, as we like to say, going to strip and dance for forty college athletes at a drinking party. The question is: Why weren't the good people of Duke and Durham—the faculty, the media, and the rest—willing to grant the same benefit of the doubt to the three young men, who, though they may have been partying and behaving boorishly, were not, in fact, raping anyone?

I thought you'd never ask.

Men bad.

2

honk if you love daddy

*Acknowledging that "Peg Leg" Bates was a helluva tap dancer
shouldn't obscure the fact that dancers are generally better off with the
full complement of nether limbs.*
— *Washington Post* columnist William Raspberry,
writing about children growing up without a father

Historians aren't sure of the precise date, but sometime around 1970 people in the United States drank acid-laced Kool-Aid, tie-dyed their brains, and decided that fathers were no longer necessary. At least not fathers of the traditional, heterosexual variety, who, generally speaking, were a drag—always issuing orders, passing judgment, saying "no" to everything fun. Indeed, the thinking went, children could get along with whoever popped over for dinner, in whatever configuration that evolved, just as long as the presiding adults were feeling peachy. If the grown-ups were happy, the children would be happy, too, we declared mostly to ourselves. Children, alas, were not consulted.

How did the Western world manage to lose its collective mind?

How did we as a society decide not just that fathers are unnecessary, but that they are, frankly, a bit of a burden, if not an outright threat to the emotional and physical well-being of their own children? If once upon a time mothers were treated unfairly in a male-dominated culture, fathers today are the victims of what seems like a revenge manifesto perpetuated through the demonization of deadbeat dads, the limits on male custody and abortion rights, the rise in artificial insemination, and beyond.

Where Did Daddy Go?

America leads the Western world in mother-only families. That stunning statement originates with David Popenoe of the National Marriage Project, which follows marriage trends in the civilized world. Although many European nations have a higher percentage of out-of-wedlock births, the majority of those are to unmarried but cohabiting couples. When children are born to a lone mother in the United States, it is more often without a father in residence and often without the father in the child's life. That was the case in nearly half of extramarital births in 2001, according to the most recent data. Partly, this high rate is owing to the high percentage of babies born to teenage mothers, 80 percent of whom are unmarried.

Since 1960, we've tripled the number of children living in fatherless homes, from 8 million to 24 million. To put this threefold increase in perspective, the population as a whole increased from 180 million to 300 million, or just 1.7 times.

Despite fifteen years of America's fatherhood movement, including attention from the federal government and even "Fathers Count" legislation, dads are still undervalued, and their role in family life continues to be diminished. Children are the ones suffering from the absence of fathers in their lives—caused either by divorce, by custody arrangements that sideline dads, or by other circumstances and, less commonly, by willful abandonment.

The National Fatherhood Initiative, first convened in Aspen in

1993 by former White House advisor Don Eberly, has amassed a staggering array of statistics outlining the problems children suffer when they grow up without their biological fathers. As just one example, teens from single-parent and even step-parent homes are more likely to commit a school crime—to possess, use, or distribute alcohol or drugs, to possess a weapon, to assault a teacher or another student—than teens from intact homes. Already I hear the tapping of e-mailers compelled to remind me that the Menendez boys came from an intact, traditional American family. Noted. That leaves a fair number of boys from intact homes who did not murder their parents. Children in father-absent homes also score lower in reading and math tests and are twice as likely to drop out of school than those who live with two parents. Children from fatherless homes are multiple times more likely to commit suicide, to have behavioral problems, to run away and end up in prison.

There are lots more where these come from, though most experienced parents don't need statistics to confirm what they already know from years in the trenches. This is not meant to be an indictment of single mothers or step-families, most of whom deserve a parade, not a critique. I am, after all, a member of both groups. And though some moms and their children are better off when bio-Dad finds other interests, a large and compelling body of evidence makes clear that children who have strong relationships with their fathers do better in every way. They're less aggressive, less antisocial, and suffer fewer negative feelings, such as anxiety, depression, and low self-esteem. They're also less poor. Poverty and fatherless households are nearly axiomatic. And nothing predicts these other problems, from drug abuse and trafficking to prostitution, like poverty. Despite this overwhelming evidence that kids need dads, rising generations of young Americans have embraced the idea that fathers aren't all that necessary. A 2001 survey by the National Marriage Project found that only 16 percent of twenty-somethings think the main purpose of marriage is having children. Sixty-two percent said it was fine for a woman to have a child even if she lacked a "soul mate."

Feminism's Collateral Damage

The trivialization of fathers was not an accident, though the larger acceptance of fathers as dispensable and disposable may have been. Like a virus that infects a community, the anti-dad message seeped into America's unconscious gradually and insidiously. I don't intend to blame all our ills on feminism, without which I probably would be publishing this book under the name Kevin Parker, but we can't ignore the role feminism played in helping shape our attitudes toward hearth and home. What is feminism if not antipatriarchy? Who is Father if not a patriarch?

Before women could be released from patriarchal constraints and achieve equality with men, they had to be liberated from the home, which was viewed largely as a prison where indentured women in aprons and high heels hovered over ovens filled with made-from-scratch Toll House cookies and stressed out about which cleanser to use on those stubborn rings around the collar. Second-wave feminists made it clear that women's liberation hinged on escaping domestic chores, including the care and nurturing of the children. We love them oh-so-much, but couldn't someone else take care of the little dickenses? (For those of you who skipped their women's studies classes, first-wave feminism got women the vote; second-wave got them employed and divorced; third-wave is busy making them porn stars. More or less.)

In a demographic sleight of hand, women's liberation created a new self-perpetuating underclass. While rich women got nannies and play groups, poor women got day care and gangs. For richer or poorer, America essentially abandoned its children to the care of strangers earning minimum wage. Today, after thirty years or so in life's assembly line, the curse of "barefoot 'n' pregnant" undoubtedly sounds like a vacation to many women. But in the post-pill 1960s and 1970s, when Lady Liberation wore Earth shoes and spoke abortion, no woman worth her smelling salts wanted to be "just" a mother, and never a submissive Mrs. playing handmaiden to Mr. Wonderful.

Obviously, there were and are exceptions to this evolutionary posture. Some women are content in their role as wife and mother, and thousands of others are taking a career break to raise their children after figuring out that "balancing career and family" was a propagandist slogan invented and perpetuated mostly by childless ideologues. But by the mid-sixties, following Betty Friedan's assertion that women were miserable and it was men's fault, the culture generally tilted toward women finding fulfillment beyond the confines of home.

If home was a prison, men were the wardens. No-fault divorce gave women the keys, feminism gave them permission to leave, and child support laws ensured they wouldn't starve. Under no-fault standards, anyone could abandon a marriage for any reason. Whereas it took two to say "I do," it took only one to say "I don't" and "I'm outa here." Some men walk out and abandon their families, certainly. But two-thirds of divorces are filed by women who, often as not, say that they're "unhappy" or "unfulfilled" or that they and their husbands are "drifting apart"—and many men find themselves suddenly bereft of not only a wife, but their children as well.

Men, who admittedly can sometimes be oblivious, are surprised to learn that their wives were miserable. Displaced dads are surprised to learn that they're allowed to see their children only on weekends, alternating holidays, and three weeks during the summer. The fact that we call this intersection of a father and his children "visitation" tells the story of postdivorce fatherhood in too many cases. Nobody thinks it can happen to him . . . until it does.

Stephen Baskerville, former president of the American Coalition for Fathers and Children and a government professor at Patrick Henry College, describes the daily experience of thousands of men in his well-researched book, *Taken into Custody: The War Against Fathers, Marriage, and the Family:*

A man comes home one day to find his house empty. On the table is a note from his wife saying she has taken the children to live with her sister or parents or boyfriend. . . . Soon after comes a knock on the door. He is summoned to appear under an "emergency" motion to a family court within a few hours. In a hearing that lasts a few minutes his children are legally removed from his care and protection, his right to make decisions about them is abrogated, and he is ordered to stay away from them most or all of the time. He is also ordered to begin making child support payments, an order is entered to garnish his wages, and his name is immediately placed on a federal government data base for monitoring "delinquents." If he tries to see his children outside the authorized time, or fails to make the payments, he can be arrested. Without being permitted to speak he is then told the hearing is over. No members of his family, the public, or the press have been permitted to be present, and no record will remain of what was said.

This Kafkaesque vignette is surreal, but it's not fiction, and it's often much worse. Ordinary men facing a divorce battle often get the short end of the custody stick, since society usually sides with the mom, thinking children are naturally better off with their mothers. In cases where domestic violence or abuse accusations come into play, men are presumed guilty. Even without being formally charged, a father can be prevented from seeing his children unless state monitors are on hand. In a matter of hours, dear ol' dad has become a defendant in his own life, required to prove himself worthy of having some degree of "custody" of his own children, while paying alimony, child support, and legal fees.

Obviously, such measures are justified in cases of real abuse. And kids have to eat while investigators find out if allegations are true. But what if he's not guilty? What if he's an ordinary, loving (if not fabulously interesting) father who just doesn't happen to get along with his wife? What if she's manipulating the system, taking a preemptive strike in a divorce? It's not unheard of. What's a decent, sane father who finds himself being treated as a criminal supposed to do under these circumstances? Pure and simple, the deck is stacked against men.

Some critics of the system have smartly suggested that accusations of abuse be shifted away from family courts, which are ill prepared to process them, to criminal courts, where assault cases properly belong. Such a shift would protect both the abused and abuser while ensuring due process. More to the point, criminal processing would hold the accuser accountable and, likely, make false accusations rare.

In the meantime, a father's "trial" before the family courts effectively makes him a slave to the state. His wages become state property, and his time with his children is determined by a family court judge, who has almost unlimited power and who operates behind closed doors out of privacy concerns. If the father fails to pay his child support on time for any reason—and there is no "good" reason—he faces jail time. It is strikingly counterintuitive to throw a delinquent dad in jail, where he can't earn money, where he will become even more in arrears and will surely lose whatever job he may have had. Although we've grown accustomed to this process as routine and acceptable—indeed, we have applauded it—the state's power in criminalizing fathers and alienating their children is an astounding development in a free, democratic society.

Baskerville makes a powerful argument that the removal of a man's children through custody awards constitutes judicial kidnapping and that the government's divorce custody machine is, in effect, a war on the family, the fathers, and the Constitution. Instead of seeking therapy for our injured hearts, he proposes that we should be asking tough questions, such as "Do we really expect parents to simply acquiesce as the government takes away their children because two social scientists say it will not harm their children?"

Although Baskerville's critics say he's sometimes over-the-top in his concerns about a racketeering government conspiring to usurp family autonomy, he speaks for thousands of men who feel not just disenfranchised, but impotent. Exiled from their homes and excommunicated from their children, they feel both robbed of their essential role as men and powerless to fight back. Nevertheless, most do as they're told, lick their wounds, and pay their bills.

Our Fathers, Our Selves

Seeing one's dad fifty days a year—the average number of days children of divorce see their biological father—can't be compared with having a father in-house, day-to-day. It's an unnatural relationship, often awkward, in which fathers try to jam the month they missed into a single weekend. Never mind the impossibility of consistency in boundaries and discipline.

Experience teaches that we develop our sense of "self" from the ways in which we interact with both our same-sex and our opposite-sex parents. Further, our success in future relationships hinges to some degree on how we navigate those first relationships. One does not need to be a psychotherapist to reckon that a girl abandoned by her father will have trouble trusting men or relating to them in healthy ways as an adult. A boy without a father will have trouble learning that he belongs to the fraternity of men and, in the absence of a strong male role model, may overidentify with Mother. How does a boy learn to be a father when he has none to show him? And finally, if fatherhood doesn't matter, how can we expect boys and young men to aspire to become responsible fathers someday? The answer is, we can't. Daughters have been especially wounded by the men bad/daddy lousy story they've heard from their mothers and the wider culture. How does a little girl reconcile her love of her first "hero" with the antihero messages all around her?

Interestingly, we seem to accept that children shouldn't be raised without mothers, but we regard the contributions of fathers as optional seasoning, as though children are little casseroles, especially tasty with a pinch of Dad, but guests will hardly notice if you leave him out.

Another rarely mentioned reason that children need two parents is that they need protection from the other parent—not just physical, but emotional as well. Often a child raised by a single parent becomes too much the focus of that parent, too much the emotional partner. Adults who need their children to fill some void in their own lives are unintentionally placing an enormous burden on their children. Boys who become little men to their mothers, and girls who become little women to their fathers, are being deprived of their rightful claim to more innocent concerns. I'm not talking about incest as we think of it, but there's such a thing as emotional incest. Boys drafted to become emotional caretakers to their mothers—often forced to measure up to an unfair standard—eventually may find ways of proving themselves imperfect.

Girls, meanwhile, are at risk of being too controlled by their adoring fathers and may have problems exercising independence or finding males who measure up as mates. One thing fathers do exceedingly well is teach their girls how to live among men. This is a skill both useful and enjoyable. It also seems to be in short supply these days. You don't suppose there's a corollary between father-deprived daughters and an inability to relate well to males of the species? Or, just possibly, that teenage girls' early sexual activity is related to a misplaced search for male attention and affection?

In fact, research tells us that girls who grow up without fathers tend to become promiscuous at early ages. Females want and will seek male affection. In the absence of a father in the house, a girl will seek male, fatherly affection outside the home. This is not genome tracking here. Two-thirds of births to unmarried teen girls are fathered by adults, usually men in their twenties. In looking for love from older men, girls would appear to be seeking father figures in their mates, confusing sexual attention with love.

Research also shows that girls without a biological father in the home tend to reach puberty earlier than girls with fathers. In a 1999 study published in the *Journal of Personality and Social Psychology,* researchers found that girls who have fathers actively involved in their lives—and who were also supportive of the girls' mothers—tended to enter puberty later. Nature is not stupid. Researchers theorize that a father's physical presence keeps his female offspring sexually immature so that she is safe from other males who would exploit her, and possibly to reduce the risk of incest. Girls also may unconsciously delay puberty based on their fathers' behavior. Without the father, she becomes more readily available to other men. The same study suggests that exposure to the pheromones of unrelated males in the household—either Mom's boyfriend or new husband—may cause girls to enter puberty prematurely. Where there is puberty, needless to say, there is the greater likelihood of sexual activity.

As for boys, what better way to learn to become men other than by observing the model of their own fathers? A boy watches how his father walks and tries to copy him. "Monkey see, monkey do" isn't just a cliché, but one of the most powerful forces of nature. He watches how he ties his shoes, combs his hair, and shaves. More important, he observes how his father treats his mother and learns in the process how he should treat women. He also learns from his father how to manage his temper, how to laugh at himself, how to get up when he falls down. Without a father and those lessons in channeling aggression, boys are more likely to become predatory males, more likely to engage in violent behavior and promiscuity. Research shows that 60 percent of rapists in this country came from fatherless homes. Here's the truth: A man who has been initiated into manhood by his father has no need to be macho. An insecure, uninitiated man takes on the symbolic, exaggerated masculine role because he has never been given the real thing.

Other men—grandfathers, uncles, stepfathers, adoptive and unrelated mentors—can and do serve as role models. Biological fathers aren't the only people who can guide a boy along the path toward manhood, but the fact that we recognize the need for a male role model merely underscores the fact that a boy needs a father figure.

The only thing better than a father figure, of course, is a father. They're really so handy to have around, one wonders why we go through such contortions to make substitutes necessary.

Some argue that mothers can do most things fathers do, but that's true only if we reduce a father's contributions to a series of mechanical drills. Fathering is more than a skill set, and besides, men and women do things differently. They talk different, smell different. They even hug different. A father can feed a baby a bottle, but he's still not a mother. And a mother can play catch in the backyard, but she's still not a guy playing ball with his son. A dad playing catch with his daughter is more than a free play period or a gratuitous gender equity exercise. It's a learning opportunity for male and female to experience fair play, to accept failure in the presence of the opposite sex, to be clumsy and foolish and cute all in the glow of deep, noncompetitive, nonjudgmental, protective, accepting paternal love. That's quite a package to ignore.

Learning to Love Dad

Anti-male bias has taken such a toll on the rising generation of wives and mothers that young women are having to unlearn some of their negative attitudes toward men. Dr. Linda Nielsen is leading the charge at Wake Forest University in Winston-Salem, North Carolina, where she teaches a charter course she developed about fathers and daughters. Nielsen, professor of adolescent psychology and women's studies and an avowed feminist, is convinced that young women today have been brainwashed by movies, music, television, and other media into believing that men are inferior to women as parents and that whatever is wrong with the father-daughter relationship is mainly Dad's fault. In some cases, especially in divorce, girls have absorbed their mothers' anger and bitterness toward their fathers. In an analysis of father-daughter relationships in 140 feature-length films, Nielsen found that fathers are generally presented unfavorably—far more so than mothers. These portrayals also run far afield of reality when compared with research in psychology and sociology, says Nielsen.

She found that filmmakers usually portray mothers and mother-daughter relationships in idealized, sympathetic ways that don't accurately reflect most American families. By contrast, fathers are treated far less sympathetically, especially in movies dealing with adultery, divorce, single parents, and alcoholism.

I visited Nielsen's class one day and found a circle of students—all female except for one male, who said he hoped to become a better father by taking the course. This is not a babysitting class, but a tough, reality-based exploration that often brings students to tears. Using statistics and hard data, Nielsen tries to show her students that sometimes girls and women aren't victims but create their own unhappiness and misfortune. She doesn't demonize mothers, which wouldn't be fair or productive, but she documents how fathers have been mischaracterized in the culture.

Students are often surprised to learn, for instance, that two-and-a-half million single dads are raising three million kids on their own or that 80 percent of married fathers in this country earn most of the money for their families. These young women began to see their fathers as hardworking, responsible men rather than as objectified wallets who are either criticized by their families for working too much—or criticized for not being financially successful enough.

Nielsen has launched a campaign to get father-daughter courses into other academic programs. Making her case in the Fall 2005 *Marriage and Family Review* journal, she wrote that fathers often have a greater impact on their daughters than mothers do. For example, the father, to a large degree, shapes his daughter's ability to trust, enjoy, and relate well to the males in her life. And well-fathered daughters are usually more self-confident, more self-reliant, and more successful in school and in their careers than poorly fathered daughters. Daughters with loving, comfortable, communicative relationships with their fathers are also less likely to develop eating disorders. In short, a father's impact on his daughter's life is far-reaching and life-long.

In Nielsen's class, students learn that they share the responsibility for having a better relationship with Dad and that fathers sometimes need permission to be more involved with their daughters. Such lessons offer dividends beyond grades, as expressed by grateful students who write to thank Nielsen for helping them discover their fathers as fellow travelers in life's journey rather than as obstacles to gratification. Most important, they learn that Dad is just human, not a superhero and not an ogre. How odd that they have to go to college to learn that.

Deadbeat, or Just Dead?

One of the cruelest pieces of propaganda in the war against fatherhood has been the myth of the "deadbeat dad." Certainly, some fathers may be first-rate losers, but the "deadbeat dad" trope has become so entrenched that all fathers are presumed lowlifes.

Here's what demonization looks like. Alabama once took a novel approach to tracking fathers in arrears and ran an ad in the state's daily newspapers featuring photographs of alleged child support violators—all men—with the headline LOST DOGS: HAVE YOU SEEN US?" The ad was the offspring of a 2000 law requiring the state Department of Human Resources to list the names, photographs, and other information of ten alleged child support violators.

Such derogatory terms are also damaging to the children the state is purportedly trying to help. What child benefits from hearing his father referred to as a deadbeat or a dog? There's ample evidence that women responsible for child support are equally "deadbeat," but you don't see posters of women portrayed as animals. Somehow in trying to be helpful, we became harmful. Those who abandon or otherwise ignore their children don't deserve our charity. But if children are, indeed, our primary concern, we might find more constructive ways to help fathers participate in their children's lives rather than demonizing them in front of their kids. Following protests from fathers' groups, the state changed the term *deadbeat dads* in the Alabama legislation to *deadbeat parents,* which resulted in one woman being included in the lineup posted on the department's website.

The deadbeat dad assumption was codified and institutionalized during the 1980s and 1990s when the federal government began a crackdown to collect money from fathers who allegedly didn't support their children. The dirty little secret here is that this crackdown was really aimed at the fathers of welfare children as a means of shifting financial responsibility from the government to fathers. In the process, the government implemented a system of collecting child support from all noncustodial fathers, not just those who are in arrears. Whereas fathers used to write checks voluntarily to the mother of the children directly—most of them in full and on time—they now have to pay the state. The state then stashes the money in a fund for distribution and collects bonuses from the federal government for its trouble.

While bureaucrats brag about clamping down on those dastardly deadbeats, what they've really done is collect money from middle-class fathers who were going to pay their child support anyway, while those who don't or can't pay continue to be in arrears, often because they're poor and unemployed. In January 2000, for instance, Health and Human Services Secretary Donna E. Shalala boasted that the government had set new records in child support collections the previous year, reaching $15.5 billion. But as Professor Baskerville points out, the figures were misleading because the increase in collections was thanks to nonwelfare cases. In fact, nonwelfare cases account for 83 percent of child support cases and 92 percent of money collected.

The real "deadbeats," many of whom are in jail, most likely won't be able to change their status. It's hard to cough up the dough when you're broke, harder still if you're behind bars. If you take a close look at the photos of most deadbeats, it's clear that these fellows are not skipping town on yachts burdened with babes. Indeed, *The New York Times* reported in 2005 that 70 percent of child support debt is owed by men who earn $10,000 a year or less or who have no earnings at all. Less than 4 percent is owed by those earning more than $40,000 per year. Even fewer are the six-figure earners who make the front pages on slow news days.

As added incentive for states to be aggressive in their collections, the federal government offers half a billion dollars in bonuses to be divvied up among states and also pays a percentage of the expenses for collections and paternity DNA testing. Thus, the child support industry has been a windfall for states and for middle-class divorcing women. Economist Robert McNeely and legal scholar Cynthia McNeely go so far as to suggest that these government policies have led to destruction of the family "by creating financial incentives to divorce [and] the prevention of families by creating financial incentives not to marry upon conceiving of a child."

Out of the happy loop are fathers, who feel indentured to the government, and taxpayers, who are subsidizing an elaborate and thriving system of collections and incentives that is predicated on an assumption that men are chumps. In the meantime, politicians feel virtuous that they're holding bad guys responsible and that women and children are being rescued.

Penalizing errant fathers has become the only form of chivalry modern woman will tolerate, but it *is* chivalry, based on the idea that Uncle Sam must come to the rescue of the nation's distressed damsels. The real result of the child support industry, however, has been the creation of a system that grants bureaucrats unprecedented access to private records and control over the lives of people, most of whom have committed no offense. As investigative reporter Robert O'Harrow Jr. wrote in *The Washington Post,* commenting on the expansion of federal child support initiatives, "Never before have federal officials had the legal authority and technological ability to . . . keep tabs on Americans accused of nothing."

Virtually Dad

More than a quarter of noncustodial fathers do not live in the same state with their children, according to the U.S. Census Bureau. When courts ruled that a custodial parent could pack up the kids and move hundreds or thousands of miles away, the notion of the other parent's absence became not only inevitable, but just one of those things. No big deal—except to the father, who usually was the one too far away to visit, and the children, who, despite whatever convenient fibs we tell ourselves, still want a father, preferably their own.

As a result of this long-distance debacle, family judges increasingly are ruling in favor of "virtual visits" as part of the custody arrangement, as though e-mailing or seeing Dad on the computer screen is tantamount to visitation. So popular is the idea that virtual visitation bills are either in play or taking shape in twenty-seven states. Internetvisitation.org offers model legislation and tips to parents, judges, guardians *ad litem,* and others on how to add virtual visitation to their divorce decrees or parenting plans. A cartoon on the website shows a happy boy seated at a computer table and chatting with his virtual dad, whose happy face fills the computer screen. In the background, his happy mom is trudging by with a load of laundry. *See, divorce is fun! Everybody's smiling.* Okay, maybe Dad's in Seattle at a convention and Joey's just getting help with his math homework. Still, the message is clear: Being virtually there is almost as good as being there. Although the site's authors make it clear that they're not promoting a parent's move away, Internet parenting surely will make such moves easier to justify.

Other websites are equally friendly. And chilling. Distanceparent .org and Virtualfamiliesandfriends.com, a blog, tell us how to com-

municate without touching loved ones, while Moms over Miles
and Dads at a Distance make staying at home seem boring. During
one virtual visit, I bumped into journalist Lily Yulianti, who has
discovered virtual babysitting. Thanks to the miracle of technology,
her husband once managed to babysit their eight-year-old son in
Tokyo from his apartment in Örebro, Sweden, five thousand miles
away by watching the child over a webcam. Apparently, the baby-
sitter was sick and Yulianti was en route home from the office but
couldn't get there for forty-five minutes, during which time the child
was alone.

"The virtual babysitting worked pretty well and on that day I felt
that we had solved a serious parenting issue in an emergency situation thanks to the Internet!" wrote Yulianti.

One can easily see the convenience of being able to chat with a
child when away from home for a spell. And children doubtless find
it reassuring to be able to summon Mom or Dad to the screen and
chat. But touching base virtually and touching are not quite the same.
The worry is that parents—and family judges—will find too much
comfort in the convenience of virtuality and children will become
virtually unnoticeable except when the instant message bell dings.
How long before that, too, becomes an unwelcome interruption?
Children raised by machines may not be a good bet for comfort and
empathy when the elder years roll around. Better get them a virtual
dog, quick.

Virtual visits can also backfire, as we witnessed in 2007 when actor
Alec Baldwin blew up at his eleven-year-old daughter, Ireland, for
missing their scheduled weekly telephone conversation. Little Ireland may not have understood the importance of the conversation,
but to a father whose participation in his daughter's life is limited to a
weekly phone call, the missed connection was infuriating and, obviously, painful. Baldwin gets no daddy points for his draconian reaction. A tape of his meltdown, during which he railed against his
daughter and called her a "rude, thoughtless little pig," was replayed

in the media for days. Without condoning his behavior, we can easily recognize his frustration.

Noncustodial mothers face the same challenges as fathers, just not in the same numbers. And deadbeat mothers never quite seized the imagination the way deadbeat dads did. No alliteration. "Miserly moms" doesn't quite trip off the tongue the same way "deadbeat dads" does. More important, there's been no comparable men's movement to fight the system. A few have tried—and a few websites have popped up to give men places to vent—but the fact is, men aren't very good at coalition building.

Baskerville cites other obstacles to men's activism, including fear of retribution. "Who is going to protest or provoke the authorities when doing so can mean never seeing your children again?" he said to me in an e-mail. "We are up against a massive multibillion-dollar federal machine. Even the civil rights protesters, for all the obstacles they faced, did not have to face losing their children or homes or the opposition of a half-trillion-dollar federal bureaucracy, along with bar associations, social workers unions, and virtually the entire psychotherapy profession."

Additionally, many fathers are hamstrung by responsibilities, principally child support payments, and don't have time or money to organize and stage protests. Baskerville is palpably resentful when he says, "We do not have the luxury of organizing demonstrations, making speeches, being frog-marched off to jail in front of the cameras, and then returning to our homes to congratulate ourselves on our selfless dedication to the glorious cause. We have had our homes invaded, our children taken away, our bank accounts raided, and many of us are a paycheck or two away from jail."

Aborting Dad

Although abortion rights are viewed largely as a woman's issue, these "rights" can be problematic from a male point of view, as Supreme

Court justice Byron White suggested in *Planned Parenthood v. Danforth.* He wrote:

"A father's interest in having a child—perhaps his only child—may be unmatched by any other interest in his life.... It is truly surprising that . . . the State must assign a greater value to a mother's decision to cut off a potential human life by abortion than to a father's decision to let it mature into a live child."

As a practical matter, abortion raises significant questions of equality and fairness between the sexes and highlights the incremental phasing out of fatherhood. How do we reconcile insisting that men be good fathers while also insisting that they have no say in whether they *become* fathers? On the other hand, how do we reconcile putting men in jail for failing to pay child support when they—like so many aborting women—may not want to be a parent in the first place? Or, as is often the case, when they literally can't afford to be fathers?

Rarely is any consideration given to the father of the unborn. Given that every baby has a father, at least technically, shouldn't men have a voice in the decision to abort? The feminist playbook has an absolute response: No. Men legally have no voice when it comes to abortion, even though the child is theirs to either love or disown. They can neither force a woman to carry a baby to term—*Hallelujah!*—nor force her to have an abortion. Ibid., chorus. Yet by law, men can be forced to become fathers against their will and held financially responsible until the child reaches adulthood. Is that fair, or is fairness mandated only when women are the beneficiaries?

It seems that where women have all the reproductive choice, men have none. We've flipped the switch on destiny. Whereas woman's biology used to be woman's destiny, today woman's biology is man's destiny, as Warren Farrell put it in *Father and Child Reunion.* We can't have imagined that men wouldn't notice or mind.

Playing devil's advocate, one can see how men may feel variously marginalized or discriminated against. Consider the following scenarios from the male perspective:

Scenario 1: Dick and Jane make woo. Jane becomes pregnant and gives birth. Jane demands child support; Dick is obligated to pay it.

Scenario 2: Dick donates his sperm to a sperm bank. Jane receives his deposit by artificial insemination and gives birth. Jane demands child support. Dick is *not* obligated to pay it.

In both cases, Dick is the biological father; in both cases, he voluntarily contributes his sperm. Why, then, should these cases be treated differently? In the first case, many a Tom, Dick, or Harry does not intend to father a child. But in the second case, any man who contributes his sperm to a sperm bank manifestly intends for it to be used to impregnate a woman. He knows that he is going halves in creating a life. Obviously, we make a contractual distinction between the two arrangements, organized around the idea that women should be able to avail themselves of any and all choices made possible by technology. But from a moral perspective, how is it that Dick is responsible for the child he unintentionally fathers and yet not responsible for the one he intentionally fathers?

This seems as good a time as any to point out that life is not fair. Nor has it ever been, especially to women, who have the larger burden when it comes to childbearing, from birth to breast-feeding and beyond. It is that extra burden—and the disproportionate share of child care that follows—behind arguments that women should be the ultimate decision maker in matters of conception. But these arguments all take place in the clinical sphere of theory. In the messy realm of reality, where heartbreak and despair keep company, the answers are not so clear. Real life is, alas, problematic.

Consider the unpleasant family history of one Tanya Meyers, age twenty-two, and ten weeks pregnant back in 2002. Meyers wanted to end her pregnancy, but her former boyfriend, John Stachokus, twenty-seven, wanted her to carry the baby to term and let him have custody of the child. Stachokus sought and was granted a temporary injunction barring the abortion. A common pleas judge subsequently dissolved the injunction and dismissed a lawsuit filed by Stachokus. Hours later, Meyers reportedly suffered a miscarriage.

The fetus—also known as a baby among those who plan their pregnancies—was no longer at issue. But the legal wrangling prior to the miscarriage provides a glimpse into the heart of conflict surrounding parental rights. From a woman's point of view, it is unconscionable that a man—a former boyfriend, no less—could prevail in insisting she give birth to his child. Women in this country, thankfully, are not required to serve as childbearing vessels for men. It may well be that Stachokus would have been a lovely parent, but his donation of sperm to the process of procreation doesn't compare with the woman's contribution. Without the moral bindings of marriage, by which men promise to protect their offspring, his vote simply has less sway.

But what about viewing this situation from the male perspective? What about the man's moral claim to what is undeniably his offspring-to-be? What about his moral right to determine whether he becomes a father? It must be bitterly ironic to men that the tables have turned so dramatically. Once upon a time, women insisted on marriage before having sex. Now many women eschew marriage, have sex as casually as men, and have children when it suits them—all under the protection of laws that also permit what many men see as extortion through child support. Some men's advocates argue that though women should make the final decision in pregnancy, men at least ought to be allowed a voice. Writing in *Throwaway Dads,* Ross Parke and Armin Brott suggest that a man should be allowed to express how having—or not having—a child will affect him. He also "should be encouraged to try to convince his partner that he is right while also allowing her to convince him that she is right ... Denying men a role in their own reproductive choices serves only to reinforce the old stereotypes that men are uninterested in children and that family issues—and fatherhood itself—are women's issues."

One could argue that no one is discouraging men from trying to convince their girlfriends and wives not to abort, but laws supporting women's right to choose make men's input irrelevant. In other words, why bother?

What's largely missing from the debate is an acknowledgment that abortion causes suffering in men. As it happens, many do suffer emotional pain and loss. On websites where men gather to confess their sorrow, headlines tell the story: "I was a coward," "I wasn't strong enough," and "Grief for an aborted son" are typical, as are heart-wrenching stories that betray a sense of involuntary complicity. The men say they consented to abortions because (1) they could; (2) society said it was okay; (3) it wasn't their body. But it *was* their baby, which these men realized too late. In some cases, they found out about the abortion after the fact, as was the case with the man who posted these poignant thoughts:

"I know I am not innocent of the thoughtless and criminally care-less conception of this child," he wrote. "That will always haunt me, as will the profound sense of being powerless to protect it. For several months after I found out, I had the strong sense that my child existed, was somewhere 'out there' and that there was no way to exercise a newly formed paternal concern. Thoughts came unbidden, like, 'Is he cold?' The reaction—nauseating feelings of helplessness and dereliction of duty. . . .

"Coincident with this was a sense of not having protected my girl-friend," he continued. "I have read enough on the subject to know that it is a violent procedure. That this woman I loved so much should undergo such a cold, soulless and brutal experience, and then have to hide it from those who love her, sickens and saddens me. And yet a strange, disquieting dichotomy not unlike that which prevailed at the time of my discovery, exists here as well. How could I comfort her when she herself made the decision, without my concurrence or even foreknowledge, to subject her body to one of those hideous ma-chines? Had she been struck by a car or fallen down stairs I would have been the first to help console and heal her. As it was, I did what

I could, but not without a sense of being divided. I knew she felt this too and that only made me pity her the more, and further the sense of division."

Reading that Web entry, I was struck by the writer's decency and empathy toward the woman. He was not the callous, uninterested male of modern mythology. The obvious question that arises is, why wouldn't we expect that men would suffer?

It is little wonder that men are confused. On the one hand, we insist that men be sensitive and invested in childbearing and child rearing. On the other hand, we insist that men not care about the "product of conception." One's a baby, we insist; the other's just a clump of cells, we assure them. Father on; father off. Emotions on; emotions off. Except, of course, it's not true that one is a baby and the other is a clump. It's all the same thing, which is what many women begin to realize once they start having babies.

Given that men can't experience pregnancy or the bonding that women experience during those nine months, their emotional involvement in a fetus—Latin for "child," incidentally—is always a choice of spirit. I've long marveled that men can become as involved as they do with something of which they are not physically a part. Or aren't they? Is it just fanciful for a man to say, "Our child is part you, part me?" Women, again, decide how men are allowed to feel about their own babies. That men more often than not charge forth to be fathers to their offspring is a gigantic miracle of heart, mind, and spirit that exposes our minimizing of fatherhood for the travesty—and the lie—that it is.

Abortion's Other Victim

There is little research on the effects of abortion on men, but the few existing studies and surveys confirm that men suffer emotionally. The benchmark study in the field was conducted by Drexel University sociology professor Arthur Shostak, whose interest was sparked by his own "bruising experience" in the early seventies when he and his then lover agreed to an abortion. Accompanying his partner to the clinic, Shostak was surprised by how deeply the procedure affected him, so he decided to study other men's reactions as well. Based on a survey of one thousand men in clinic waiting rooms, Shostak found that the majority felt isolated and angry, as well as concerned about their partners. Half of the single men had offered to marry their partner if she would have the child, but only 25 percent of the men said they had offered to pay to raise the child.

Many of the men surveyed also were distressed about the child itself. More than one in four thought that abortion was equivalent to murder, while 80 percent said they already had begun thinking of the child that might have been. Even so, 45 percent of them said they had encouraged the woman to have an abortion. They later reported negative feelings and relationship problems, which they associated with the abortion. Many also reported feeling that they had no way to express feelings of guilt, shame, or regret, figuring that those emotions were off-limits to them.

In an interview with *M.E.N.* magazine, Shostak explained why men's feelings about abortion remain a taboo subject. One, some feminists think that involving men will exacerbate what they view as a power struggle—"a potential front in the eternal battle of the sexes. It's perceived as a zero sum situation." Shostak, who despite his own experience is unflinchingly pro-choice, thinks this attitude is shortsighted and counterproductive. "The progress we can make in gender relations is not going to come through repression of difficult subjects," he told interviewer Don Kruse. "It's going to come through their airing."

Another obstacle is men themselves, who are reluctant to talk about abortion. By leaving men out of the discussion, Shostak says, we are undermining manhood and manliness. He contends that making something as serious as abortion an "invisible nonevent for the male partner is not a contribution toward clarifying manhood. Manhood is a matter of rights and responsibilities."

In follow-up interviews with male participants in abortion,

Shostak found a lack of resolution, a "seething discontent," and a sense among men that they were second-class citizens. The men also felt that they would not be consulted in future family-planning decisions, which caused them to feel less trustful and less willing to commit.

Shostak favors abortion reforms that aren't likely to gain much traction among feminists. He thinks men should be involved in the decision-making process and makes no distinction between married and unwed, saying, "If you are a co-partner in the beginning of life, I think you should be a co-partner in its ending, in its resolution." Moreover, given that those seeking abortion tend to be recidivists— 35 percent of women and 25 percent of men are abortion repeaters— Shostak believes that involving men will help reduce abortion. He also urges abortion providers to take advantage of men's three-hour presence in the clinic to educate them about contraception.

The sense of powerlessness described by Shostak has prompted a new, if mostly symbolic, twist in abortion's history—a lawsuit titled *Roe v. Wade for Men,* which seeks equal protection for men in reproduction issues. The 2006 suit was filed by the National Center for Men on behalf of twenty-five-year-old Matthew Dubay, a computer technician in Saginaw, Michigan, who was ordered to pay $500 per month to a former girlfriend who gave birth to a baby girl after telling Dubay that a medical condition prevented her getting pregnant. Dubay felt betrayed—even tricked—and unfairly burdened by a financial debt for something over which he had no control.

The lawsuit argued that while *Roe v. Wade* gave women control of their reproductive lives, nothing in the law changed for men. Women can have sexual intimacy without sacrificing reproductive choice and without fear of forced procreation—just as men did through centuries of domination. Funny how different the shoe feels on the other foot. One could argue forcefully that women do not always have control of their reproductive lives. "Oops" works both ways, and the responsibility of conception precedes the act that leads to that some-times inconvenient miracle.

A press release related to the lawsuit notes that while women have control of their lives postconception (except when they don't), "men are routinely forced to give up control, forced to be financially re-sponsible for choices only women are permitted to make, forced to relinquish reproductive choice as the price of intimacy."

While women are probably not choking back tears, such thinking has supporters in the equity bleachers. Sociology professor Frances Goldscheider of Brown University coined a term that speaks to angry men: "financial abortion." (And you thought abortion couldn't get any uglier.) Goldscheider makes the strictly egalitarian argument that men should have the option to disinvest in their progeny with proper notice. If women can decide to be or not to be a mother, then men should have an equal right to be or not to be a father. The only problem with her argument is that government would have to pay for the children whose mothers couldn't afford them, and we've seen where that leads. Arguments that advance cyclical dependency, lead-ing to new generations of children without fathers, aren't likely to earn many supporters.

Most women would argue that raising a child is tougher than writing a check. Given that women bear the burden of pregnancy, childbirth, and a greater part of the nurturing, they arguably should have the ultimate decision-making power over whether a pregnancy is carried to term. It is, after all, her body, not his. Men can't ever quite grasp the overpowering nature of pregnancy. To a woman, the idea that another individual or institution should have the power over a decision related to such a personal transaction is at the heart of feminists' passion in protecting "choice."

Nevertheless, by simultaneously ignoring men in the decision making—and indenturing them through child support—women have engaged men's warrior spirit. Men have watched the success of the women's movement and have been pecking away at their own keyboards. They've found the male counterpart to Norma McCorvey, the lead plaintiff in *Roe v. Wade,* and asked that men be granted equal protection of the laws that safeguard the right of women to make family-planning decisions after sex. The National Center for Men argues that fatherhood must be more than a matter of DNA and that a man must choose to be a father in the same way that a woman chooses to be a mother. A reproductive rights affidavit filed with a U.S. district court in Michigan reads, in part: "I will not recognize the moral authority of a court to strip me of my constitutional right to reproductive choice. I will challenge any court order that seeks to impose a parental obligation upon me against my will by asserting my right to equal protection of the law."

There wasn't much honorable about the suit, which was dismissed, but then honor is a vanishing virtue in our modern world. Women relieved men of that burden decades ago. It is, frankly, hard to feel sympathetic toward a man who, in the name of gender equality, prefers to allow his own child to grow up without a father rather than live up to his half of the responsibility. Men lose big points with women, meanwhile, when they pretend that forking over money each month is equivalent to the 24/7 job of hands-on parenting. But such is the extent to which we have commodified children. We don't want to pay for something we're not getting—or that we're not interested in "owning"—even if it means a real human being suffers because of it. Abortion is the ultimate expression of that commodification, of course. Men's objections may be fairly viewed as a justifiable response. On the one hand, they lose a child, thereby eliminating one of man's central roles (if not his most critical) in society. On the other, their value to the born is measured and quantified only in dollars and cents. Woman is arbiter of the life force, while man is reduced to sperm and a wallet.

It is one of life's crueler ironies that men and women in the clutch of passion—and sometimes even love—should create one of life's most heartbreaking predicaments. The reduction of our sexual relationships to banal intersections of eggs and sperm independent of any connection to family has changed the nature of the human connection. We've transformed lovemaking from the joy of sex to the job of sex—from an aria to an oil change.

Roe v. Wade for Men does not represent one of humanity's best moments, but it does illustrate the level of frustration among many men.

Even pro-choice women can understand men's sense that they matter only to the extent they can provide income for women, who hold all the credit cards. If we were to make a list of rights and responsibilities regarding childbearing, the men's column is long on responsibility and the women's long on rights, though both share equally in the decision to have sex. Now, there's a sentence to still the human libido. Nothing like reducing life's greatest pleasures—once considered the ultimate expression of human bonding—from making love to the ol' heave-ho. All of the above would be at least mitigated if we still insisted that marriage be a precursor to childbirth. There's no guarantee that those marriages would survive, but at least each child would enter the world with two parents, who, for better or worse, would be held equally responsible for his or her well-being.

Hey, Wait, That's My Baby!

Women also have the advantage when it comes to adoption. A married father can contest an adoption without much trouble, but an unmarried father has his work cut out for him if he wants to claim his biological child before an adoption takes place.

Many laws vary from state to state, many have "putative father registries," wherein unmarried fathers can file their names for notification should a child of theirs be placed for adoption. Legally, a reasonable effort is supposed to be made to locate the biological father, but even being registered isn't a guarantee of parental rights. The father, assuming he's found, has to prove himself fit by certain criteria, such as whether he supported mother and child during the pregnancy—an unlikely finding if the "father" didn't know Mom was pregnant. The court finally makes a determination according to who can provide the most stable, permanent home for the child—the father or the adoptive parents. Usually, the latter prevail.

The mother can thwart putative fathers in a variety of other ways. She could sign the adoption papers with a different name, such as her maiden name (the mother's name is used to search the putative father registry); she can marry or get another man to acknowledge paternity; she can anonymously leave her baby at a hospital or place the child out of state. In other words, men who sire a child in such a situation are not likely to have much success in being that child's father. I'm not a fan of postbirth paternal claims. I figure if men can keep up with their car keys, they can keep up with their DNA. The notorious 1995 case involving Baby Richard, which prompted laws limiting paternal claims, highlighted the terrible consequences when men and women wage war over conflicting procreative rights.

Baby Richard made headlines when, aged four, he was taken from his adoptive parents and returned to his biological father. The child had been surrendered four days after his birth by his unmarried mother, Daniela Janikova, who had told the father and estranged boyfriend, Otakar Kirchner, that the baby had died at birth. When Otakar learned otherwise on the fifty-seventh day after Baby Richard's birth, he immediately began proceedings to recover his son. In a weird twist, Otakar and Daniela reunited and were subsequently married. Unfortunately, the courts moved so slowly that the child was well established with his adoptive parents when the breathtaking ruling was delivered.

Most people, including me, recoiled in horror at the sight of this young child being wrenched, crying, from his adoptive parents' arms and handed over to a man who, though related biologically, was essentially a stranger. The case was enormously controversial, and outrage was evenly distributed among adoptive parents, birth mothers, biological fathers, and anyone with a heart. Otakar was reviled for causing so much pain, despite the fact that he began proceedings when his baby wasn't yet two months old. Few, meanwhile, gave much thought to Otakar's pain.

Looking back, our tempers cooled by time, it is possible to view the case differently. I have no idea if the Kirchners are good parents. Baby Richard's therapist, Karen Moriarty, wrote a book in 2003 reporting that the boy is a happy, well-adjusted, straight-A student attending Catholic school. The more relevant question is, what would we have had Otakar Kirchner do when he learned that he had a fifty-seven-day-old son in the world? Shrug and walk away, thus ratifying our cultural consensus that men are no good? Was he wrong to fight for his own flesh and blood? It's not as though he waited until the child was four years old and then decided to disturb his life. The lower courts ruled that he should have contested the adoption within thirty days according to the law, rather than waiting close to sixty days. But he couldn't reasonably be blamed for not knowing his son was alive when he had been told otherwise.

Indeed, Otakar tried to exercise his paternal rights but was thwarted by legal technicalities and by adoptive parents who loved and desperately wanted to keep their baby. Understandably, they held out hope until the last possible moment that the courts would rule in their favor. They lost, and few but the father and Daniela could find cause to celebrate. The truth is, Baby Richard's father should have been regarded as a hero—a stand-up guy who wanted to be a good father—who fought for the right to be a parent to his child. It is worth noting that such cases are framed as father's rights vs. mother's rights, when the only right that matters is the child's right to his parents.

The Baby Richard story is not an everyday tale, but it was a vivid demonstration of how wrong things can go in a world that devalues the role of father. If Otakar had been treated fairly in the first place, by both the child's mother and the courts, Baby Richard would not have had to endure the fate he was handed.

Not all fathers deserve our defense, obviously. Sometimes fathers win custody when they shouldn't. Sometimes fathers who should don't. What's clear is that they are treated with suspicion until they can prove themselves worthy, while mothers are presumed by virtue of their biological connection to be the better parent. I can happily argue that babies need their mothers more than they need their fathers during infancy, even at the risk of alienating the dads who feel I'm in their court. Baby also needs his or her father, but in the earliest stages of life, baby needs him principally to guard the door and take care of mother so that she can take care of baby. Most men know this instinctively, because most men—contrary to what sitcom writers suggest—are not stupid. They get it. Most men would be delighted to play their masculine part in this little pas de trois, protecting mother and child, if only women would let them.

A World Without Fathers

For a fuller understanding of where fatherlessness leads, one need look no further than the African American community, where 70 percent of babies are born to unwed mothers. It is probably not a coincidence that young black men occupy a disproportionate number of prison cells. Or that among African Americans, 91.4 percent of expulsions from prekindergarten are boys. Where there are no fathers, in other words, the probability of dangerous boys increases. The profound hunger for male identity and the male fraternity to which all males long to belong leads to the predictable gang phenomenon where exaggerated male behavior—macho and misogynistic in the extreme—is acceptable and encouraged.

Unwed motherhood, a relatively new trend in the African American community, is a function not so much of feminism as of good intentions and culture. Through welfare programs such as Aid to Families with Dependent Children, begun in 1935 as part of the New Deal and predicated on a no-man-in-the-house policy, the U.S. government inadvertently made unwed motherhood profitable and father abandonment predictable. Welfare reform in 1996 under the Clinton administration was aimed in part at ending this counterproductive effect, but the damage had been done. Between 1950 and 1996, the percent of black families headed by two parents dropped from 78 percent to 34 percent. Compare this with 1890, just twenty-five years after the Civil War, when 80 percent of African American households were headed by married couples. In the 1960s, only 23 percent of black babies were born out of wedlock.

Today's out-of-wedlock birthrate is also tied in part to cultural trends specifically within the African American community, where young people aren't encouraged to marry, though recent surveys show that 77 percent of black adults ages nineteen to thirty-five say they would like to get married. Yet fatherhood is considered so passé that the name "baby daddy"—usually used for the ghetto caricature of an unwed father—has gone mainstream. Novelist Maryann Reid found this trend so disturbing that she wrote a book, *Marry Your Baby Daddy,* and founded a nonprofit organization, Marry Your Baby Daddy Inc., aimed at getting African Americans to marry each other. Promising to pay for the wedding ceremony, Reid raised $90,000 in goods and services from local businesses and went looking for ten couples to sign up. Her phone began ringing immediately. Most callers weren't women fantasizing about the dream wedding, but men in search of family. Imagine that.

Writing in *The Christian Science Monitor,* Reid noted that some women among hundreds she interviewed for her book reported that their men—once marriage became a real possibility—became more responsive, took more initiative in household matters, and were suddenly more interested in their future. When men were treated respectfully, and likewise held responsible for civilized behavior, they seemed to respond in kind.

I don't mean to suggest that men can be trained to behave, though come to think of it, that's what civilization is mostly about—channeling male energy in ways that benefit the larger society and shift self-interest toward the common good. Anthropologist Margaret Mead noted that a civilization is gauged by whether it can socialize men to become fathers. Although we're no longer fending off saber-toothed tigers—and women are no longer helpless against marauding tribes (at least not in the United States, at least not for now)—generations of civilized societies have concluded that two-parent families are best for children. David Blankenhorn, author of *Fatherless America,* points out that men, given their inclination toward promiscuity and "paternal waywardness," are not ideally suited to fatherhood. "Because men do not volunteer for fatherhood as much as they are conscripted into it by the surrounding culture, only an authoritative cultural story of fatherhood can fuse biological and social paternity into a coherent male identity.

"Anthropologically, human fatherhood constitutes what might be termed a necessary problem," he writes. "It is necessary because, in all societies, child well-being and societal success hinge largely upon a high level of paternal investment: the willingness of adult males to devote energy and resources to the care of their offspring."

If teaching men to be fathers so that women and children can thrive is our aim, one might ask, what would be the goal of unteaching men to be fathers? Not only do we no longer value fatherhood, but we also have effectively released men from a cultural identity that tied them to a higher moral purpose. Relieved of that purpose—and otherwise marginalized—men are not likely to respond in ways that are going to please or profit women.

Wherefore Art Thou, Father?

The future of fatherhood hangs in the balance as other cultural currents have combined to cast doubt on the necessity of fathers in the child-rearing equation. The push for same-sex marriage, even if advanced for the right reasons (commitment to significant other and equal rights under the law), necessarily devalues the contribution of at least one parent, most often the father, given women's superior advantage in procreation. The past decade or so has produced several books and studies aimed at "proving" that children can get along without Dad. The pièce de résistance was a 1999 study published by the American Psychological Association, "Deconstructing the Essential Father," which made the case that male fathers are, well, not essential. Is there any other kind, you ask? During saner times, this would be a rational question, but today fathers come in all flavors, and the male heterosexual kind seems least in favor.

Anyone can be a father, according to authors Louise B. Silverstein and Carl F. Auerbach, psychology professors at Yeshiva University in the Bronx, New York. The two researchers weirdly blame "neoconservatives" for the push to make heterosexual fathers seem essential, while asserting that gay and lesbian parents are just as good as the old patriarchal model. Although kids do need parents—in fact, as many parents as possible—they needn't be biological, they say. No agenda *there*! No, wait, there *is* an agenda, and the authors honorably admit it.

"We acknowledge that our reading of the scientific literature supports our political agenda," they write. "Our goal is to generate public policy initiatives that support men in their fathering role, without discriminating against women and same-sex couples. We are also interested in encouraging public policy that supports the legitimacy of diverse family structures, rather than policy that privileges the two-parent, heterosexual, married family."

"Privileges"? The world has become profoundly strange when the idea that children need both a mother and a father has to be defended, or when "privilege" is used as a verb to mean marginalizing "diverse family structures." Generally, I have avoided discussing same-sex marriage and other gay and lesbian issues except where impossible to ignore. One book can tackle only so much. But when biological fatherhood is dismissed as little more than an optional lifestyle choice, passivity is not an option. Biological fathers *do* matter, and they *are* essential and children *do* take their cues from their parental relationships—not exclusively, but in important ways that ensure psychotherapists will not be found in food stamp lines. Nevertheless, Silverstein and Auerbach insist that what matters is only that a child have a quality relationship with reliable parent types.

As one raised among enough parent types and an extended family large enough to qualify for at least one congressional seat, I am something of an authority on this matter. Parent types are lovely, but parents are better. If we define "essential" as meaning you can't get along without, then the authors are right. Will boys still grow up to be men without a biological father on the premises? Yes, but mere survival isn't our standard for a healthy childhood. Can stepfathers do the job as well? As a stepparent, I would never insist otherwise. But the real targets of such research are the heterosexual father and the idea that a "traditional" family model of married mother and father is the best configuration for healthy children.

We know a mother and father are best, yet we seek ways to prove otherwise in order to ratify our personal preferences. That's fine as long as we admit it, but to insist that there's a "good" reason to minimize the importance of fathers is plainly about agenda and not about children. I'll concede that loving families do not necessarily have to be blood kin. "Love" is the key word, and most of us are lucky if we have one solid adult who loves us unconditionally. That doesn't mean, however, that just one should be our goal. It is worrisome that we seem content to set the family bar according to the least we can do rather than the best we should aspire to. That we fail sometimes, or even often, doesn't mean we were wrong to try or that we should accept failure as inevitable.

To try to prove that fathers are unnecessary is a dubious goal on its face. There's ample evidence supporting the commonsense understanding that father involvement benefits children both immeasurably and in measurable ways. Children with involved fathers are better students, more self-assured, less likely to get in trouble, and, not least, they know who their father is and, therefore, who they are.

That's not nothing.

3

faux pa and the
yadda-yadda sisterhood

What men offer today is obsolete.

—Rosanna Hertz, author of *Single by Chance, Mothers by Choice,* 2006

Nothing quite says "Men Need Not Apply" like a vial of mail-order sperm and a turkey baster.

While men historically were necessary to the creation of babies and to their protection against a hostile world, today's world is hostile toward men, who are no longer considered necessary for much of anything. In the high-tech nursery of sperm donation and self-insemination—and in the absence of traditional shame attached to unwed motherhood—babies now can be custom-ordered without the muss and fuss of human intimacy.

It's not fashionable to question women's decisions—especially when it comes to childbearing—but shame attached to unwed motherhood did serve a useful purpose once upon a time. While we happily retire the word *bastard* and the attendant emotional pain for mother and child, acceptance of childbearing outside of marriage represents not just a huge shift in attitudes, but, potentially, a restructuring of the future human family. By elevating single motherhood from an unfortunate consequence of poor planning to a sophisticated act of self-fulfillment, we've helped fashion a world not just in which fathers are scarce, but in which men are superfluous. How did this happen?

Anyone older than thirty can hardly bear to hear the name Murphy Brown again, but the famous sitcom character of the 1980s and 1990s spurred on the modern trend of unwed motherhood by moving it out of the ghetto and placing it in the middle of America's parlor. Brown, played by the gorgeous Candice Bergen, wasn't some welfare welsher, after all. She was One of Us, the quintessential modern woman—attractive, hip, funny, smart, and accomplished. I like that in a woman. She was also single and pregnant. The night she became an unwed mother, thirty-four million Americans watched and got the message. So what if there was no male partner in the picture? Did women really need men? a nation asked itself. And the answer as it echoed across the land was a resounding "No." CBS boasted a 35 percent market share that night, and Bergen became a cover girl on women's and news magazines, won another Emmy, and even was awarded an honorary degree by the University of Pennsylvania. In the fantasy world of situation comedy and canned laughter, a child could do fine without a dad.

Few dared suggest otherwise, especially after witnessing the backlash against then vice president Dan Quayle when he singled out Murphy Brown as contributing to the erosion of family values. With his comment, Quayle unleashed a national debate about the nature and structure of family and prompted another *Murphy Brown* episode in response, titled "You Say Potatoe, I Say Potato," referring to Quayle's infamous misspelling of "potato(e)" during a school visit. We all learned from that exchange between Hollywood and Washington that one swims against the feminist tide at one's peril. Quayle was made to look foolish—despite the fact that he was right—and unwed motherhood took off as not just acceptable but fashionable.

Having a baby out of wedlock is hardly news, and Hollywood didn't invent it. Lots of women get pregnant without meaning to, and lots of guys pull a vanishing act when the little zygote starts dividing. Furthermore, many of the same people who were offended by Brown's having a baby outside of marriage would have been far more offended had she opted for an abortion. Suddenly, America came face-to-face with her conflicted feelings about abortion and the hypocrisy suggested by disapproval of single motherhood. As the pro-choice retort goes: "Conservatives only care about children *until* they are born."

But Murphy Brown made a more significant contribution to the larger conversation about the American family: She attractively delivered the message that men are not essential for family. Murphy (and her nanny) could handle childbirth and child rearing without the actual father in the picture. That she probably could—and did— isn't the point. Lots of women can, do, have, and will always raise children without fathers, whether out of necessity, tragedy, or other circumstance. But that fact can't logically be construed to mean that children don't need a father. Or that going the Murphy way is just as good as any other. The fact that some children manage with just one parent is no more an endorsement of single parenthood than driving with a flat tire is an argument for three-wheeled cars.

For most of recorded history, human society has regarded the family, consisting of a child's biological mother and father, to be the best arrangement for the child's well-being and the loss of a parent to be the single greatest threat to that well-being. There's bound to be a reason for this beyond the need for man to drag his woman around by her chignon. Journalist Midge Decter said in a 1993 speech: "Families are not something good, like chocolate cake; families are absolutely necessary. They are necessary not to make you happy but to make you human."

Being human is no modest goal, yet Americans are increasingly inattentive to what humanity requires. The debate about family, as Decter also notes, is silly on its face. "It is in fact not a matter of flippancy at all but rather of astonishment that we should have gotten ourselves into the kind of mess where we should be speaking of family as if its existence were something to have opinions and theories about.... Families ... just *are,* the way nature just is. Sometimes they are good news and sometimes, let us not forget, they are bad news, but they are not up for debate."

How did we come to this? By multiple avenues, but all roads led to the idea that adults should always be happy no matter what. Thanks to the culture created by such notable tracts of self-justification as *Creative Divorce: A New Opportunity for Personal Growth,* popular in the seventies, American parents were able to convince themselves that as long as they were happy, their children would be happy. It was a good bedtime story for adults, many of whom *are* happier after divorce—80 percent of divorced women and 50 percent of divorced men say so—but not so much for children. While parents often celebrate divorce, as illustrated by greeting cards featuring champagne bottles and "new life" proclamations, cards for children of divorce tend to express sentiments of regret, as in, "I'm sorry I can't always be there for you."

Children, as a matter of fact, are not overly concerned with their parents' happiness and shouldn't be. Rather, their thoughts tend to center on more pressing concerns, such as Am I hungry? Am I thirsty? Am I getting what I want? If Mom and Dad are fighting constantly, that's annoying and we all wish they'd stop. But better they should fight in the kitchen than that they should sleep with a stranger in the bedroom. Confucius would say this if he were alive.

Murphy Brown's Body Politic

Sanctification of the single mom got another boost when Jodie Foster appeared on the cover of *People* magazine in 1998 with the chirpy headline AND BABY MAKES TWO! Actually, no, baby makes three. Mom, dad, baby. But here we were celebrating an out-of-wedlock pregnancy as though we were witness to a virgin birth. Foster is doubtless a sperm donor's dream date—beautiful, intelligent, educated, successful, rich—and she has every right to procreate as it suits her. What was jarring wasn't so much her decision to play out life as she chooses, but our celebration of single motherhood. Foster became one more imprimatur stamped on single motherhood by choice while the message was clear: Single moms aren't just good. They're *glam*!

The magazine piece was written with the sort of breathless, go-girl giddiness that brings morning sickness to the menopausal, while Foster's decision to go it alone was presented as just another step toward feminist self-actualization. Her parenting qualifications needn't be debated—none of us is qualified—but *People*'s description of Foster's parenting bona fides played into the new mythology of parenting as hobby and fathers as optional.

As the article reported, Foster plays well with children. When a close friend gave birth in Paris, Foster knew exactly what to do. She sent flowers. *Get out!!* Then she flew over to help and was positively fabulous with the older children as she performed her *Sesame Street* "Ernie" impersonation. As all parents know, there's nothing much else to bringing up children. A few flowers here, a few cartoon character impressions there, and the rest is just so many diapers.

The list of unwed and pregnant celebrities is now long and expanding. Recent additions include Nicole Richie, Halle Berry, Jessica Alba, and Jamie Lynn Spears—younger sister of Britney. Matthew McConaughey blogged in 2008 that he and his girlfriend, Camila Alves, "made a baby together . . . its [*sic*] 3 months growin [*sic*] in her womb and all looks healthy . . . we are stoked and wowed by this gift from God."

Being stoked and wowed is a fine thing, but pregnancy outside marriage in the real world isn't usually considered cause for celebration. Marriage doesn't guarantee a successful family, as divorce statistics indicate, but research shows that children born to married couples have a better shot at leading well-adjusted lives—free of delinquency, crime, and substance abuse—and that they have the lowest odds of living in poverty.

The problem isn't that celebrities, for whom poverty is less of a concern, choose to behave irresponsibly, or that they opt for alternative ways of being related.

How to Become a Single Mother

As I write this phrase—"how to become a single mother"—it occurs to me that when people used typewriters and carbon copies, nobody ever typed those words. Not so long ago, the idea of purposely becoming a single mother wasn't just ridiculous, it was the central theme of prayers feverishly offered along with promises never, ever, ever to do *that* again. Now becoming a single mother isn't so much an accident as, for some, a goal.

It's impossible to know how many women are choosing to be single mothers because the data don't distinguish between unwed mothers who become pregnant by accident and those who elect to have babies without benefit of marriage. We do know that between 1999 and 2003, the number of babies born to unmarried mothers between the ages of thirty and forty-four increased by nearly 17 percent. The largest sperm bank in the United States, the California Cryobank, reports that in 2005, single women made up one-third of its business. That translates to 9,600 vials of sperm. Or, put another way, 9,600 love affairs that never took place.

The woman most often credited with organizing single motherhood is psychotherapist Jane Mattes, who in 1981 got pregnant while unmarried and decided to become a mother. More power to Mattes, who after all could have aborted for about a millionth the trouble of bearing and raising a child. Realizing that there were probably other women out there who hadn't met Prince Charming and who still might want to be mothers, Mattes created Single Mothers by Choice (SMBC) and wrote a book by the same name. The book is filled with practical advice on everything from making the decision to become a single mother, to conceiving, to how to deal with family, friends, and the inevitable "daddy" questions.

Today, SMBC hosts eleven Internet Listservs and boasts an international membership of four thousand, including women from Australia, Switzerland, and Israel. In 2005, the organization took in twice as many members as ten years earlier. Single mothers by choice, in other words, do not appear to be a passing fad.

Mattes makes it clear that her book and organization aren't about male bashing or advancing feminism. She simply aims to help women who, for whatever reason, have missed out on what feminist writer Robin Silbergleid calls the "heteronarrative" arc, wherein boy meets girl, they fall in love, and babies ensue. In fact, Mattes urges women to surrender the romantic male-female fantasy and grieve the heteronarrative as part of making their decision to become an SMBC. Even so, she concedes that becoming a single mother isn't the optimum childbearing arrangement. It is a decision of last resort often made necessary by the ticking of a woman's biological clock or the unavailability of acceptable men.

Mattes's position seems reasonable. She at least acknowledges that daddies are best without making single women feel that they're doing something wrong by conceiving alone. But some feminists disagree with that view, including Silbergleid, who finds Mattes's "last resort" premise offensive. In Silbergleid's view, single motherhood should be celebrated as equal to any other family configuration. Writing in the journal *Americana,* Silbergleid expressed disappointment that Mattes formed her group around "a tale of hard luck and missed chances, rather than realized dreams."

As the pendulum has swung from woman as chattel to woman as Mother Goddess, we've veered off track toward just another extreme. In the radical middle, where most people dwell, mothers and fathers continue to do yeoman's work in trying to make the sucker float, as Pat Conroy once described family life. Most are too busy balancing checkbooks and arranging for child care to indulge in debates about matriarchal ascendancy or deconstructed fatherhood. But what transpires among the intelligentsia has a way of filtering down, and soon the world is an unfamiliar place where children grow up without fathers and the pathologies we used to consider rare have a stranglehold on the next generation.

Forty-Year-Old Wake-Up Call

Certainly, having a child is a dream of many women, regardless of their marital status. Many simply run out of biological time and feel they have no recourse other than to go it alone and hope for the best. Part of the blame for that circumstance belongs to the feminist you-can-have-it-all culture that led women to believe they could procreate successfully into their forties. That turns out not to be true, which many women discover when they try to get pregnant. In women over forty, the fertility rate per month is only about 5 percent, according to the Southern California Center for Reproductive Medicine. Even with in vitro fertilization, the pregnancy rate is only about 10 percent per try. Embryo biopsies, meanwhile, show that at least 90 percent of a woman's eggs are genetically abnormal after forty, while the miscarriage rate is 33 percent.

Alexis Stewart, Martha Stewart's then forty-two-year-old daughter, put a human face on that statistic recently when she talked to *People* magazine and Oprah about her difficulties getting pregnant. She began trying when she was forty-one, divorced, and single and spends $28,000 a month on fertility treatments, she told Oprah. Alexis blames the culture for misleading women and doesn't care what people think.

"We get distracted because now we have jobs, and now we have other things to do. Medicine seems miraculous—you can do anything you want," Stewart told Oprah. "Movie stars have babies late. It seems all possible, but you don't hear the stories of the people who can't have a baby."

News that women have trouble getting pregnant after forty has prompted an interesting backlash from feminists. Caryl Rivers, a journalism professor at Boston University, sees an antifeminist agenda to push women back into the 1950s mold. "The subliminal message is, 'Don't get too educated; don't get too successful or too ambitious.'"

I may be missing something here, but every little thing is not a gender issue. Every personal decision need not be political. Perhaps I'm granting ordinary humans too much benefit of the doubt, but young men and women are capable of making childbearing and career decisions independently of what their choices may portend for the future of feminism. Or the patriarchy. If sometimes the patriarchy benefits—if men have wives who don't hate them and children who know who they are—is it not possible that matriarchs may benefit as well? Does one always have to be up and the other down?

Women who claim to speak for others seem to be haunted by some heeled, coiffed, and aproned feminine specter—terrified that some woman somewhere might be amusing herself with a Sunbeam Mixmaster, looking forward to her husband coming home for a dinner she prepared while the children were playing in the next room. If there's one, there may be others, and next thing you know, we're all living in Stepford, USA. Better, presumably, that she should come home exhausted from work, toting Chinese takeout and sending the kids off to instant message their porn buddies while she pours a glass of wine and looks for the child support check.

How perfect that Alexis Stewart—daughter of America's most feminine feminist and iconic homemaker—should be the one to tell other women they've been duped. Getting pregnant, bane of the *Sex and the City* class, isn't so simple once we need reading glasses. And men, objects of scorn for desperate housewives, are not so easily replaced with the latest cosmopolitan cocktail—sperm served straight up in a glass vial—cherry optional.

The Baby and the Bathwater

In trying to shed ourselves of an often cruel prejudice against unwed mothers and their illegitimate children, we also seem to have shed our good judgment. Single motherhood may not be all bad, but it certainly isn't all good. As Theodore Dalrymple, the retired prison psychiatrist and British social commentator, noted, one prejudice simply replaced another. The current prejudice is that there is nothing wrong at all with creating children out of wedlock. "Unfortunately," writes Dalrymple, "mass-bastardy is not liberating for women."

Dr. Steven D. Johnson, a Cincinnati obstetrician, has observed the fallout from fatherless pregnancy. In an e-mail to me, he noted that while pregnancy can be difficult for a woman in a supportive relationship, it can be overwhelming for a woman without. Discussing our willingness to use science to replace the natural role of men, he wrote: "We've applied our advanced reproductive technologies to women who are merely looking for a sperm donor without asking ourselves whether this is appropriate. The role of the father in the rearing of the child has been trivialized."

Feminists like Silbergleid are contemptuous of men who protest their minimized status in child rearing, categorizing their dissent as neurosis. Men's objections to the growing popularity of single motherhood stem, she says, from "paternal anxieties"—the fear that technological advances are making men irrelevant and that single mothers are undermining the hallowed patriarchy.

"Single mothers, of course, yield a substantial threat to the weakening patriarchy," Silbergleid writes, "particularly as donor insemination makes it possible for the male role in reproduction to be reduced to a single cell from a frozen vial, and the male role in the household virtually eliminated."

Well, yeah.

Under the circumstances, paternal anxiety seems a perfectly reasonable response. Imagine what kind of "maternal anxieties" we'd witness were men able to remove women from any role in reproduction and if women's role in the household were virtually eliminated. We may not have to imagine long. Some men are already hiring surrogates to give birth to their offspring. Others have entertained the idea of outsourcing the problem of procreation. Philip Greenspun, a never married, forty-four-year-old MIT computer scientist, wonders on his blog why men couldn't be more like women when it comes to innovative reproduction.

"What stops a high-income older man from hiring surrogate mothers to produce kids and an au pair or two to take care of them when he is at work or otherwise unavailable?" he asks.

Answering his own question, Greenspun acknowledges some of the obstacles to men, including the reluctance of courts to enforce surrogate motherhood contracts. But Greenspun is a scientist and, therefore, pragmatic.

"In an age of outsourcing Java coding, something for which many months of training are required, to the Third World, why not outsource surrogate motherhood?" he asks. "Suppose that a man has a budget of $50,000 per child. A smart, healthy, college-bound woman in the U.S. would probably reject that amount, only slightly more than the cost of one year at a top university. Consider, however, a woman with a good genetic patrimony in a country where the average income was $5,000 per year. Ten years of salary for 9 months of work! A bit of labor (literally) today and enough capital to buy a house and perhaps start a business. Perhaps that $50,000 is beginning to sound attractive. Not to mention all the other advantages of production in a foreign country. Obstetrical care and hospital fees are vastly cheaper in any country other than in the U.S."

Already, poor women in India are serving as hired incubators, carrying babies for wealthier infertile couples in the United States, Taiwan, Great Britain, and elsewhere. The pregnant surrogates live in group housing and enjoy room, board, and health care, while their outsourced fetuses develop. Additionally, they take home pay equivalent to what most would earn over a fifteen-year period, according to a 2008 Associated Press story.

Commercial surrogacy is legal in the United States and in several other countries, but India leads the industry as impoverished women flock to clinics to sign up for artifical insemination. Greenspun's scenario suddenly seems less far-fetched. Modern women already choose not to breast-feed their babies to preserve their busts. What's to stop them from opting out of pregnancy to avoid those stretch marks, not to mention the enormous pain of childbirth? And what's to stop men from enjoying the same privileges?

With thinking like Silbergleid's gaining mainstream acceptance, it was inevitable that ruminations like Greenspun's would follow. Nowhere in such feminist discussions is any consideration given to the possibility that men might be feeling anxious not only because the patriarchy is crumbling, but because they value their children and love being dads. Whatever compels men to provide their sperm for a stranger's use, I can't say. But paternal anxiety seems to me a healthy reaction to being expunged from the family. In latest developments, women may not even need men for sperm donations, given new technological advances that make artificial sperm possible. Recently, scientists have successfully created live mice using sperm created from embryonic stem cells and are hopeful that human sperm can be similarly manufactured. Though such advances may prove helpful to infertile males, it is also conceivable that artificially produced sperm could further eliminate the need for real males. We've already seen that where there is a way, there is a will.

Two other recent tomes paint a bleak picture for the future of fatherhood. In *Single by Chance, Mothers by Choice: How Women Are Choosing Parenthood Without Marriage and Creating the New American Family,* Wellesley College women's studies professor Rosanna Hertz asserts that fathers simply aren't necessary. While conceding that we still need an egg and sperm to get started, she argues that the core of the family is mother and child and that men are, in a word, obsolete. She based these conclusions on interviews with sixty-five single mothers, some of whom involved men in their children's lives, but only as a means of introducing their children to "male privilege." This was especially important for the daughters, wrote Hertz, so that they would be able to recognize male privilege when they encountered it later in life. What these daughters will do once they encounter male privilege is anyone's guess. Hijack a Black Hawk and strafe Cincinnati?

Cornell University's Peggy Drexler makes the case in her book *Raising Boys Without Men: How Maverick Moms Are Creating the Next Generation of Exceptional Men* that boys are sometimes better off being raised by single mothers as well as in lesbian homes. Drexler concluded from her interview subjects that men aren't just unnecessary, they're frankly in the way much of the time. Writes Drexler: "Sometimes it's actually easier having no partner to negotiate with about parenting, even under painful circumstances. Single mothers get to do it their way, no ifs, ands, or buts. . . . No discussion about parenting methodologies. No crossed signals or being played one off the other by a budding Machiavelli. For a super-organized person like Ursula [one of Drexler's interview subjects], this was a major plus. No compromising on plans—at least not with her partner. The decisions, the choices, the priorities, were all hers."

Any mother can identify with Drexler's point—living alone precludes debate about myriad potentially conflicting issues. But the reward of always right is a weak argument for dispensing with father. In one of her more jarring remarks, Drexler suggests that fathers may be overtouted: "In our society, often we idealize and elevate the role of father in a boy's life without giving credence to the fact that actual fathers can be destructive and a boy may be better off without his father. . . . Sometimes a father can be an aggressor who berates the mother, is hypercritical of his children, or—in less dire circumstances—is simply not a good model."

We also know that actual mothers can be destructive and aggressive, that they sometimes berate the father and are sometimes hypercritical of their children. Where is the book by a male psychotherapist titled *Raising Girls Without Mothers,* wherein single dads by choice point out the many reasons why women are simply not necessary and are, in fact, sometimes not that pleasant to have around? No one would be demanding statistics to prove what is patently obvious—or experts to disprove the lie. We know that children need their mothers, yet we hardly flinch when a psychotherapist justifies raising children without fathers simply because some men are not fit fathers.

Drexler presents Brad, the son of two moms and a donor dad, to make her point. Like many children in Drexler's book, Brad is positioned as the wise child who is both objective and insightful when it comes to adults. He's especially sage regarding the male whose seed Mom borrowed for his creation. It seems clear that we are to infer that such premature insight is due to the boy's having been raised primarily by wise, calm, and thoughtful women. Brad sees Donor Dad one month in the summer and two weeks during the year, from which he has been able to conclude that—brace yourself—"men scream more. They get angry faster."

This summation was based in part on a visit during which Brad's biological father slapped Brad's biological half-brother when the younger boy accidentally broke a pool table. Without any other information, we might reasonably conclude that Donor Dad is a short-fused jerk. But is he an abusive father? How hard did he slap the boy? Was it a whack on his hindquarters or across the face? You don't have to favor child slapping (and I don't) to grant Donor Dad another shot at parenting—or to concede that sometimes even the best parents lose their cool. Maybe it's not easy being a donor dad who sees his son only now and then. Maybe it's discombobulating? Drexler brings closure to the discussion by helping Brad articulate his feelings.

"So it sounds like you're more careful with him than with either of your moms," she says to Brad.

"Yeah," he says.

Roger that.

Books on single motherhood probably aren't crowding out Nora Roberts and Danielle Steel on bedside tables, but they do contribute to academic debates and are welcome fodder for idea-starved newspaper feature writers. A few stories here and there, and soon the idea infects the culture that single motherhood is just another option on womankind's delicious menu of choice, while men become footnotes in the annals of family history. Someday, men may give up the fight for a place at the family dinner table. But meantime, they are justified in wondering why they're supposed to be Superdad one day, and What's-his-name Sperm Donor the next.

Googling Mr. Sperm

Rarely is the commodification of men and children more vivid than when women go online to pick a "father" for that special date with themselves. *New York Times* reporter Jennifer Egan, who followed several women through Sperm World, compared buying sperm on the Internet with buying shoes.

Reading Egan's article, I am riveted by Daniela, a six-foot-one-inch blond, thirty-eight-year-old German woman who was in the market for impregnation. She had opted for the sperm of a friend—known donors have many advantages, including fresher fluids (I can't believe we're talking like this) and, therefore, more live sperm. The downside of a known donor is that in most states they have parental rights regardless of what the adult participants might prefer. Daniela was fine with that, as she wanted her child to have a father. She said to her donor friend, "You don't have to pay for the child, but if you want to have it with you or you want to participate, you're more than welcome."

Doubtless, "it" would be relieved to hear that Dad could participate in its life should he be in the mood someday. As it turned out, the sperm didn't take, which led Daniela to the Internet. Daniela is a thoroughly enlightened gal—a diversophile, if you will—and also practical. Thus, she decided she wanted to be inseminated by a man of a different race. Says Daniela, "I would probably choose somebody with a darker skin color so I don't have to slather sunblock on my kid all the time. I want it [there "it" is again] to be a healthy mix. You know how mixed dogs are always the nicest and the friendliest and the healthiest? . . . I want a mutt."

Such deep insight into human nature is rare. A mutt named "It" doesn't exactly make one want to haul out the embroidery needles and whip up a sampler. Physical traits aside, what exactly does one know about a person based on his donor profile? You get height, weight, pigmentation, hair, interests, hobbies, and education. Is that enough information to choose a mate? What about personality, moods, those intangibles that create or negate chemistry? What about that je ne sais quoi? Daniela worries about those things, too, hence her initial preference for a known donor.

On the Internet, she finds a couple of promising prospects. One is Indian, dark, straight black hair, brown eyes, six feet, and only 150 pounds. She likes this one because if "it" is a girl, "it" will want to be skinny. She can eat what she wants and, importantly, Daniela says, "you don't have to get in fights about food."

The next fellow is a mix of Chinese, Peruvian, and Italian. You can't get more multiculti than that. But wait. Has he read Henry James? Why, *yes*! And he likes Hesse and Lorca, too. This one has potential. Yet another fellow, a dreary old Caucasian, doesn't make the preliminary cut because he's a research assistant in psychology. Daniela sums up her resistance: "You don't study that if you haven't touched upon it somewhere." I don't know. Guys who have sought self-awareness through analysis are usually pretty good company given that, among other things, they tend to like to talk and occasionally will listen. But Daniela is a woman who knows what she wants.

Karyn, another woman featured in the story, keeps a picture of her donor in her apartment. She fell in love with her Jewish spermador at first sight on a website that featured photos. Karyn realizes it's silly to be in love with a stranger who sells his sperm, but he's so *cute!* She even sent a copy of the picture to her father so he could meet his new son-in-law. Or would that be sperm-in-law? Karyn keeps the photo on a coffee table and glances admiringly as she passes by. "It's almost like when you date someone, and you keep looking at them, and you're, like, 'Are they cute?' But every time I pass, I'm, like, 'Oh, he's really cute.' It's a comforting feeling."

It's not quite a cuddle between the sheets, but you can't have everything. Or maybe you can. Another woman featured says that being artificially inseminated has been sexually liberating. She no longer has to worry whether boy toys would also be good dads. This woman's description of a recent date between inseminations should take the pucker out of any man's kisser:

"It was one of these dates where the guy's just telling you his sad story and his complicated relationship with his mother." (*They're all complicated, honey.*) "In my previous dating life, I would have been, like, I'm not going to get seriously involved with a man like this. I'm going to get rid of him. This time I was, like, I think he's hot, so if I just keep listening, maybe eventually we'll have sex. And we had great sex. It was really hot."

From catty to caddish, some women have surpassed the worst kind of men in their callous attitudes toward the opposite sex and the procreative pleasures of human intimacy. While single women pursue sperm vials online and men are little more than sperm in a cup, Woody Allen's orgasmatron can't hit Walmart shelves soon enough.

Before we leave Daniela and Karyn to their solitary pursuits, one telling vignette bears recounting. Daniela has just forked over $450 for an eighteen-pound white canister containing the sperm from her Chinese-Peruvian-Italian donor when she steps into an elevator and strikes up a conversation with a container on two legs—her term for a male human. He is a workman. Cradling her canister, marked with an orange BIOHAZARD sticker, Daniela notices that the fellow's fly is open. Looking down at the poor man's crotch, she says, "You're unbuttoned, you know that."

Blushing crimson, he averts his eyes and buttons up.

What more perfect denouement in this banal exchange of body fluids than the public humiliation of a man who, having haplessly left himself vulnerable and exposed, wilts beneath the castrating gaze of a Nordic goddess en route to impregnate herself?

The Biological Imperative

Sperm-donor children are a relatively new addition to the human community, and they bring new stories to the campfire. I interviewed several adults who are the products of sperm donation. Some were born to married but infertile couples. Others were born to single mothers. Some reported well-adjusted childhoods; some reported conflicting feelings of love and loss. Overall, a common thread emerged that should put to rest any notion that fathers are not needed: Even the happiest donor children expressed a profound need to know who their father is, to know that other part of themselves.

The search for identity is part of being human, from the first moment a baby notices that his left hand is, in fact, part of himself, to adulthood when he seeks to find himself through work, relationships, and especially family. Self-knowledge is daunting enough when you know who your parents are, but imagine knowing that half of your genetic self came from a stranger pleasuring himself to earn money for the weekend. Even those individuals conceived to fulfill a married couple's desire for children often find themselves feeling lost.

How could we expect donor-conceived children not to want to know the man whose DNA they carry? People from *whole* families are so fascinated by the mystery of their origins that they pay to have their DNA analyzed to trace ancient ancestors. Al Sharpton's life was rearranged in a fundamental and poignant way when he learned from genealogists that his ancestors had been slaves owned by relatives of segregationist South Carolina senator Strom Thurmond. The knowledge of his roots made Sharpton see himself in a new light, he said. Suddenly, he realized why his name was Sharpton—the surname of his family's former owners—and he wanted next to know whether he and Thurmond might be related. Ultimately, Sharpton said it didn't matter whether he and Thurmond were related by blood. "Still, I want to know the truth," he wrote in the *Los Angeles Times*.

To know, apparently, is to be.

In a letter to Dear Abby, a fourteen-year-old girl who was donor-conceived wrote of her identity concerns. "It scares me to think I may have brothers or sisters out there, and that he [my father] may not care that I exist," she wrote. Abby, bereft of empathy, basically told the girl to take a chill pill and get over it. The sperm donor thought he was doing a "noble deed," she said, and there is "no way to trace his identity." That may be the first time anyone has called Onan's deed "noble."

For other donor children like "Cass," an eighteen-year-old college student who asked to remain anonymous, Abby's glib answer rings false. As the daughter of a single mother who ran out of biological time, Cass figured out that she was a sperm-donor baby when she was about eight years old. She has been struggling, often silently, ever since. Although her mother is sympathetic to Cass's desire to know her father, she is intolerant of Cass's disapproval of her decision to procreate with donor sperm. Researching together, mother and daughter have learned that Cass has seven siblings. Articulate and thoughtful beyond her years, Cass thinks people are hardwired to want to know their parents.

"Some [donor children] disagree with me and say, 'Oh, I knew of people who had a horrible father,'" Cass recalls. "And I say, well, you had a chance to know. Biologically, we should have a father. Socially, there needs to be the relationship between a man and woman as husband and wife."

Single mothers reading this won't like Cass's position. I can sympathize. I feel fairly certain that if I were unmarried and childless at forty, I might decide to become a single mother, too. I'd like to think I wouldn't—that I'd move to Paris and go boating on the Seine—but I'm not sure that would solve the unsolvable urge to create life. Nevertheless, painful or not, it seems we should at least look closely at what we're doing when we create children without fathers and face the hard questions of whether this is the right road. At least we ought to recognize that what makes one life better does not constitute a universal truth.

Tom Ellis, a mathematics doctoral student in Great Britain, is well-known to regular readers of donor children websites. At age twenty-one, Tom learned that he and his brother were both donor-conceived. His parents told them on the advice of a family therapist, whom they were seeing as their marriage unraveled. At first, Tom didn't react, but months later he hit a wall of emotional devastation. He says he became numb, anxious, and scared. He began a search for his biological father, a search that has become a crusade for identity common among sperm-donor children. "It's absolutely necessary that I find out who he is [in order] to have a normal existence as a human being. That's not negotiable in any way," Tom said. "It would be nice if he wanted to meet me, but that would be something I want rather than something needed."

Not all donor-conceived children feel as Tom and Cass do, and many would say they're wrong. Infertile couples often seek donor help, and the resulting families get along just fine. Nevertheless, Tom is convinced that the need to know one's biological father is profound—and that it is also every child's right. What is clear from conversations with donor-conceived children is that a father neither is an abstract idea nor is he interchangeable with a mother.

As Tom put it: "There's a mystery about oneself." Knowing one's father is apparently crucial to that mystery.

4

gelding the american male

Have you considered castration as an option?

—Katie Couric on the *Today* show, interviewing an abandoned bride

What Lorena Bobbitt lacked in nuance, she made up for with precision. The dubious victor in America's dirtiest and most symbolic battle in the gender wars, Mrs. Bobbitt became an eponym for castration when in 1993 she expressed her marital ennui by separating Mr. John Wayne Bobbitt from the spire of his steeple. As everyone over the age of twenty knows (whether they want to or not), Mrs. Bobbitt left the house with her husband's severed anatomy and tossed it from the window of her car as she sped away. Littering has never been trashier.

Mr. Bobbitt's dismemberment is memorable not only for the certifiable horror of it, but also because the incident inspired one of the weirdest moments in boy-girl history. Rather than being appalled by Mrs. Bobbitt's actions, a startling number of women embraced news of John Wayne's comeuppance as gratifying and overdue. Mrs. Bobbitt, who used a kitchen knife to maim her sleeping husband, became, if briefly, a symbol of feminine retribution, a just cut against the cruelty of man toward woman since the beginning of time.

Poor Mr. Bobbitt's real-life nightmare—every man's most primitive fear made painfully manifest—became a feminist cause célèbre, the punch line in late-night jokes, as well as inspiration for a few forgettable songs and even some remarkably banal movie lines, most notably Brad Pitt's peculiar recitation in *Fight Club:* "You know, man, it could be worse. A woman could cut off your penis while you're sleeping and toss it out the window of a moving car." Ah yes, ye olde "penis" and "moving car" legend. Somehow that's not the way I imagine men discussing two of their favorite toys in the midst of proving their manhood in a fight club. Ultimately, Mrs. Bobbitt was forgiven her transgression. Charged with "malicious wounding," she was found not guilty on grounds that she was temporarily insane on account of her having suffered abuse at the hands of her husband. Whether Mr. Bobbitt was abusive may remain a secret of the Bobbitts' mystery marriage. But fear of abuse, as it turns out, wasn't what provoked Mrs. Bobbitt's attack. Rather, she was motivated by her uncaring spouse's most grievous offense: not knocking her about, but failing to escort her to the finish line. He habitually went first, apparently, leaving poor Lorena stranded in anticlimactic limbo.

Well, dang, woman, why didn't you say so in the first place? It was bad enough that Mr. Bobbitt allegedly forced her to have sex when she wasn't in the mood, but the insult of premature happy-boy was more than a liberated woman could bear. The selfish thing had to go. *Off with his appendage!*

Emasculation is rarely so vivid, but Mrs. Bobbitt's flirtation with infamy brought into sharp focus an anti-male spirit that had been simmering beneath the surface of radical feminism for decades. In the extreme feminist view, man's best friend is the cause of most of the world's troubles. What more expedient route to improving men and society than by removal of the offending member? On a certain level, there is, perhaps, some logic to the idea that separating men from their most distinctive feature would bring an end to earth's tribulations. Sort of like "fixing" Sparky so he'll calm down, quit chasing Fifi, and leave the fire hydrants alone.

Beyond the bedroom, emasculation takes subtler forms. From television commercials and Internet ads that mock manhood to cultural cues that diminish maleness (along with boyness), it would seem that we're trying to point the American male in another direction—away from traditional masculinity to something more closely resembling Adam's rib: Woman. What women seem to really want from men meanwhile is a better girlfriend—one with broad shoulders who can come to the rescue in a pinch, but who is otherwise equally at home with a DustBuster and a weed whacker.

The Viagra Dialogues

Gelding a human male doesn't require surgery, as clever women know. Tell a man he's inadequate and eventually he may fulfill the prophecy—if not much else. The onslaught in recent years of male-enhancing drugs and paraphernalia may be helpful to some men, but must we know about it? Here I am minding my own business, watching the news and tossing a salad, when suddenly some stranger with an undertaker's voice is chatting about the downside of a possible four-hour erection. Is this necessary? Not just the longevity, but the discussion.

I confess to being chronically embarrassed by TMI—too much information—from television commercials, beginning years ago with those Hallmark mother-daughter beach chats about feminine hygiene. I missed that little chapter in mothering, having gotten most of my intimate information from that Very Special Girl Scout meeting, which convinced me that sex and childbearing were out of the question—but which did not, in fact, prepare me for sitting in the den decades later with my boy toddler and two new teenage stepsons watching a tampon commercial. Four sets of male eyes turned my way, whereupon I did the enlightened motherly thing, pulled out a pad and pen, sketched a diagram of the female landscape, and vastly increased the probability that these boys would never seek a wife.

"I always wondered how that worked," said my new husband. He was only half joking.

Ignorance about things womanly—and the understanding that some things are none of a guy's business—was once one of man's more charming traits. No more. By the time my son had reached ninth grade, he knew more about chlamydia than I did. That's because here on Planet Lamaze, there's no such thing as TMI; everybody's a gynecologist. Between being frog-marched through the swamps of feminalia while most boys are still content to fixate on the miracle of mammaries, and incessantly reminding men that they're sexually inadequate.

If talking incessantly about men's sexual stamina doesn't send the old boys into a fetal curl, those still standing can power up the laptop for an hourly e-mail reminder of the many ways in which they are deficient. "Size does matter," men are now told by countless purveyors of enhancers, extenders, swellers, and whatnots—a *Ripley's Believe It or Not!* of torture instruments designed to make men bigger and better. This is no small market. If you Google "penis enlargement" (I did so that you don't have to), you'll find close to 250,000 links.

That's a lot of extensity—and even more insecurity. If you're not feeling inadequate yet, fellas, just stick around. We'll have you reduced to a shadow of your former self in no time. Of course, women have been reminded for aeons about their inadequacies in the mammarian region and have responded by seeking surgical augmentation. Lots of it. Everybody can be Anna Nicole now, and an alarming number of women seem to think that's a good plan. But a woman's bra size is a subjective, aesthetic judgment, sort of like wearing earrings. Some like studs; others like hoops. In the end, jewelry and breasts are optional accessories, whereas a man's equipment is fairly critical to, well, everything.

Whether faced with disapproving scrutiny by their would-be lovers or left alone to consider their many shortcomings, men may be forgiven their decision to seek alternative sources of companionship of the pixelated variety. Computer romance with a virtual woman, after all, carries exactly zero risk of criticism or failure. Not only that, she doesn't even talk back unless you pay her to, and then she says what you want to hear. And when you say it's over, unlike in the real world with a real woman, it really is over.

Midwifing Men into Women

Those men who do somehow find themselves engaged with a real woman often become husbands, significant others, and, as nature prevails, fathers. No longer is it enough that men should protect the hearth, bring home the bacon, and support their offspring. In the age of the sensitive male, it is also necessary that they participate in and bear witness to childbirth. Thank the sixties, when it was decided that having babies shouldn't be endured only by women, but be a shared experience. The thinking was that men who participate in their children's births would be more invested in them. (Personally, I'm partial to the wigwam way. Hand me a stick to bite and get lost. I'll send some smoke signals when the work is done.) Given that men have no natural role whatsoever in this process, birthing consultants handed the guys a stopwatch and said, "Count!"

Count what?

Her contractions.

Oh, okay. Breathe, honey, breathe. One, two, three . . .

Yes, yes, I know, childbirth is a beautiful thing. And a man counting while his wife puffs and grunts through the agony of contractions is sharing a deeply moving, spiritual experience. That's the story, anyhow, and hardly anyone wonders if it's really true. I'm just observing here. Would a man dare protest that he really didn't want to share that exquisite moment with his beloved? Ask writer Rick Marin, who wisecracked to his wife's birthing class that he had tried to get out of attending, but the doctor wouldn't let him. "You could hear crickets chirping," he wrote in *The New York Times*. "I stopped short of tapping an imaginary microphone and asking, 'Is this thing on?' But I got the message: Such heresies are not to be uttered."

At this stage of our social evolution, few of childbearing age remember a time when men didn't go into labor with their wives. Today, 90 percent of fathers witness their child's birth. Even Prince Charles attended the birth of his first son, William (and maybe Harry, but by then I'd lost interest), emerging afterward to comment, about fatherhood? "It's a rather grown up thing, I've found." Well, it bloody well is. And while one can hope—or insist—that fathers bond with and be invested in their offspring, it was a marketing coup unparalleled in human history that got men believing they were needed in Labor & Delivery. Quicker'n you can say "Attagirl," the question "Why can't men be more like women?" became a command to midwifery. Suddenly couples, not just women, were pregnant. They gathered with other couples they'd never met before in bare rooms where men cuddled their engorged partners with pillows and feigned fascination with films showing other women sweating through the gynecological splendors of childbirth. I may be wrong here, but if *I* were a guy, I'd be thinking: Never again.

Whatever hormonal emissions steal a woman's modesty during these raptures, meanwhile, are apparently airborne and contagious. How else to explain the video virus infecting otherwise normal men who, though they would manually dismember any other man who tried to steal a peek at their wife's pudenda, don't hesitate to post photos of their wife's crowning achievement as baby's head tunnels through the birth canal and out the trapdoor? Or to share a home movie?

The absence of sexual content in birthing photos and videos does not, I repeat, does not make the miracle of birth any more appealing to Other People. Everyone's birth is a truly awe-inspiring event, and every child is precious (though mine is more precious than yours, it goes without saying). Nevertheless, trust me when I tell you that no one is interested in seeing the birth of your child. No one. "Seen one, seen'm all" doesn't come close to covering the appropriateness of privacy at such times.

Just in case even one new age dad is not sufficiently offended at this point, allow me to broach an inconvenient truth that must have occurred to more than one male in the past thirty years. Men are not really needed in the delivery room unless they're doctors. Dad has made his contribution—and it was the best ever, *promise!*—and now it's time to pace the hallway and make phone calls to the two or three other people who are interested in current events. The truth is, even the mother doesn't have much to do with the birth process. I don't mean to diminish the experience for those men and women who benefit from extreme sharing, but surely some men in their private moments must consider the possibility that they've been conned into playing a minor role in a feminist morality play. For what lesson does a man learn in the final hours of labor—witness to his wife's torture, martyrdom, and postpartum resurrection—than that she is an Amazing and Brave goddess/creator, while he is but a clock watcher, voyeur to miracles, third wheel in the cycle of life?

Companion to my TMI aversion is a preference for the end-over-means school of maternity specifically and womanhood generally. Just because you like steak doesn't mean you want to slaughter a cow. Viewed in the right light, female architecture can seem like the cathedral at Chartres. Or, if you crank up the kliegs, like the Vatican tunnels. Whatever feminine mysteries remain to lure men from the embrace of their La-Z-Boys is not long for a feminized world that thinks coed bathrooms are progressive manifestations of equality. And while no one could reasonably argue that men shouldn't help with child care as much as possible—or participate in birth if they really want to—the Lamaze mandate does seem to conceal among all the heavy breathing a punitive subtext that goes something like this:

*You got me into this mess, buddy. No sitting in the waiting room with
your stinking cigar feeling proud of yourself. We're in this together! Now
you're so good at math, count, dammit!*

House Husbandry

Once we had employed men to deliver the babies they helped con-
ceive, it was then necessary to drape them in aprons. In 1983, Michael
Keaton made "Mr. Mom" a household term to describe the inept father who doesn't know how to run a household with the same efficiency as Wonder Wife. Gender swapping as a vehicle for comedy is
as old as human theater, and watching a man try to mother babies is
a natural. It was funny, if also tragically sad, when Robin Williams
pretended to be a woman in *Mrs. Doubtfire* so that he could pose as a
nanny and spend time with his children after he and his wife split.
Notice that a man is acceptable only when he's a woman. It was also
amusing when Dustin Hoffman pretended to be a woman in *Tootsie,*
though let me be the first to say, "All right already."

The film *Mr. Mom* was based on a real couple about a man who
loses his job and stays home to tend the house and kids while his wife
works outside the home. Predictably, the household falls apart under
the charge of Dipwad Dad, while the world profits immeasurably by
the addition of Wonder Wife, who is as competent working for an
ad agency as she was making truffled risotto at home. Naturally, she
has to fend off a sexually harassing boss (because all men are sexual
predators), whom she efficiently punches in the nose. (Which is okay
because women hit men only in self-defense, which is often required
because men are all brutes. Or so goes current mythology.)

Before another generation was out of diapers, Mr. Mom was no
longer a comedy gag; he was a cliché. He was also a "trophy husband." *Fortune* magazine reported in a 2002 cover story that featured
several high-powered women and the stay-at-home husbands who
made it all possible. Behind every powerful woman is . . . a happily
emasculated man. The magazine cover shows a pleasant-looking

chap wearing an apron that stops at his knees, revealing bare legs below, with his hands gently caressing his two adorable little girls. A Ron Howard look-alike, he wears glasses and the expression of a man at peace with his role in life: smart enough to think outside society's stereotyping gender box, man enough to wear an apron and give his ego a rest.

Inside, we meet Bill, who makes coffee and breakfast for his wife, Anne. There's a certain angst that impinges on the open mind upon reading this narrative, not because men can't do house and women can't do office, but because it is so contrived and overproduced. A reader is justified in feeling as though she's watching the birth of a cliché through a delivery room peephole. Here's how the story reads:

"While she's doing battle, Bill is home tending the gardens, running errands, managing the social calendar, planning the weekend, and playing golf. When Anne gets home, Bill is waiting . . . (with) dinner on the table. He's capable of a killer beef Wellington, though on weeknights he keeps things simple with chicken or pasta salad. And though he'd love some scintillating conversation, he usually lets Anne flop in front of *Wheel of Fortune* or *Jeopardy!* and fall asleep."

Okay, I admit it. I want to marry Bill. Who wouldn't? And there's nothing wrong with any of it—women working, men diapering. Whatever works. What raises a red flag is the didactic tone of such stories and the implication that if you don't play house the new way, you're either a troglodyte or a witless Stepford wife. These movies and stories aren't just randomly occurring snapshots of modern American life. They're choreographed vignettes aimed at redefining sex and gender. Making men and women interchangeable requires taking women out of the home and putting men in their place. As long as we're all happy and having a good time—and taking our Prozac— we hardly notice the nausea that comes from being manipulated into behaving in ways that are for many unnatural. Pretty soon, women are unhappy with husbands who don't know or care who stocks the best arugula and men are dissatisfied with women who aren't motivated to scale the corporate ladder. In nearly every respect, including sexually, we've set standards that most Americans can't meet and raised expectations that can only spell disappointment for millions.

———

Lifestyle used to be a section in the newspaper where readers browsed recipes, gardening tips, and fashion ideas. Today, lifestyle is a political statement. We've taken the apron-men and power-women and turned them into cultural icons of virtue and courage. It isn't enough that modern men and women help each other out because they love each other and because it makes sense. Enlightened men share recipes and are fluent in hormone replacement therapy—not to mention the best walk-in manicure salon—while enlightened women kick ass at the gym and shatter glass ceilings with a strategic *thwap!* of their brass *huevos.* Those who cling to more traditional roles, meanwhile, are considered either not too bright or cult members. Or both.

As we devalue the strong masculine type, we reward the feminized male. In 2006, Joe Molnar, a logistics manager from Buffalo, New York, won the "Mr. Good Housekeeping" contest sponsored by *Good Housekeeping* magazine. The story about Molnar begins: "How many husbands would steam-clean all the carpets, then save the water so their wives could see how much dirt they got out?" Um, that would be exactly one by my count, Joe. Mrs. Molnar insists that Joe is not "an obsessive-compulsive neat freak," even though, okay, he did take a lint roller to the cat. Joe, you're the man, not to mention the cat's meow, but your wife is wrong. You *are totally* obsessive-compulsive, but that's okay. Some of us alphabetize our spices, so we're cool with the lint thing.

What else does Joe do? He washes dishes, vacuums, launders, and hand-scrubs the floors. He even spent the previous year's tax refund on that carpet steam cleaner he had been coveting. *Good Housekeeping* also published cleaning tips from husbands. Are such articles a threat to American life as we know it? Probably not. As a former newspaper feature writer, I'm familiar with the story process. You find three guys cleaning house, you've got a trend. Five guys, you've got a contest. Ten, you've got a cover story. But these "trend" stories do bleed into the culture, and what was really, in fact, ten guys doing something rather unusual suddenly becomes de rigueur. *See? Everybody's doing it. Why aren't you?*

In another time, men may have cleaned house because the house needed cleaning. Or donned aprons to cook because lots of men enjoy cooking and aprons are practical splatter blockers, not fashion statements. Men also may have taken care of the kids because somebody had to. My father was one of those. He probably didn't love every minute of it, but he also didn't feel he was doing something revolutionary, constructing a new "gender paradigm," two words that never escaped his lips. He was doing what was necessary. Pass the butter and hold the laurels. No one outside of snake-handler country really thinks women have to stay home and take care of the babies every waking moment, forsaking their hard-earned careers and depriving the country of half its brainpower, but it's silly to make enemies of men and women because their interests and priorities do not dovetail in precisely the same ways at precisely the "right" times as choreographed by social engineers. Sane couples work these things out. In my house, whoever is best at a given job generally does it. Hint: If you don't want to do something, be lousy at it.

It's God's Fault

None of these trends takes human nature into account. Research indicates that whatever social architects might design, men and women simply do not view housekeeping and babysitting in the same ways. Women, it turns out, enjoy both more than men do. (Again, I'm just reporting.) This doesn't mean that women *love* housekeeping or that they should do more of it than men. It just means that they hate it less than men do. Or, perhaps more accurately, that they have a lower tolerance for what results when no one is tidy. If you've lived among men, you know that they have an uncanny ability to avoid looking directly at a jumbo trash bag parked by the back door and can step around or over said jumbo trash bag for days and sometimes weeks. Just as mysteriously, they can fail to notice its absence when, finally, someone else escorts the sack to the Dumpster.

Those are my anecdotal observations, but social scientists have discovered much the same. The finding mentioned earlier was the conclusion of an unintentionally amusing study of university professors aimed at finding out how parental leave policies and gender role attitudes impact the distribution of child care responsibilities. Researchers didn't set out to be funny, but toss 184 earnest, tenure-track PhDs in a study about child care and funny doesn't need an invitation.

Steven E. Rhoads, a public policy professor at the University of Virginia, author of *Taking Sex Differences Seriously,* and principal investigator on the Family, Gender, and Tenure Project, selected college professors for his research because they were the most likely people to be enlightened and—are you ready?—less likely to be burdened by archaic notions of traditional gender roles. We learn from the study description that high intellectual ability is linked to rejection of "traditional sex-role ideology." The researchers also figured that women professors, given their proven ambition, would be motivated to achieve equality in the domestic arena. Then a funny thing happened. Even these 184 tenure-track academics found themselves behaving like unenlightened blokes.

Men just weren't that interested in washing dishes and babbling with baby. And women "simply like childcare more than men and are reluctant to cede many child-care duties to their husbands," wrote the study's authors. Babies, apparently, prefer their mothers, who are more attentive, more responsive to physical cues, and better babblers. This is a temporary condition tied to hormones, by the way. Some of these preferences shift as children grow older and discover leapfrog—at which fathers are ridiculously better. Most parents, including some academics, already knew all this, but it's helpful when social scientists can toss out some stats to validate the obvious. The study's authors finally settled on several conclusions that are hard to read with a straight face. One goes: "Perhaps when parents make decisions about how to divide childcare duties they are at least partially responding to cues from their children. If infants consistently convey a preference for mothers over fathers, then the continuing dichotomy in the performance of infant care could be viewed, at least in part, as a response to the needs of infants."

The entire study is full of such tortured punch lines. Here's another: "If mothers derive more pleasure from caring for children than fathers, it will be hard to bring fathers' level of participation in childcare up to that of mothers." (Please hold your applause until the end.)

And another: "Our study suggests that it is unlikely that either changing the attitudes of men and women about appropriate gender roles or offering paternal leave to male professors will bring about equality between the sexes in the amount of childcare that they do, at least when the children are infants or toddlers. . . . It seems that neither opportunity nor ideology is sufficient to bring men's time spent on infant/toddler care up to the level of women."

Finally, in what must have been a frightening revelation: "There are aspects of having children that can never be made equal between the sexes." Because? You'd better sit down:

"Pregnancy is a condition and breastfeeding is an activity that must be borne by women."

These are complicated concepts, so allow me again to translate: There's no way to make men into women. In his book *In Search of Nature*, Harvard zoologist E. O. Wilson wrote that much of what we ascribe to men and women as socially constructed roles are deeply embedded in our genes. He is clear in saying that "what is" isn't necessarily what should be—what he calls "the naturalistic fallacy of ethics"—but that much of "what is" in human nature is largely the heritage of our Pleistocene hunter-gatherer forebearers.

"No solid evidence exists as to when the division of labor appeared in man's ancestors or how resistant to change it might be during the continuing revolution for women's rights," Wilson wrote. "My own guess is that the genetic bias is intense enough to cause a substantial division of labor even in the most free and most egalitarian of future societies."

You can be sure I'm not making a case for only women doing housework or suggesting that only men can do the heavy intellectual lifting. But changing man's nature is problematic. Even more challenging, apparently, is changing woman's nature.

Ironically, the push to apply gender-neutral ideology to parental leave policies may ultimately hurt women and children. Given that women give birth and also breast-feed, they arguably need time off to be mothers. Even in several Scandinavian countries, where, according to the Rhoads study, people accept gender neutrality as the norm, extended postbirth leaves are for mothers only. However, if feminist agitation results in companies extending equal leave to both men and women, then postbirth leave may "tilt the playing field further against women rather than leveling it," the University of Virginia authors concluded. As men gain family time, women may lose some.

Beware What You Ask For

Some American dads have become so thoroughly feminized that they've started whining. A single dad wrote in *The Washington Post* that he felt excluded from advertising aimed only at moms and kids. He wanted advertisers to understand that slogans such as "Choosy Moms Choose Jif" hurt his feelings. *He's choosy, too!*

With such fragile feelings adrift in the culture, we might expect the next cycle in our evolutionary psychodrama to present dads who feel bad about their lack of equipment at baby-feeding time. We laughed when Robert De Niro attached a fake breast to his chest to feed the baby in *Meet the Fockers*. It was a funny gag, but we may be gagging soon as comedy becomes reality. In the most efficient homes, men already feed babies with expressed breast milk so that baby isn't deprived of Mother's nourishment, even if her whole person is busy brokering a corporate merger in Bangladesh. Coming soon to a store near you are bottles with nipples custom-contoured to resemble Mom's own breast. Really. Baby will never know the difference. And perhaps Dad won't, either. It's a concept.

In France, men already are fantasizing about the day they can give birth. A 2005 newspaper story was headlined FRENCH MEN YEARN FOR PREGNANCY, and no one was surprised. A telephone poll of five hundred fathers found that 38 percent would like to have carried their children in their wombs (science permitting) and given birth. *Les garçons* may not have long to wait. In the not distant future, men may be able to implant a fake uterus in their bodies and give cesarean birth. This is clearly far-fetched, but so was Dolly the cloned sheep a generation ago. Already, scientists have discussed the possibility of transplanting wombs so that transsexual women can give birth. Why not heterosexual men? Artificial wombs could be open for occupancy by 2020 or sooner. The wombs are being created from endometrial cells with the idea of helping infertile women and premature infants in intensive care. But it doesn't take much imagination to envision a time when fake wombs will be available for convenience.

Naturally, attentive feminists are concerned that these future contraptions could interfere with abortion rights. And you thought they were worried about our humanity. Writing in *The New Republic,* Sacha Zimmerman suggested that the availability of artificial wombs could lead to those wacky pro-lifers extracting unwanted babies (otherwise known as fetal tissue) and implanting them in fake wombs, there to grow them to completion. Zimmerman's concern seems outlandish, but maybe not. Yesterday's science fiction is already today's memoir. Already several states have granted "personhood" status to fetuses in criminal cases where an unborn child has been destroyed in the commission of a crime. As technology advances our understanding of fetal growth, enhancing the perception of fetal autonomy, it is easy to imagine a time when women with unwanted pregnancies might opt for prenatal adoption. Instead of having to complete the pregnancy—or endure the unpleasantness of abortion—they could simply transfer the developing fetus to a surrogate womb. In a more draconian sci-fi scenario, might pro-life states justify rescuing a fetus when women seek to terminate a pregnancy? Stranger things are bound to happen as we grapple with powers that pit technological utility against our own humanity.

Anything is possible, and everything seems to want a turn at filling nature's ever-popular vacuum. If for now improbable, it is not inconceivable that men could rent or implant a womb as easily as a woman—laws permitting. And why wouldn't they? No wife, no criticism, no child support, no garnished wages, no visitation or custody dispute. If men are no longer needed in a world of sperm banks, women become unnecessary in a world of artificial wombs. More to the point, men weary of being used as sperm donors and human ATMs finally could enjoy a level playing field in the reproduction sweepstakes, rid at last of the plague of paternal uncertainty. Fake wombs don't mess around.

Terminating Girly Men

While scientists explore ways of making men biologically equal to women, the fashion industry has been focused on making men *look* like women. Once gays paved the way for heterosexual men to get in touch with their feminine sides, presto, metrosexuals were everywhere. Almost overnight, it seemed, American men were storming spas and elbowing their way into pedicure salons. They shopped till they dropped, scooped up fashion magazines, and memorized designer labels.

Two metrosexual encounters:

EPISODE I
I'm sitting at a restaurant counter in a Washington, D.C., hotel and the fellow next to me starts chatting. We cover the usual territory—where ya from, whatcha do?

"Great coat," he says. "Great color for you."

"Thanks."

"Nice shoes, too," he says, pointing to my loafers. "Ferragamo?"

"Fer-what? Oh yeah, I dunno, maybe. Why? How'd you know?"

"Oh, I have them, too."

"Ah."

EPISODE II

I'm visiting my son's school, wearing a tweed blazer, when I notice a father wearing the same jacket.

"Hey, nice jacket," I say as he passes by.

"Oh, wow, where'd you get yours made?" he asks in the stage whisper of a co-conspirator, and whips open his jacket to show me the label inside.

"Um, I didn't, but I love that—'Where'd you get yours made?' I'll have to remember that one."

"You did *not* buy that off-the-rack!" he huffs with a look of disbelief. You'd have thought I had confessed to putting ice in my Chardonnay. He was obviously crestfallen that his tailor-made jacket had found its way into something as pedestrian as a store—where ordinary people traffic.

That conversation wouldn't have taken place twenty years ago, not even ten years ago. A man might comment that you look nice, but he wasn't interested in where you bought your clothes. All these centuries, have men been stifling the urge to shop, nursing a secret desire for highlights and silk tips? Were those "waiting" couches parked outside ladies' dressing rooms for bored husbands instruments of torture for men who were really lusting to try that sequined halter top?

Pierre François Le Louet, managing director of the French consumer-forecasting firm NellyRodi, announced in 2005 that the masculine ideal is being modified. In a report to Fashion Group International in Paris, Le Louet said that "the traditional male values of authority, infallibility, virility, and strength are being completely overturned" and that today's males are more interested in "creativity, sensitivity, and multiplicity." Those alpha studs Arnold Schwarzenegger and Sylvester Stallone are being replaced by the twenty-first-century man who "no longer wants to be the family super-hero."

"We are watching the birth of a hybrid man. . . . Why not put on a pink-flowered shirt and try out a partner-swapping club?" asked Le Louet. Just because, Pierre, just because. An accompanying photograph in *The New York Times* showed one of those new hybrids—a male-ish lad of indeterminate age sporting bright red Orphan Annie hair and wearing Peter Pan knit pants, a red-and-green-striped T-shirt, suspenders worn backward—reminiscent of a boy dressing up like Daddy.

Doubtless, few American boys are longing to wear red Annie hair or to dress like leprechauns, but one can easily see what's up. The feminization of males isn't accidental, nor is the objective innocent. This particular fashion is a lurid marriage of pedophilia and feminization. The manly man is being traded in for a girly boy. I leave it to others to surmise to what end.

Soon thereafter, French designer Jean-Paul Gaultier—the man credited with introducing eye makeup for men—presented unisex collections in Paris that also blur gender distinctions. Both male and female models teetered around on platform heels in his spring–summer 2007 show. Gaultier defended the new girl-boy, saying that there are boys interested in dressing this way "and who can pull it off. I try to fulfill their desires."

He has a point. But it doesn't seem like the fashion industry really has men in mind when designers start fitting males for high heels. Feminists long ago figured out the purpose of heels, which was to elongate women's legs and hoist their rumps in the air to enhance the impression of sexual accessibility. Why would we want to do that to males? Now there's a question for the new millennium.

In the Bravo hit *Queer Eye for the Straight Guy,* five gay guys brought the closet to heterosexuals, amusing audiences by showing male slobs how to spiff up their act to attract the babes. It was a good stunt for laughs, but it also underscored the sense that heterosexual males needed to be made over into something less, well, heterosexual. Body hair, for which most boys hold an impatient vigil, was suddenly viewed as unsightly. Men filed into waxing salons in search of the less manly look. Or would that be the more boyish look? The smooth, hairless male may have run its course by now. Once the curmudgeonly Christopher Hitchens submits to the latest fashion trend, one can be fairly sure its time is nearly past. Hitchens wrote in the December 2007 *Vanity Fair* of his spa foray—and his submission to the tortures of body hair removal—to celebrate his recent U.S. citizenship.

Sure enough, some retrosexuals are rebelling and have begun seeking hair transplants from head to chest, trying to recapture the manly look they once eschewed. Fashion fickleness, once the purview of adolescent girls, seems to have seized males no longer confident of their manliness.

Obviously, concepts of manhood and masculinity shift with the times. A generation ago, only a ponytailed dude would do the trick for a righteous hippie chick. Once upon a time, men in ruffled shirts and powdered wigs were considered wildly macho, and clearly, men in skirts didn't start last year in Milan. The difference today is that fashions are intended to make men look or seem like women. Put another way, the designers of boy-skirts flashing on Paris runways do not have Bruce Willis in mind. Or, then again, maybe they do.

In Search of Manliness

What is manliness, anyway? The fact that we have to ask suggests that something has gone awry in the garden. In his book *Manliness,* Harvard professor Harvey Mansfield distilled manliness to "confidence in the face of risk" and an "easy assumption of authority." He tied manliness to the Greek *thumos,* or "animal spiritedness," which the Greeks sought to balance with reason and self-control. Mansfield's defense of manliness was modest, he said, because manliness is fifty-fifty good and bad. Good manliness corresponds to honor, nobility, and heroism (Achilles); bad manliness involves violence, foolishness, and stubbornness (terrorists). Too much manliness is bad, though too little can be dangerous, too. One begins to wonder, is it manly to discuss manliness?

When it comes to physical manliness, all assumptions are off. Men who try to buff up for the girls may be missing the mark, as women these days apparently are more attracted to unmanly men. Above the neck, women prefer feminine faces because they associate them with less aggression. Daniel Kruger, a social psychologist at the University of Michigan, altered composite pictures of men's faces, making some more masculine and others more feminine, and asked 854 undergraduate students to respond to them. The more masculine faces (square jaws, thinner lips, exaggerated brow ridges) were thought to be more likely to get in fights and to be unfaithful; the more feminine faces (smaller chins, fuller lips, larger eyes) were judged to be better husbands and good with children. We know they're better with accessories, but looks sometimes deceive. Remember: Jeffrey Dahmer had one of those "less masculine" faces and no one would call him a good dinner date.

As Mansfield tried to make clear, manliness really has more to do with attitude than with looks. Here's what manliness isn't. It isn't about size, brute strength, aggression, or any of the other characteristics we sometimes associate with traditional masculinity. The hypermasculine male and our attraction to him, in fact, may be a reaction to the feminizing trend in popular culture. Is it possible that our yearning for the masculine is so profound that we overreact when it's missing? Or that we are drawn to exaggerated examples to compensate for the void? The success of Tony Soprano comes to mind, as does the dangerous attraction of glamorous violence. If *Dirty Harry* was a reaction to Alan Alda, perhaps über-dad and godfather Tony Soprano is a macho backlash against the inept fathers who populate network television.

Manliness also isn't about huntin' 'n' fishin', though some manly men enjoy the outdoors and outdoor sports. Nor is it about riding horses, clearing brush, or waging war, as manliness is often misunderstood—mostly by presidents and their consultants. *Washington Post* writer Ruth Marcus dismissed Mansfield's call for manliness, saying that we needed not more, but less of it. She pointed out that the "undisputed manliness of the Bush White House" has gotten us all in a whole heap o' trouble, not to mention a war.

Bush, after all, famously clears brush at his Crawford, Texas, ranch—"backstopped by a quail-shooting fly fisherman comfortable with long stretches of manly silence—very *Brokeback Mountain,* except this crowd considers itself too manly for such PC Hollywood fare," wrote Marcus. She noted that Bush, when asked about *Brokeback Mountain,* the movie in which two male wranglers fall hard for each other, said he'd be happy to talk about ranchin,' "but I haven't seen the movie." The implication of Marcus's *Brokeback* commentary was clear. By not seeing the movie, which millions of other men also declined to see, Bush was further confirming his legendary lack of intellectual curiosity. My guess is that if Bush had watched *Brokeback,* he might have concluded that those cowboys were two sad puppies. Both men came from such bleak emotional landscapes, few empathetic souls would have denied them whatever small pleasure they could find under the stars. In any case, Bush, along with other men who resisted the call of the mountain, surely can be forgiven if watching men romance each other isn't on his must-see list. The feeling many men expressed about the controversy surrounding the film was that they were being manipulated by cultural puppeteers. See the movie and be cool; don't see it and you're a homophobe. Similarly, war is not some sport to prove manliness, though manly men often come in handy. Manly men are not bullies, show-offs, braggarts, or swaggerers—all of which are ungentlemanly behaviors and suggestive of insecurity, which is consummately unmanly. Remember, confidence in the face of risk. Of course, one can be overconfident, often without justification. Whatever one's opinions of the Bush administration's policies, Bush's election to the presidency offers an instructive example of how manliness sometimes works. Bush won the presidency against Al Gore and reelection against John Kerry in part because enough Americans considered him to be more manly than his effete opponents. That perception, justified or not, had nothing to do with his fighter pilot swagger or his tough "bring it on" talk, both of which were more frat-boy than manly.

So how did a college cheerleader beat two Vietnam vets? Call it "the *Brokeback* factor." Bush oozed Regular Guyness, and his perceived manliness had mostly to do with his lack of interest in the vanities. A YouTube production comparing John Edwards's interest in his hair to Bush's captures the concept. Edwards, who famously spent $400 on a haircut, sits not just primping before a TV appearance, but "fluffing," as Robin Givhan noted in *The Washington Post*. Prize poodles primping before the Westminster Dog Show have fluffed less. Bush, on the other hand, ran his hand over the top of his head once and looked goofy. Poofy or goofy: your choice.

America may never fall for a regular guy again, but that's the way it was post-Clinton. Gore, on the other hand, forfeited any claim to manliness when he hired feminist author Naomi Wolf as wardrobe consultant to help him convey Alpha Maleness. She dressed him in earth tones—neutral browns and greens—which made him about as manly as a wilted salad. It's not that he didn't look good in his new threads; it's that manly men don't chase fashion or hire consultants to make them *seem* manly. Shouldn't someone have told him?

Kerry was the quintessential presidential candidate—ruggedly attractive, his face looking sculpted by Rushmore's chiselers. Tall and country club tan, he was a decorated war veteran, smart, thoughtful, and well read. But Kerry's manliness ended with the résumé among so-called Ordinary Americans. Like Kerry, I'm a T. S. Eliot fan and I've always thought I should have been a pair of ragged claws scuttling across the sands of silent seas. But someone should have told Kerry—or he should have known—that reciting passages from "The Love Song of J. Alfred Prufrock" to Maureen Dowd, who reported it in a column, was not going to help him with the guys. "Do I dare to eat a peach?" Kerry mused to Dowd. "Should I wear my trousers rolled?" [*sic*]

Uh, no, John, you don't dare. And no, you shouldn't. For some reason, it would have been all right if Mansfield had recited "Prufrock." Somehow you get the feeling that Kerry was gazing out the window of his private jet as he let the words tumble from his slightly moistened lips onto Dowd's notebook. I don't know how Mansfield would have done it, but I suspect with a wink of self-awareness at the preciousness of the moment. Manliness is tricky.

Gelded by Any Other Name

The ultimate act of emasculation is, of course, the elimination of man's central role as father. Back in the day before fathers were held in suspicion, children knew something about what fathers did. He was the law, and kids obeyed it. He was also the line between his family and a hostile world. As long as Father was around, children slept peacefully in their beds. There was never any confusion about what a man did with respect to his family. He took care of them. He protected them. He made sure they had what they needed to thrive. He checked the locks one last time and made sure the flashlights had batteries. He kept the pantry stocked and the water bottles filled. Just in case another depression came. Manliness wasn't a fashion statement; it was a state of being.

My father, like most, was a man long before we kids entered the world. He had a whole history of manhood and masculinity before we knew him. But he couldn't be a father until we showed up. Being a father was far and away the manliest thing he ever did. Because ultimately, being a father means sacrifice and putting everyone else ahead of oneself. When we take away a man's central purpose in life and marginalize him from society's most important institution—making him ridiculous and superfluous in the eyes of his children—we do nothing less than strip him of his manhood. If we did the same to women, taking their children and rendering motherhood obsolete, Lorena Bobbitt wouldn't be one nutty woman with a knife.

She'd be a movement.

5

the vagina diatribes
and the sacred clitorati

The story of your vagina is the story of your life. . . .

—Eve Ensler, author of *The Vagina Monologues*

Say what?

—Kathleen Parker, author of *Save the Males*

SMALL-PRINT WARNING: GIVEN THE UNAVOIDABLY EXPLICIT NATURE
OF THIS CHAPTER, READER DISCRETION IS ADVISED.

From Adam's rib to Eve's vagina in just a few short millennia.
Who says time doesn't fly?

Actually, it's been only a couple of decades since vagina worship
grabbed America by the throat and forced it not to throw up. In a bat
of mascara-denied lashes, women have gone from keeping their
knees glued together to squatting over mirrors and delivering oleagi-
nous soliloquies about their familiars.

Well, you know what they say about familiarity.

Somehow, feminism as first conceived has morphed through the years into a worship of woman's interior anatomy, scaring men half to death and possibly confusing them beyond retrieval. Weren't guys supposed to avoid talking about vaginas in public? And weren't women supposed to be above that sort of thing? If ever, no more.

Today vaginaism has joined the pantheon of modern isms and boasts a cult following. After centuries of modest dormancy, vagina worship is today a fertile field of cultural study, a professional pose, the vestal vestibule itself an objet d'art, a vessel of admiration and envy. Volumes have been written, poems scribed, plays performed, monologues mouthed, and parties organized around the sanctification of what once was a very private parlor for the occasional well-chosen visitor.

It's not as though women's bodies had been ignored all those centuries. They were rather lushly admired by painters and sculptors, beginning with that fat little fertility broad posthumously named "Venus" by some generous curator, aka the goddess of Willendorf. Yet for some reason, earlier artists didn't feel compelled to expose the stalactites and stalagmites of the vaginal cave. Some may call that denial; I call it civilization. Undergirding this celebration of the feminine, however, is a bold-faced subtext of antipathy toward the masculine—the male figure, the male weapon, and the male God—the triad of patriarchal oppression. To become fully liberated from the patriarchy, women had to not only eschew the phallic, but embrace their sacred vessels. This is all fine and good, we hasten to add, because we prefer not to enrage thousands of proud vaginas. But if you're a guy, crowds of women celebrating epiphanies about their units is not likely to damage the perception that women are sometimes a tad unstable.

Even Freud, who articulated the notion that women were envious of man's best, noncanine friend, could not have imagined Eve Ensler. The author of the wildly successful *Vagina Monologues* apparently tapped into a deep, hidden reservoir of female pain—centuries of suffering at the mercy of man and biology. While women who perform the *Monologues* celebrate their very intimate selves in a raunchy display of narcissistic self-parody, men are supposed to play along and pretend that women are perfectly rational and absolutely to be trusted with management of the free world. Vaginas *have* always ruled, after all.

Through the *Monologues,* in which women of various ages and backgrounds tell stories about their formerly private parts, women claim to have found some hidden part of themselves and reclaimed their anatomies from the patriarchy. Infatuation with one's sexual nether region is not unfamiliar to men, needless to say. But coming from women, who previously had been modest about such things, public self-admiration leads to cognitive dissonance. *Are we supposed to talk about this or not?* To my sons, I would have to say: *Nyet.* Let's keep our privates—and our private thoughts about our privates—to our private little selves, shall we? But millions of women around the world do not share my nostalgia for the unspoken. And guys haven't a clue how to respond, except, no doubt, to wonder silently: Does this mean we get to have more sex?

Isms and Ologies

The origins of this curious path to self-realization can be traced to the early seventies and possibly the strangest-ever coffee table tome, *Our Bodies, Ourselves,* wherein newly liberated women discovered and celebrated their pubicity. Pictured for the first time outside medical textbooks were ordinary naked women in all their cellulited glory. The book covered everything from anatomy to sexuality to abortion to lesbianism—the latter a distant early warning that feminism was being hijacked by women who were not precisely interested in bonding with the opposite sex. In the nonjudgmental Thorazine voice popular among the mellow, peace 'n' love crowd at the time, deeply caring doulas coached readers about how to have an abortion (with the warning that sometimes you'll feel bad afterward, but it passes); or, alternatively, how to have a baby and be a parent in a commune.

As a young, liberated woman at the time, I owned my own copy and feigned fascination with these new discoveries. Budding feminists were not supposed to question—ever—whether something as beautiful as childbirth or as deeply moving as group contractions was perhaps best kept under wraps and enjoyed in privacy. In one especially memorable photographic series, we watch a woman giving birth, free at last to gaze into the hirsute abyss of God's little oven, and marvel that children ever get conceived after a glimpse of this process.

I knew I was supposed to glory in the nakedness of emotion and the slippery beauty of bonded birth, and I'm sure I made all the right murmurings. But I'm also certain that I was thinking: What have we got against sheets? Few women are modest at the birthing point for reasons that become clear when it's your turn, but something of woman's mystery got lost in that period, and it's been missing ever since. The mystery of why males pored over the glossy, airbrushed pages of Hef's bare bunnies, on the other hand, was thus and forever solved.

Women's discovery of their bodies, themselves was not to go unheralded. Having felt objectified by men as sex objects through the centuries, women were reclaiming their vaginas with rare enthusiasm. Or was that vengeance? Young women of my generation were suddenly the proud owners of their own specula, plastic replicas of the heavy metal versions employed by gynecologists for the annual cervical review, invariably performed in those days by men. (In solidarity with the sisterhood, I fully endorse the gradual trend toward women gynecologists. I mean, why try to explain cramps to a man when you can just roll your eyes at a woman and get your pain pills?)

All across the nation, women were suddenly getting a gander of what only their doctors had seen before. Not quite Disney's Body Wars, but equally amazing, if not awe-inspiring. For those women not quite able to grasp the concept, Vulva Sherpas were invented. In possibly the most insipid photograph in feminist history—also featured in *Our Bodies*—a young woman is lying on the floor sans britches and with her speculum properly situated. Another woman is perched in the bird's-eye seat, holding a mirror so that her supine sister can view Her Very Own Self. The mirror holder's expression seems to say: *See, I just knew you'd love your vagina if you ever got to know her!* I've been recovering from that photo for thirty-five years. Nary a peep from men, who, polite as ever, figured women knew what they were doing and that, moreover, this new shared fascination seemed a promising development.

From sister helpin' sister came the vagina mirror party in *Fried Green Tomatoes,* in which Kathy Bates joins a gathering of other culturally oppressed women to admire their vulvas. Their bottoms unsheathed beneath skirts, the gals gamely perch over mirrors as the group leader guides them through one of the most memorable scenes in movie history: "And tonight, we're gonna begin to explore our own femaleness by examining the source of our strength and our separateness. Our vaginas. So if y'all will just slip off your panties and straddle your mirrors."

Alrighty.

However men and women may be alike, it's a certainty that no man ever had to be urged to get to know the source of his strength. Or would that be his "precious"?

The vulva workshop—leave it to women to organize and make work out of their sexual organs—has been enjoying a brisk business the past thirty years thanks largely to renowned feminist sexologist Betty Dodson, who teaches women how to pleasure themselves. (There is yet another sentence that makes no sense to men. Women have to be *taught*?) During Dodson's still-popular group tours of female anatomy, women pose for portraits (yes, of that), preen and prune, and then join in helping one another achieve the Big O. Sorry, but there's no separating this kind of talk from what feminism has wrought. So what do you call a group of women displaying their sex organs, massaging one another, and having group orgasms? Bingo! A lesbian orgy!

But because they're women scuttling male oppression through self-expression, we're supposed to pretend that it's, oh, I dunno, feminist liberation sexology. Throw in an ism and an ology and you can justify nearly any narcissistic perversion. In her book, *Sex for One,* Dodson identifies self-pleasure as a meditation on self-love. Because women are compelled by feminist ideology to celebrate themselves, they aren't allowed to suggest that (1) loving oneself does not require a mirror and a flashlight; (2) self-pleasure is not, alas, brain surgery; and, finally, (3) most women do not intend to live without men, which is the sacred subtext of vagina worship.

It was a very short trip, indeed, from Dodson's and Bates's self-actualization to Eve Ensler's spectacularly successful celebration of women's intimate parts now galactically known as *The Vagina Monologues.* Ensler isn't just a cottage industry. She's a commercial megalopolis that stretches from Off Broadway, where her play debuted in 1996, to more than seventy-six other countries—including Afghanistan and Bosnia—but not to China, where public vagina talk is, at least for now, frowned upon. Mao wasn't wrong about everything.

The monologues, which are based on some two hundred interviews with women, provide a window into the female psyche, a treacherous place for males to visit. Touted as a celebration of the you-know-what (enough with the v-word), the monologues can also be viewed as diatribes against men. That some women have been hurt by men is not in dispute. But the undertone, which isn't so "under," is decidedly anti-male. Indeed, some of the monologues advance the idea that women love women better than men do. In "The Woman Who Loved to Make Vaginas Happy," a dominatrix talks of giving women pleasure. She used to be a lawyer, but this was more fun. "There was nothing like this in tax law," says the monologist after describing her arsenal of props, including whips, handcuffs, rope, and dildos.

The most controversial piece, "The Little Coochi Snorcher That Could," concerns the lesbian seduction of a teenage girl that many critics view correctly as a child rape. In the vignette, a "southern woman of color" relates several memories related to her "coochi snorcher." (I'm just getting started and already I want to wash my mouth out with soap.) There's never any explanation offered for this affectionate name, though I have to say it's a relief not to have to say you-know-what again. In the monologue, the woman, whom we'll call Regina, recalls being raped by a family friend, Alfred, in the basement while visiting her father. (Who is drinking with his buddies: bad daddy.) Avenging the crime, Regina's daddy does the manly thing and shoots the SOB. As a result, Alfred is paralyzed for life, and Regina's mother bars her from seeing her father for seven years. That's too bad, because maybe Bad Daddy could have parceled out a little justice when his daughter was again raped, this time by a twenty-four-year-old woman with the implicit consent of the child's mother. Personally, I think Dad deserves an award for doing the fatherly thing and dispatching the man who hurt his little girl.

It is an artful trick of perception to make Dad the bad guy for avenging his daughter's deflowering, while Mom is given a pass for allowing her daughter to be statutorily raped by a woman. We can all see that forced sex by a man and consensual sex with a woman do not meet the same definition of "rape." Even so, the moral of the story, as Regina articulates it, is profoundly anti-male: The beautiful lady with the nice apartment taught her a new way of thinking about her coochie snorcher, she said, "so I'll never need to rely on a man."

In 2000, Robert Swope, a Georgetown University student writing for the school newspaper, *The Hoya,* suggested that it might not be in women's best interest to celebrate what amounts to a rape in the *Monologues.* Swope posed his concerns as a question: "Is there such a thing as a good rape?"

Big mistake, Bob.

For his audacity, Swope lost his place as the lone conservative voice in the paper. Editors pulled the column before it ran, and Swope was dismissed when he complained. True to his journalistic calling as a troublemaker, Swope had written another column the previous fall questioning how the Georgetown University Women's Center, which supports women who have been raped, could give a standing ovation to the *Monologues,* given its celebration in "Coochi Snorcher" of what he considered a "rape." He began that column with this question: "What do you get when you glorify . . . the rape of a

minor, promote lesbianism, insult heterosexuals and attack men?
Answer: an event by the Georgetown University Women's Center."
Then he asked, "Why is rape only wrong when a man commits it, but
when it's by a woman committed against another woman, who just
happens to be 13-years-old, it is celebrated and a university club spon-
sors it?" (In an earlier version of the play, the child was 13. Her age
was later changed to 16.)

You have to admit, the boy had a point. He also had a bull's-eye on
his back. He was quickly targeted by outraged faculty, including the
associate dean. His column was called "hysterical" and "scurrilous,"
and he was banished into the outer darkness. So much for free
speech. Among the very few who commented on Swope's behalf was
Georgetown alumnus William Peter Blatty, author of *The Exorcist.*
In a scathing letter to the editor of *The Hoya,* he wrote: "With all that
the demon says and does in my novel, never until I read of *The Hoya*'s
and [GU president] Leo O'Donovan's support of *The Vagina Monologues,* and their suppression of Robert Swope's article, have I truly
appreciated the meaning of the word 'obscenity.' "

The message to Swope and any other male who attempts to question the sanctity of the anti-male message of *The Vagina Monologues* is
that he will be disabused of his opinion soon enough. Exorcised, perhaps, or reprogrammed. Only those who play along will get along,
while those who cooperate may even be allowed to become vagina
boys. Yes, you read that right. At performances of the *Monologues,*
evolved boys hip to the charms of the liberated vagina are sometimes
allowed to be ushers. When Christina Hoff Sommers attended a
Monologues performance, she was escorted to her seat by a young
man wearing a name tag that read "Hi, I am Vagina Larry."

I'm worried about Larry and all other young men who have to
bite their tongues and pretend that what is false is true, that what is
ridiculous is profound, and that they're supposed to walk past a forty-
foot inflatable vagina at Arizona State University as though there
were nothing remotely unusual about that, for example. And yes,
they did create just such a dirigible. At the University of North Car-

olina at Chapel Hill, coeds wore T-shirts that read "I Heart My Vagina" and at Roger Williams University, "My Vagina Is Flirty." At Florida State University, young women could attend an orgasm workshop.

One of the bigger crowd pleasers in the *Monologues* invites women to reclaim one of the English language's ugliest words: "cunt." Let me just say I'm glad my grandmothers were able to miss this chapter in American history. Glenn Close made the cunt-a-logue famous when she got 2,500 people to stand up at a 1998 celebrity benefit and chant the word. "Cunt, cunt, cunt, cunt, cunt, cunt, cunt!" And then everybody felt liberated and cunts were happy everywhere.

I suppose one had to be there, but the grown-up in me struggles to imagine dressing up for a high-end adult party and reveling in the great unexplored pleasure of saying a really, really bad word in public and collapsing in giggles. I've seen nine-year-old boys in the backseat of my car do that. As women are shouting "Cunt!" at the top of their lungs, little boys everywhere must be thinking: There's something wrong with Mommy. We'd certainly think something was wrong with Daddy if he and 2,500 of his buddies packed a stadium and started shouting "Dick!" at one another and clutching their sides with hysterical laughter. We'd have them arrested and put in jail.

Ensler's fascination with vaginas was born, she says, of having grown up in a brutal home and a violent society. She admits to being "obsessed with women being violated and raped, and with incest. All of these things are deeply connected to our vaginas." Indeed, they are. But in Ensler's world, *every*thing is connected to the vagina. After the huge success of her monologues, she said her whole life had been changed. For the first time in her life, she was fully "inside" her vagina, she said.

"Inside your vagina?" asked a bewildered interviewer, echoing what other normal people were thinking.

"I'm in my life. I'm in my seat. I'm in my core. I'm in my power," said Ensler. "Talking about vaginas all the time has really given me that confidence and strength."

Not talking about vaginas gives me strength and confidence, but to each her own. Women just shouldn't expect men to reward them with straight faces if they continue to obsess about their beloved units. To her credit, Ensler has turned her fixation into good works, trying to save women from violence, especially those in countries where genital mutilation and public stonings are routine. She's raised many millions for programs that help victims of domestic violence through her February 14 V-Day movement, though it's lamentable—a misdemeanor, if not quite criminal—that she has usurped the only day of the year when romantic love between men and women is celebrated. Valentine's Day is no longer about hearts; it's about wounded vaginas. And, of course, bad men.

Vaginas on the Plain

I don't mean to pick on Ensler, but her play has had a profound impact on American culture and especially on the next generation of young men and women entering adulthood. *The Vagina Monologues* is staged to growing audiences on about five hundred campuses where performance of *TVM* is almost mandatory. To reject the play—or to fail to appreciate its artistic integrity—would be tantamount to approving violence against women. You have to admit, X-rated drama is an unexpected twist on public virtue. Performances at colleges and universities are usually preceded by a week-long celebration that includes blanketing of campuses with vagina propaganda—pamphlets, displays, sculptures, and other, frankly aggressive vagina-mongering.

With deep gratitude, we turn to the College Republicans at Roger Williams University in Rhode Island, where playful young men created Penis Day and *The Penis Monologues*. Administrators put a swift end to the boys' fun. Offended by a good-natured and much-needed spoof, they apparently had no problem with campus girls randomly handing out questionnaires asking, "What does your Vagina smell like?" and posting flyers with slogans such as "My Vagina Is Huggable." Yes, parents, this is what you're paying for. The problem for the males may have been their mascot—a gregarious penis named Testaclese—who chatted briefly with university provost Edward J. Kavanagh.

Kavanagh apparently mistook Testaclese for a mushroom and enjoyed a friendly exchange. When Testaclese handed Kavanagh an honorary "Penis Warrior" award and the provost realized what he really had been talking to, his sense of humor failed him. P-Day planners also plastered the school with their own slogans: "My Penis Is Majestic" and "My Penis Is Hilarious." And, indisputably, he is. In one flyer, Testaclese is reclining on a couch reading Michael Barone's *Hard America, Soft America,* with the caption "My Penis Is Studious."

Turnabout would seem fair enough play in an equality-obsessed world, but that's not how the game is played. Girls can do what boys do, but clearly boys cannot do what girls do. True equality, of course, will be possible only when women can take themselves as unseriously as the young men at Roger Williams do. In the interim, which may not be short, Ensler's monologues will continue to be taken Very Seriously as thousands of "vagina queens" and "vagina warriors" wage war on a phallocentric world.

Clash of the Icons

In 2003, the Harvard University crew team built a nine-foot, anatomically correct snow phallus in Harvard Yard. It was intended as a joke, it should be unnecessary to say. Not long after erection of the phallus, angry feminists destroyed it, launching an amusing debate on campus about sex and art. Jonathan H. Esensten, an associate editor of the *Harvard Crimson,* wrote a column questioning what might cause such "iconoclastic fanaticism" and offered a pleasant history of the phallus as happy symbol in various cultures.

"Perhaps the phallus-breakers of Harvard Yard were reacting with bourgeois conventionality in labeling challenging art as subversive," wrote Esensten. "Or maybe they were acting on some radical women's liberation agenda that requires the destruction of visible symbols of male virility."

Student Amy E. Keel responded in a letter to the editor that she and her roommate dismantled the sculpture because they found it offensive. "Neither I, nor any other woman, should have to see this obscene and grossly inappropriate thing on my way to class. No one should have to be subjected to an erect penis without his or her express permission or consent."

I can't find fault with that sentiment, but tell it to the vagina queens. It's true that an assertive penis can do far more harm to an unwilling woman than a passive vagina can do to an unwilling man, though it's helpful to remind ourselves that we're talking about a snowman. The idea that a nine-foot snow penis is a symbol of male dominance while a forty-foot inflatable vagina is a celebration of all that is glorious and lovely is a fashionable conceit that begs to be pricked. So to speak.

Surely, too, we've heard enough about vaginas for at least another two hundred years. Alas, we can expect no such reprieve as Ensler's army continues to grow. There are a lot of vaginas out there. And you thought Wahhabism was a problem. This much we know: If men were running around reciting soliloquies to their very own selves, no one would hesitate to say that they had lost their minds. But women, no matter how they complain, still enjoy special status in the culture, and we can expect for the foreseeable future to be awash in vaginaism, nary a word of protest permitted. Already, Ensler's dreamscape—a dark torment of personal injury—has been absorbed into the mainstream. We're all victims now, vaginas on the plain seeking out other vaginas with which to hold hands and gaze unlongingly into the silky night of a manless moon.

Ohmigoddess

It should come as no surprise that the vividly narcissistic vagina-worshipping phenomenon would morph into the woman-centered, self-genuflecting goddess movement. The complete dismantling of the patriarchy isn't possible, after all, as long as God is a male. Moreover, how can women ever be fully equal to men as long as Eve (the other one) is the cause of humankind's fall from grace?

Women weary of the male God have found solace in the sacred feminine and the feminist-religious theory that in pre-Christian times, we humans lived in a female-centered universe. Unseriously distilled, goddess history goes something like this: Women ruled, all lived in harmony with the earth, peace reigned, and everybody knew where her G-spot was. Then about five thousand years ago, men took over, installed male-dominated hierarchies, made God a "heavenly Father," and now we have terrorism and global warming. More or less.

Did women really rule once upon a time? And does it matter? Historical accuracy is hard to come by, as written records were pretty patchy five thousand years ago. Most deductions about goddess worship in earlier eras are inferences based on thin evidence—feminine statues, funeral rites that seem to indicate gender equality, time measured as cyclical rather than linear. And, of course, no missiles. Critics of the goddess theory point out that although some early human organizations may have paid homage to womenfolk, a few feminine statues do not a civilization indicate. There may have been a time when women were revered and spoiled—I think it was the 1950s—but no matter. People have a right under our patriarchal system of government to worship as they please, and witches are fine by me. Yet goddess worshippers and their feminist sisters (and the occasional brethren) remain steadfast, intent not only on dismantling the patriarchy, but on replacing it with a matriarchy.

The need to self-identify with God as female, meanwhile, underscores the narcissism of the goddess movement—I am female, therefore God must be female—and an undercurrent that is decidedly anti-male. The feminist concern, not unjustified in fundamentalist communities, by the way, is that male-centered religion grants men permission to dominate women. Whatever the random male funda-mentalist fanatic may believe about woman's place in the world, in this country he doesn't get to beat his wife or have her executed if she "dishonors" him. He can try, but then he goes to jail. And the lit-tle woman, having been awarded free will by her Maker, can walk out whenever she chooses. Such are the fruits of America's tree of knowledge.

Fortunately for goddesses, Western civilization's separation of church and state also allows them to form covens and read chicken entrails, if that's their preference. Most Americans are fairly relaxed when it comes to how others choose to worship, as long as the doxol-ogy doesn't include "Death to the infidels!" No matter what Pat Robertson comes up with to explain intemperate weather or terrorist attacks, no one really worries that Southern Baptists are going to blow up buildings, shouting "Blessed assurance, Jesus is mine!" But lately, goddesses have become a little annoying, as fanatics inevitably do. Where once these gals were quiet fringe-surfers, they have be-come mainstream, thanks to Madison Avenue and Dan Brown. God-dess books abound, as do goddess seminars and vulva support groups. Put three or more women together in the ladies' room and you're likely to hear the word *goddess*. There are goddess pillows and god-dess T-shirts (I own a "Wine Goddess" T-shirt myself). I even went on a goddess hike once with a group of goddesses (I think we were ahead of the curve), who, upon encountering a chain gang of a dozen men with chain saws about two miles up the Appalachian Trail, began praying feverishly that a troop of gods, otherwise known as our husbands, would soon arrive.

The notion that the world had misplaced its sacred feminine self got a secular jolt with Dan Brown's blockbuster novel *The Da Vinci Code*. His story (plot spoiler for those just emerging from comas) was that Jesus and Mary Magdalene married, had a child, and created a bloodline that continues today. The church, evil bastion of patriarchy that it is, conspired through the centuries to conceal this dark secret to preserve the patriarchal order of the church and to keep women in their rightful place of subjugation. I like it. It's a good yarn and the book was a true page-turner, though I was insistently bothered that no one ever ate a meal or took a rest stop during the entire epic-in-a-day. About three-quarters of the way through, I also was beginning to feel seriously played. Whether Brown's story is true, or even truthy, has occupied religious scholars and goddesses ever since.

Debunking Brown has become an industry unto itself, a counter-movement to the goddess movement. Is the alleged John the Apostle really Mary Magdalene sitting to the right of Jesus in Leonardo da Vinci's *The Last Supper*? Or is he just an effeminate, "biblical-era metrosexual," as John J. Miller wrote in *The Wall Street Journal*? Was Mary M. pregnant at the crucifixion? Was Mary really the Holy Grail, and was her daughter really the mother of the Merovingian dynasty of France? Yes, and LBJ shot JFK. And George W. Bush brought down the World Trade Center towers with a remote control device he keeps hidden in a secret box made to look like a child's book called *The Pet Goat*.

Though the blurring of fact and fiction has been problematic for church leaders, *The Da Vinci Code* confirmed what goddesses had believed all along. As one of Brown's characters put it: "Almost everything our fathers taught us about Christ is false."

Those fathers. Always lying.

Brown clearly sensed and capitalized on a tipping point. He merged the secular culture's antipathy toward males (and especially male authority) with the feminist/goddess movement's search for the sacred feminine, tossed them with the current lust for conspiracy theory, and voilà—sixty million copies in more than forty-five languages, a movie, and riches, oh-the-riches. Brown was a god among goddesses. But wait a minute, do goddesses need gods?

The surprise trinket hidden in Brown's crackerjack book is the subtext that women, even those descended of Jesus, need men after all—to help them break codes, to protect them from albino monks, and to ferry them toward their rightful destiny as daughters of God.

Sophie Neveu, the protagonist and descendant of Jesus, was pretty weak for someone whose ancestor could walk on water. Perhaps Brown, rather than being a goddess liberator, is just another patriarchal seducer, a Testaclese disguised as Vagina Dan.

The Holy Grail

The effect of these trends toward honoring women's parts and reclaiming the earth from men has been the creation of a cultural environment in which males can be properly blamed for everything wrong with the world. When college campuses become incubators for anti-male sentiment—and when dissenting opinion is censored and punished—we have sacrificed truth and free speech and surrendered to a totalitarian groupthink that makes us vulnerable to ideologues in their various incarnations.

Once graduated, young men and women will probably come to terms over vaginal tokenism and ice penises. But a generation weaned on male bashing and goddess worship may have difficulty clearing the hurdles ahead as they navigate marriage and family life. Fundamentally, the Holy Grail of goddess feminism is not, alas, the vagina, but the mirror. And the corresponding religion is more properly known as the cult of narcissism. The object of goddess worship is, after all, the worshipper herself. One's own inner goddess. *Moi!* In the absence of a church to call her own, the goddess turns to the temple of her familiar. But as women seek new ways to express their narcissism and invent new matriarchal myths to sustain them, we might remember that for every alluring Georgia O'Keeffe pistil in nature, there is an important-looking stamen nearby.

celebrity sluts and america's ho-down

A crude culture makes a coarse people, and private refinement cannot long survive public excess.

—Theodore Dalrymple, British commentator and psychiatrist

If man was once tortured by the Madonna-Whore conundrum, he has been released. We're all hos now.

No offense to the rock star Madonna, who deserves much credit for raising sluttery to an art form. Ever the iconoclast, Madonna made gazillions strutting around in her lingerie, while the little girls who emulated her got stuck with bad boyfriends and a drawer full of faded undies. At least those who still wear them. Thanks to misguided celebritarts Britney Spears and Lindsay Lohan, panties are officially passé. Both babes revealed their inner sanctums to gazing bystanders—eight-year-olds in Lohan's case, as she strutted her stuff at the 2006 Kids' Choice Awards. Lohan's presentation was a moon to Spears's sun, which one hopes will soon set.

Poor guys. It's little wonder boys and young men are confused by

constantly shifting and conflicting signals about how they should behave toward the lovelier sex. Torpedoed by cultural messages that are
relentlessly sexual, by pole-dancing moms and prostitots decked in
baby hookerware, they are nonetheless expected to treat females
as ladies. Except don't call them "ladies," which is insultingly patriarchal. Depending on a woman's mood, a male is expected to know
exactly when to respond to her wiles by issuing a devastating compliment; or when to pretend he hasn't so much as noticed her strategi-
cally plunging décolletage. Above all, he must be sensitive to her
vulnerabilities—except when she's feeling empowered. The deal is
basically this, fellas: Females can flaunt their foliage when, where,
and how they choose, and you males have to be psychics to respond
appropriately.

The rise of America's slut culture would seem, on the one hand, a
boon to males, whose legendary attraction to visual stimulation has
rarely been so eagerly indulged. On the other hand, the sight of so
much flesh from coffee through cocktails must be discombobulating,
especially to young males who report being perpetually aroused.
Such males may be forgiven if they're not sure when greeted by a
comely lass whether to grab a sword or a sheath—of the latex variety.
Or perhaps a shield. To walk down any street in almost any town or
city today is to be taunted by a parade of approaching midriffs featuring pierced navels and retreating "tramp stamps"—tattoos that rise
like bait from too tight, low-riding britches.

A casual glance along America's urban sidewalks today confirms
that age is no obstacle to ho culture. Older women no longer see a
leather miniskirt and ask themselves, "Am I too old for this?" Nor
does it seem that it's ever too early to start little girls thinking about
sex and teaching them to dress the part. Edgy four-year-olds can opt
for T-shirts that say "Future Porn Star" or "I Faked It." Budding
tartlettes can find bustiers, stilettos, and "pleather" pants in toy stores,
as well as itsy-bitsy lingerie sets of lacy panties and bras. Bratz
"bralettes"—bras for those who don't need them—come in thirty dif-

ferent styles, including padded ones for girls not quite ready for implants. In 2003, girls ages thirteen to seventeen spent more than $157 million on thong underwear. Wedgies R Us.

Little girls in training to drive boys wild can practice with hooker dolls. Bratz Babyz features baby dolls dressed in leather and lingerie, while Mattel offers "My Bling Bling" dolls—Madison, Chelsea, Barbie, and Nolee. Statuesque and glitter-lipped, the bling girls are essentially streetwalkers. Tall and leggy, they wear knee-high boots, bustiers, and miniskirts and deck themselves in bling: the big jewelry, flashy cars, and ho chic glamorized by gangsta rap and being sold to middle-class tots who can play ho at home until they're old enough to hit the streets. Accessories include a purse, makeup, cell phone, and a small compact I can't quite identify. Perhaps a fancy condom case? Or maybe a discreet container for an evening's stash of coke.

Those tired of playing with dolls can play the real thing with Halloween Pimp 'n' Ho costumes. Brands on Sale, a California-based company, began selling Pimp 'n' Ho costumes for kids in 2003, taking advantage of a trend that has become a cottage industry. It's just a costume, of course, and little trick-or-treaters don't even know what "pimp" means, but the grown-ups who shell out $40 to $60 for a costume do. Doubtless it's adorable when a little girl dressed like a ho knocks on a stranger's door: *Trick or treat! Got candy?*

Although kiddie ho costumes and baby "porn star" T-shirts probably don't pose a threat to the Oshkosh franchise, the "joke" is part of a larger trend in which children are being sexualized at ever-younger ages. More curious than an infant girl wearing a shirt declaring that she faked it are the mothers who participate in their children's sexualization. Somehow I don't think many dads are pimping their baby girls as orgasm fakers. As a rule, dads don't do the shopping for little tyke wardrobes. Why would a twenty-first-century mother in a post-postfeminist world enable the marketing of her daughter as a sex kitten? The explanation may in part be simple ignorance or lack of awareness. Dress-up is fun, and little girls in grown-up garb are adorable. JonBenét Ramsey was never cuter than when she batted those mascaraed lashes and cut her Lolita eyes at the judges.

On the other hand, we might find clues to the sexualization of girls in the success of Randy Blacker, a businessman in Fresno, California, who sells the "Lil' Mynx Dance Pole"—a portable prop for pole dancing at home. Girls tend to imitate moms, and moms are busy doing their own thing these days. Apparently, women weary from the nine-to-five drill like to relax by faking intimacy with an inanimate pillar that never goes limp. What was once the domain of bad women in dark places is now the realm of good women in search of their inner slut. At fitness clubs and gyms, women show up for class in lacy tops and barely-there bottoms with garters stretched around legs strapped into four-inch stacked boots. A quick online review of some of these exercises in self-awareness exhausts the cringe reflex. For women too embarrassed to bump and grind in front of others, there's a robust selection of DVDs and videos for an at-home workout. All promise that exotic dancing will help women find their "inner beauty and grace."

For the budding teen stripper, there's the Peekaboo Pole Dancing Kit, including an instructional DVD with sexy dance moves. The kit also teaches how to pick a "Peekaname" (the indispensable stripper nickname), how to set the scene, what to wear—all designed to unleash one's repressed lap-dancing diva. The Peekaboo brand also offers a lap-dancing kit, a tickle ring, and a pole dancer game. From Candy Land to Pole Dancing. Is it any wonder that attentive parents want to lock their girls in a tower and hide their sons?

The trend of scant clads has been a marvel to behold to those of us weaned on Hepburn & Hepburn in the Age of Absolutely Not. That's what parents used to say when a girl wanted to wear makeup to school, or ditch her white socks and shave her legs too soon, or wear a too-short skirt. In less than a generation, girls went from sitting with their ankles crossed demurely to displaying their wares with the pride of a first grader showing off a new tooth. By the turn of the millennium, America was populated by a generation of girls whose knees had never met, even casually.

Women and girls pretending to be strippers 'n' hos may be a sign that all remaining obstacles to personal expression have been eliminated, but I'm not sure this is where feminism intended to go. Yes, early pro-sex feminists such as Germaine Greer once insisted that sexual liberation was critical to women's broader liberation and fulfillment. But even she acknowledged in her later works that the sexual revolution was a lie. It never happened. "Permissiveness happened, and that's no better than repressiveness, because women are still being manipulated by men," she told *The New York Times* in a 1984 interview following the publication of *Sex and Destiny*.

"Today's society is preoccupied by sex to a point where it dominates our culture. Women act as if sex is a social duty. They don't even know if they want it or not, but everyone's doing it, so they do it too."

She hadn't seen nothin' yet.

My chief disagreement with Greer's assessment would be that women, if they are manipulated by men, are having their share of the fun without taking any of the responsibility. Among the many conflicting messages men must process in their social interactions with women is that women who play ho are not necessarily inviting sexual attention. "Look but don't touch" has never been more rigidly enforced or more confusing. The usual signals to men that a woman is sexually available have been redefined. Strutting her stuff is a woman's prerogative—even to the extent of showing up at the office in what amounts to a teddy—while men aren't supposed to notice.

There's nothing inherently wrong with cleavage—most women covet and most men admire it—but the idea that guys aren't going to notice or be aroused is delusional. Yet to glance where the eye, against all reason, isn't supposed to wander—or to comment "Hey, nice blouse!"—is tantamount to professional suicide in some cubicles. Men aren't crazy to wonder why it's sexual harassment to compliment a woman's appearance, which she clearly hoped you'd notice, but it's not sexual harassment to wear provocative clothes that get men's minds off their business. Once women sexually objectify themselves, it becomes harder to insist that others not.

Raunchier than Thou

Being a slut isn't just fashionable these days, it's practically mandatory. Yale student Katherine Hill wrote about her Halloween travails in the *Yale Herald* in 2003: "My biggest problem is that I'm a college girl, which means that any costume I come up with has to be slutty, skimpy, or otherwise sexually provocative—which basically rules out all of the mu-mus and bridesmaid gowns the Salvation Army has to offer. 'You could be a witch,' my friend Brady told me the other day when I whined to him about my lack of options. 'But you're in college. So you have to be a slutty witch. Or you could be a nurse. But you're in college. So you have to be a slutty nurse.'"

Women may choose to present themselves promiscuously these days, but even so, we're not supposed to call them "sluts" anymore—a central canon of feminist orthodoxy. There's even a body of work now dedicated to slut culture and slut etiquette—"sluttiquette"—the operating tenet of which goes something like this: Just because a gal *acts* slutty doesn't mean she *is* slutty. Maybe this is what we get for raising children the pyschologically sensitive way, by which parents never tell their children they're *bad;* they're just *acting bad.*

But aren't we what we do?

If guys need reference material to help them navigate the boundaries of sluttiquette, we've got books. In *Slut!: Growing Up Female with a Bad Reputation,* Leora Tanenbaum explains why being a slut is acceptable, while calling someone a slut is not. One is a choice, which is to say a sacrament; the other is ad hominem, unfair, and not nice. Other books of the genre—*Fast Girls: Teenage Tribes and the Myth of the Slut,* by Emily White, and *Manifesta: Young Women, Feminism, and the Future,* by Jennifer Baumgardner and Amy Richards—more or less argue that girls are as entitled as boys to enjoy carnal pleasures without risking reputation. As a female of the species, I hear their

point and share their pique. The double standard has been annoying since the beginning of time. But as a mother of sons, I've got
bad news. It's not going to change—ever. Easy girls (note I did not
say sluts) are fun for a night or a weekend—and many if not
most men will gladly enjoy what's offered—but such lasses usually
won't be invited home for Mom's takeout. And guys being guys will
use the s-word behind women's backs as soon as they're out of hearing range.

No one, apparently, mentioned these unhappy truths to the star-
lets of *Girls Gone Wild*, video productions in which inebriated young
women bare their breasts—and sometimes other features—for
smirking guys with cameras. Entrepreneur Joe Francis was just
twenty-four with a degree in business administration when he recognized a bonanza in filming drunk girls willing to expose themselves
and created a $100 million empire.

Some girls just flashed; others played girl-on-girl; still others
found their way back to the RV and a casting couch. Their spring
break shenanigans are memorialized for all time—just $9.95 a tape.
For their trouble, the gals got a hangover and a cheap souvenir. What
a deal. Not all Francis fillies woke up filled with remorse. But the
night is young. Maybe someday a bridesmaid will whip out a video at
the star's rehearsal dinner. Or maybe someday her son's pals will enjoy
viewing "Mom" in her younger days. Boys already have a term for
that particular interest—MILFs, or "mothers I'd like to f——." Nice
work we've done.

Except for potential future embarrassment, no one has suffered
any real damage for their filmed escapades, argue fans of *Girls Gone
Wild*. Nobody made them do it, and the girls featured in the films allegedly signed consent forms. Even if true—and no matter how we
rationalize this silliness—nothing much has changed when women
reduce themselves to sex objects in exchange for T-shirts and trinkets.
It's difficult to make the case that women are gaining ground by exercising sexual autonomy when they're essentially allowing themselves to be used. How did women get so off message? And how are

young men supposed to view women in such a hypersexualized, self-denigrating climate?

It's no wonder that guys view our daughters as two parts "t" and one part "a" after a no-holds-barred week at the beach during spring break. Sure, titillation is fun, but raising pigs was never the goal of any mother I know. The explosion in women's overt sexuality, however, has fed the modern male's perception that women are sexually insatiable and men have simply responded in kind. The downside for women is that, thanks to those who choose a path of exhibitionism and promiscuity, no woman gets treated like a lady.

Eeeny-Meeny-Miney-Ho

Males may be further confused by media trends that seem to suggest women are never happier than when they're pleasing men. The media have helped de-stigmatize the sex professions by their prominent coverage of what otherwise would be published in the yellow pages. Strippers and porn stars regularly make the covers of reputable magazine and newspaper sections, giving the impression that these professional gals are just like any other. We might privately think that stripping is a base profession, but the mainstreaming of the nasty arts has contributed to a blurring of the lines between what is healthy and appropriate and what is dangerous and sleazy. Media outlets may be tapping into the twin human appetites of exhibitionism and voyeurism to sell papers and airtime, but the everydayness of these features may help convince a rising generation that there's no reason not to strip for men's pleasure as long as there's lucre in the transaction.

In 2004, a *New York Times* story on a Vegas stripper named Trixie featured this breathless headline: A LIFE AS A LIVE! NUDE! GIRL! HAS A FEW STRINGS ATTACHED. Trixie is from a small midwestern town—aren't they all?—and stands six-feet-three in her seven-inch heels. She boasts fake blond hair, fake lashes, fake green eyes, a fake tan, and fake breasts. Despite suffering "stripper foot" from those skyscraper shoes, Trixie is happy—and we're supposed to care. More to the point, we celebrate stripping as we might any other career path, just another day in the life of a gal on her way up. Or down, depending on the price.

Stripping does come with considerable perks, including book contracts, so that a literary-minded girl might see the pole as a shortcut to the publishing house. The stripper/porn star memoir has become the newest publishing genre—chick lit in a plain brown wrapper, bodice rippers for the literal-minded. In the first five years of the new millennium, porn stars Jenna Jameson, Traci Lords, and Christy Canon all wrote about their lives of self-discovery under the hot lights. In 2006, two other memoirs hit the shelves: Sarah Katherine Lewis's *Indecent: How I Make It and Fake It as a Girl for Hire* (Seal, 2006) and Diablo Cody's *Candy Girl: A Year in the Life of an Unlikely Stripper* (Gotham, 2006).

Women's stripping for men's pleasure is hardly the stuff of novel or scandal. It's an old routine. Today's enlightened strippers see themselves as empowered—taking back their sexuality and using it to their own ends. But the dirty little secret is that what many of these performers share is an intense antipathy toward men, whom they find repulsive. Stripping for them is an act of revenge. Men may not care what motivates women to display themselves, and strippers may not care what men think of them. In a way, the strip joint is the coldest war theater in the battle of the sexes. An unnatural, sexually charged détente hangs by a G-string, thanks to the hulky bouncer, but hostility bubbles just beneath the surface of the exhibitionist's studied smile and the voyeur's appreciative leer.

By eroticizing her disgust toward men, the feminist stripper finds pleasure in her audience's pathetic vulnerability. In this setting, at least, she has all the power, while he is reduced to impotent bystander. Everyone may be getting just what he or she wants. She gets revenge money; he gets visual pleasure. But undergirding the transaction is palpable hostility and a tease to violence. The popular culture's embrace and glamorization of a seedy business that dehumanizes its participants while coarsening the broader environment surely undermines the humanity we hope for in our children.

Do I think strippers and their admirers should be punished? No, I think adults should be able to participate in activities of their choosing as long as they do no harm. But if we think that the commercialization of women's bodies and the mainstreaming of human objectification are harmless, we aren't thinking very hard. Inevitably, what we accept into the culture via books, magazines, movies, radio, television programs, and now Internet entertainment trickles down into the parlor and down the hall into the nursery. What was once kept from children is now on America's coffee tables and on our iPods. It should surprise no one that children thus exposed long-term might have trouble relating to others in any but superficial and self-gratifying ways.

Men won't be clamoring to my door for further insights into these matters, I am fairly certain. And gals making hard cash for shedding and sharing their wares won't be grateful for my concern. Thus I leave these affairs to others' sorting with two questions: When you bring your baby girl home from the hospital, will you hope with all your heart that she grows up to be a stripper? Will you look into your infant son's face and think, Damnation, I hope that boy can find a stripper with a nice rack to pimp someday?

The Porning of America

The mainstreaming of pornography is no longer a concern, but a reality. Once the world of lowlifes, back alleys, and organized crime, pornography has morphed into a family business where anybody can be a star. Internet porn sites are loaded with amateurs posting their own pictures on dot-com sites such as YouPorn and PornoTube for strangers who pay nothing and get what they came for. The user-generating, free porn industry has become so popular that the $12 billion adult entertainment industry is suffering a financial crunch. YouPorn, which began in September 2006, boasted fifteen million unique visitors a day by May 2007 and was growing at a rate of 37.5 percent per month, according to *Portfolio* magazine. (A unique visitor is a statistical measure meaning each visitor to a website is counted only once in a given time frame, even though each may visit several times.)

While teenagers and grandmothers busy themselves with videocams, *Playboy*'s website offers "Naughty Amateur Home Videos" and has a casting call for "hotties." Its "Amateur Spotlight" focuses on "Women of Wal-Mart"—their prices are low, but their sex appeal is high. Porn is for everyone! In a celebrity profile of comedian Kathy Griffin, *Entertainment Weekly* asked questions about tattoos, favorite divas, and the best way to gain thirty pounds for a movie role. The final question was fill in the blank: "My porn name is . . ."

What? You don't have one? (Hint: Combine your first pet's name with the street you lived on as a child. That would make me Gigi Shipp.)

If men aren't sufficiently confused by women's conflicting messages of ladylike ho, then America's pornaffair must leave them spinning. On one level, they know that porn isn't right. Sex is the ultimate intimacy, and voyeurism, until recently, wasn't something of which many were proud. Now, voyeurism is a group activity enjoyed with popcorn. The wrinkle in the satin sheets is that women, though some may also enjoy porn, don't really want their men to think of them with pornographic ways or to compare them with the "stars" in porn videos. Yet at the same time, being a good feminist means feigning solidarity with porn stars, who must be viewed as consummating the ultimate feminist expression—exercising autonomy over their bodies and profiting from men's desire rather than merely being objectified by it.

Pro-sex feminists like the eminently sensible Wendy McElroy, author, columnist, and Web mistress of ifeminists.com, argues that porn is good for women. In her book *XXX: A Woman's Right to Pornography,* McElroy notes that porn provides sexual information and therapy for women, some of whom reach adulthood without learning how to pleasure themselves. (And this would be because they're . . . imagination-challenged?)

Once again, freedom of choice includes the freedom to choose unwisely. Which is fine. Just don't expect men to join in arguing forcefully that women who perform as porn stars are desirable after the first, oh, ten or twelve minutes. Or however long it takes. Bulletin: In 2005, *Time* magazine found that porn films—which constitute two-thirds of the films rented by hotel guests—were viewed an average of twelve minutes. Just a tidbit between appetizer and entrée for those dinner parties that just can't seem to lift off.

Porn is so pervasive as to be almost inescapable. It is also nearly impossible to nail down accurate figures for usage and profits. In 1998, there were 28,000 X-rated websites, generating about $925 million. Three years later, the number of websites had exploded to 280,000. Every day, 260 new porn sites go online. In 2005, *Time* put U.S. porn sales at $20 billion annually. Suffice it to say, sex really does sell.

Whether pornography is a legitimate choice for the few remaining women who are not in law school en route to becoming television legal analysts is less compelling than the more important question: Is porn harmful? Today's research on the effects of pornography suggests that our oversexed culture is having a devastating effect on relationships. A 2000 MSNBC.com survey found that nearly 80 percent of porn consumers were spending so much time on the Internet that they were risking their jobs and their relationships. Al Cooper, a sex therapist at the San Jose Marital Services and the survey's author, said that most of those people had no sex addiction problems before discovering cybersex.

While it's easy to imagine the harm that might come to women as a result of a pornified world—beginning with the increasingly prevalent view that women are usable, discardable objects—little concern is focused on men. Certainly men, who constitute 72 percent of online porn viewers in the United States, by and large don't seem to feel they need to be saved from porn. But what of our male children? What kind of world are we presenting to them? Boys today are marinating in pornography, and soon they'll be hooking up with our daughters. In 2001, the Pew Internet and American Life Project found that 15 percent of boys ages twelve to seventeen—and 25 percent of boys fifteen to seventeen—had accessed adult sites by faking their ages. The actual numbers are likely much higher, given the amount of porn spam that finds its way into in-boxes. If the rising generation of young men has trouble viewing the opposite sex as anything but an object for sexual gratification, we can't pretend not to understand why.

But it's just sex, we keep hearing. What's the big deal? If ever there were a word that should never be paired with "just," it's "sex." That's like saying, "Oh, it's just enriched uranium." Enriched uranium can be used to produce electricity that keeps a city's lights burning. Or it can be used to build bombs that extinguish light for the foreseeable future. Sex has been known to start wars and shape history. If it were "just sex," we wouldn't use it to sell everything from car wax to hamburgers. Thus, before we can sanely evaluate where porn leads us, we should probably acknowledge that it's not just sex.

My O's Better than Your O

Women's liberation may have made women more accessible as sexual partners, but it also made them more threatening to men, wrote Christopher Lasch in *The Culture of Narcissism*. The perception of women's sexual insatiability was first advanced in popular culture by the Masters and Johnson report on female sexuality, which highlighted women's superior ability to have multiple orgasms while Superman over there was napping. "Sexual 'performance' thus becomes another weapon in the war between men and women; social inhibitions no longer prevent women from exploiting the tactical advantage which the current obsession with sexual measurement has given them," wrote Lasch.

Or, as the hero of Joseph Heller's *Something Happened,* Bob Slocum, put it: "I'm sorry they ever found out they could have orgasms, too."

Women's orgasmic superiority may yet prevail, but the playing field otherwise has been leveled by the advent of a little blue miracle pill named Viagra and various offspring. And guess who's taking it? Not just middle-aged and elderly men, but college men, who increasingly are reporting sexual dysfunction and performance problems. A 2006 study at Northwestern University, the first of its kind, found that 13 percent of young men had experienced ED (erectile dysfunction), and 6 percent said they had used ED medication.

College counselors confirm that ED, never a problem fifteen years ago, is a frequent complaint. Keith Brodie, former chairman of the Department of Psychiatry at Duke University, told *The Washington Post* that he hears ED complaints from as many as a quarter of the students he counsels. Others quoted in the story report similarly rising rates, including one urology professor who tells his students that 30 percent of his patients with ED are under age thirty.

There could be several explanations for the rising incidence of impotence among young males, including alcohol, drugs, stress, and generally poor health. Many arrive at college on antidepressants or antianxiety medications that tamp down sex drive and inhibit normal responses. But researchers don't discount the sexual aggressiveness of young women and the effects of massive doses of pornography as potential contributing factors. One female college student told the *Post*: "I know lots of girls for whom nothing is off-limits. The pressure on the guys is a huge deal."

Robin Sawyer, who teaches human sexuality at the University of Maryland, told the *Post* that he had spoken with a young man who hadn't been physically aroused in more than two years. "He was 20 years old, good-looking," said Sawyer. "I told him once he was in a relationship, things would get better. He said he could never get to the relationship because when he went out with a woman, she wanted to have sex almost immediately. He never got comfortable enough to tell them he had a problem [with that], so he stopped dating."

Women's sexual assertiveness may be an advance for women in some ways, but for guys "it has come at a price," said Sawyer.

"It's turned into ED in men you normally wouldn't think would have ED."

Indeed, emerging research seems to suggest a correlation between female sexual assertiveness and pornography in our culture and a decrease in young men's libido. Clinical experiments show that men who look at porn are much more likely to have ill-timed hallelujahs and sexual dysfunction, says Dr. Mary Anne Layden, co-director of the University of Pennsylvania's Sexual Trauma and Psychopathology Program at the Center for Cognitive Therapy. The result of so much overt, graphic sexuality is that men are desensitized and become sexually less potent.

"It could be that looking at pornography diminishes the ability to perform with a real woman." Layden told me. "Porn is a one-way street, focused only on what you want without needing to take into account what the other is feeling or wanting. You have the ability to click and click until you find exactly the image that will stimulate you at the moment. It takes harder kinds of images to stimulate you over time as tolerance develops. All of this makes for problems with performance with real women."

Men accustomed to a visual relationship with a woman who always says "yes" and for whom orgasm requires nothing more than a zap in the microwave are going to have problems with a live woman, who operates more like a Crock Pot. Other research has found that men who watch a lot of porn, viewing women as insatiable and men as hypermasculine, begin to lose touch with reality as well as their ability to have a real relationship. In her book *Pornified,* Pamela Paul quotes porn researcher Dolf Zillmann: "The massive exposure of men to portrayals of women as sex-crazy creatures who move from partner to partner is thought to make women seem unworthy of attention and care in an enduring relationship." To put it bluntly, real women are boring compared with porn actresses.

Porn is also highly addictive, according to Layden's research, though some disagree with her findings. In one University of Pennsylvania study, brain scans of men watching porn were compared with brain scans of drug addicts who were watching people consume cocaine. The same parts of the brain were bright with activity and to the exact degree, says Layden. One difference between coke addicts and porn addicts is that the porn addicts are harder to treat, says Layden. For one thing, you can't detox a porn addict the way you can a drug addict. The images are in the brain forever. Porn addicts are also more likely to relapse.

Not surprisingly, given the saturation and availability of porn, the number of sex addicts is escalating. Does this matter? Only if you think antisocial behavior is undesirable. Porn, says Layden, is the best delivery system we could design to produce toxic behavior. It's free; it's available 24/7; and it's piped into our homes. Men who become sex addicts also suffer a higher rate of substance abuse and suicide. Some 40 percent lose their spouses, and 59 percent suffer financial reversals. About 27 percent either lose their jobs or are demoted, and as many as 40 percent lose their professions because of excessive porn use.

Of perhaps greater concern, Layden's own research shows that extended exposure to porn causes disturbing shifts in perception among both men and women. In one study, men were shown imagery of sex and violence in rape videos. Later in the study, they asked the men to arouse themselves without touching, and the men reported using rape and torture images to get an erection. Thus, says Layden, we've trained men to get erections from images of rape.

Not all porn is violent, of course, so there's no reason to assume that all men who watch porn will then find gratification in violent imagery—or that they will act violently in a sexual relationship. But the experiment demonstrates that imagery does have an effect on the brain and that violent porn, where it exists, does have the effect of sexualizing violence.

Of much greater concern is the effect of porn on boys, whose sexual templating comes increasingly from pornography. We tell boys that their self-esteem is tied to the amount and kind of sex they have—the more the better. All of us, male and female, come into the world hardwired to want to think, "I'm enough," as Layden puts it.

Our culture tells boys and girls that the factors leading to that feeling of "I'm enough" are more sex, better sex, more flesh, bigger breasts. Porn stars shave their bodies; boys and girls in high school shave theirs. Boys see porn stars with large breasts; girls get breast implants. Since 1998, as the porn industry has exploded, the number of breast implants has increased 700 percent.

"We've sent them [women] the message that you have to have breasts that are never meant to be on a person with a thin frame," says Layden. "That's now normalized because all the porn stars have fake breasts. Everybody wants to be 'enough,' but you never get enough of what you don't need."

Meanwhile, college men using Viagra to cover for loss of sexual power report a lack of self-esteem because they're not up to the Olympian task of all-sex-all-the-time. They are similarly insecure about their bodies, as not every fellow is qualified to be a porn star. If they've watched a lot of porn, they've also witnessed a whole lotta hotamighty. Male porn stars now routinely take Viagra to enhance their performance, which has been a brutal development for porn actresses. (I have to say, I never really wanted to know this much about porn, but it's impossible to talk about relationships between men and women today without also talking about porn.)

Absent from all these discussions of sexual mechanics is any mention of our humanity—that intangible thing that can't be measured or compared, implanted or chemically infused. The victory of Technos over Eros is a recipe for the elevated levels of depression and anxiety we see among young men and women. And hookups—one-night sexual encounters devoid of intimacy or the promise of a relationship—are the complete antithesis of human connection. The despair that passeth all understanding is waking up in bed with a stranger who doesn't even know—or care enough to ask—one's last name.

That orgasm doesn't take you very far. Eventually, people learn that life is not a pubic triangle. Once sex is free of all considerations except what pleasure it brings in that moment, then what? Well, we're nothing but beasts. Theodore Dalrymple puts it this way: "It is precisely the envelopment of sex (and all other natural functions) with an aura of deeper meaning that makes man human and distinguishes him from the rest of animate nature. To remove that meaning, to reduce sex to biology . . . is to return man to a level of primitive behavior of which we have no record in human history. All animals have sex, but only man makes love. When sex is deprived of the meaning with which only the social conventions, religious taboos, and personal restraints so despised by sexual revolutionaries . . . can infuse it, all that is left is the ceaseless—and ultimately boring and meaningless—search for the transcendent orgasm."

The hookup culture prevalent on college campuses—and even in high schools and middle schools—has institutionalized what amounts to animal behavior and produced fresh vocabulary to accommodate new ways of relating: "friends with benefits" and "booty call." FWB I get, but "booty call"? I had to ask a young friend, who explained: "Oh, that's when a guy calls you up and just needs you to come over and have sex with him and then go home." Why, I asked, would a girl do such a thing? Why would she service a man for nothing—no relationship, no affection, no emotional intimacy? She pointed out that, well, they *are* friends. With *benefits*! But *no obligations*! Cool. When I persisted in demanding an answer to "why," she finally shrugged and said, "I have no idea. It's dumb." Here's a bumper sticker to put the skids on hooking up: "Friends don't let friends have sex with people who don't care about them."

Guys have no idea why a girl would do that, either, but they're not complaining—even if they're not enjoying themselves that much, either. In researching her book *Unhooked,* Laura Sessions Stepp of *The Washington Post* found that males ultimately find hooking up unsatisfying, but they are unlikely to decline a freebie, slower to recognize the problem, and less able or willing to articulate the nagging feeling that this—whatever-it-is—isn't quite right. For both male and female, hooking up has become almost a rite of passage for incoming freshmen and then a habit before anyone bothers to ask themselves whether they're having fun yet. "What comes as a surprise to some young people who hook up is that hookups, like relationships, can cause pain," says Stepp.

It's All Ball Bearings Now

Hookup sex, besides being emotionally unrewarding, can become physically boring. Once sex is stripped of meaning, it becomes merely a mechanical exercise. Since the hookup generation is also the porn generation, many have taken their performance cues from porn flicks that are anything but sensual or caring. What little I've seen reminds me mostly of a construction site in Dubai—lots of big cranes and loud pounding, but not much to warm a human heart.

The biggest problem for both sexes—beyond the epidemic of sexually transmitted disease—is that hooking up is essentially an adversarial enterprise that pits men and women against each other, as Stepp points out. Some young women, now fully as sexually aggressive as men, have taken "liberation" to another level by acting as bad as the worst guy. Stepp told a story at a 2007 panel discussion on campus sex about Nicole and James. After they hooked up, Nicole jumped out of bed and said, "See ya." When James asked where she was going, Nicole said she was returning to her dorm because "I got what I came for."

Where does this revenge spirit come from among young women who never had spent a nanosecond in Betty Friedan's angst-filled kitchen? Perhaps Nicole learned her moves from a male George Washington University student Stepp also ran across, who carried a condom in his wallet with a little piece of paper that read "Toss the bitches." So we're all enemies now, and where does that get us? If everybody is out to get theirs and to hell with the rest, then we can't expect much in a family way for the next generation. Nevertheless, most young people say they expect to marry someday. Among American high school seniors, 82 percent of girls and 70 percent of boys say that "having a good marriage and family life" is "extremely important" to them. These percentages are slightly higher than in the late

1970s. As these kids hit college and the marketplace, however, and begin enjoying the benefits without obligation of hooking up and shacking up, the call of commitment gets lost in a din of iniquity.

No one reading this book thinks that casual sex is a new development, but the world today is a far more dangerous place for the sexually adventurous than it was a generation ago. In the past twenty years, the United States has seen an explosion of STDs—more than two dozen varieties—some of which are incurable viruses that are also potentially life-threatening. Meanwhile, we know from centuries of experience that "slutty" behavior from women will never evoke gallantry from the opposite sex. It has ever been that girls set the standards for behavior, not only for themselves but for boys. Carol Platt Liebau, Harvard law grad and author of *Prude,* says that when girls begin behaving more coarsely, so, too, do boys.

"And now, because so many young girls have been told that it's 'empowering' to pursue boys aggressively, there's no longer any need for boys to 'woo' girls—or even to commit to a date," she wrote me in an e-mail. "The girls are available (in every sense of the word) and the boys know it."

Young women might be surprised to learn that their male counterparts are often as insecure about their bodies as they are—and far more concerned about sexual performance. Sexually aggressive women are a terrifying attraction that insecure men often view as something to conquer. This is primitive terrain here and nothing to play with. It is possible that the recent increase in sexual assault is related to our sexually aggressive culture? Arguments once advanced that a more relaxed sexual environment would lead to a decrease in sexual assault have regrettably been proven false. Despite our best efforts to pretend sex doesn't matter, we seem unable to evict jealousy, possessiveness, and other complicated emotions from the house of humankind. Dr. Miriam Grossman, a UCLA psychiatrist and the author of *Unprotected,* has treated thousands of young men and women who suffer a range of physical and emotional problems related to casual sex, which she blames on sex education of recent years that treats sex as though it were divorced from emotional attachment and as if men and women were the same. She asserts that "there are a lot more victims of the hookup culture than of violence [date rape]."

Men, meanwhile, have feelings, too. Although they're less comfortable sorting through them—and generally won't if no one insists—I've listened to enough of them to know that our hyper-sexualized world has left many feeling limp and vacant. Our cultural assumption that men only want sex has been as damaging to them as to the women they target. Here's how a recent college graduate summed it up to me: "Hooking up is great, but at some point you get tired of everything meaning nothing."

Thoughtful mothers don't raise their sons to be sexual predators or to treat women as receptacles for male aggression. So how do we reconcile the world of porn they're bound to encounter with the image of the young ladies we hope they'll meet and marry? To millions of mothers of sons, the commodification of sex through porn and the objectification of women is a tragedy for men as much as for women. Layden makes a profound statement about the effect of porn on men when she says that porn is essentially hate speech about men.

"The sex industry spreads the myth that male sexuality is viciously narcissistic, predatory and out of control. It is not just strippers who come to think of all men as sexual 'pond-scum.' This myth about men makes it difficult for women to give men the trust and respect that they are due and damages the image that men have of themselves and of male sexuality."

To Layden's words, I would add these e-mailed comments from a friend and mother of sons:

"I just think men's great possibility for nobility, self-sacrifice, and greatness is reduced when their whole focus becomes their penis. Some men literally never recover and become addicted to the sensation. I can almost see it in men's eyes, and I feel so sorry for their poverty. I'm not naive and realize that men would laugh out loud, but I think women's vision of what a boy can be actually shapes what he becomes. I just love men so much and think so highly of them and am not so cynical. I remember a friend of mine, who is so masculine and handsome, saying that he was with a group of guys flirting with a young woman around 20. They were clearly lusting over her and he wanted to take off his jacket and make sure she got home safely. The difference between 'just men' and a gentleman."

Man to Man

My friend was right when she said men would laugh at her concern—or any suggestion that men need to be saved from pornography. Who wants that job? Far be it from me to concern myself with the nation's erectile function. Thus I defer to a man—University of Texas at Austin journalism professor Robert Jensen—who began studying pornography in the late 1980s. Somebody had to do it. Jensen, who admits to having been a casual porn user as a younger man, was interested primarily in First Amendment issues related to pornography but became a feminist in the process of his research.

Once he began watching as a feminist anthropologist—viewing porn actresses as human beings instead of objects—Jensen's former pleasure turned to grief and revelation: When men objectify women, he realized, they also objectify themselves. They "check out" and turn off the emotional reactions typically connected to sex with a real person. What is sacrificed in the process is their humanity. The trick, he says, is to get people to see porn honestly and, even tougher, to see themselves honestly: "How do you persuade people that a rich and decent life involves more than delivering an orgasm in an efficient manner?"

The tipping point for Jensen came when he attended a porn industry convention in Las Vegas as part of a documentary project. After spending a full day bombarded by constantly streaming video, surrounded by sex toys, porn practitioners, and purveyors, he told his colleague, "I need a drink." They went to a bar, ordered, and sat down to talk. When they tried to articulate what they had experienced, Jensen began to weep. He has written and spoken about that moment when, he says, he was simply overwhelmed by the "concentrated inhumanity of the pornographic world," which he says reduced women to "three holes and two hands."

It's not that he had seen or heard anything new. It wasn't as though he had experienced an epiphany about the meaning of pornography. "It's just that in that moment, the reality of the industry, of the products the industry produces, and the way in which they are used—it all came crashing down on me," says Jensen.

"My defenses were inadequate to combat a simple fact: The pornographers have won. . . . The pornographers not only are thriving, but are more mainstream and normalized than ever. They can fill up a Las Vegas convention center, with the dominant culture paying no more attention than it would to the annual boat show. And as the industry has become more normalized, paradoxically, the content of their films becomes ever crueler and more overtly degrading to women. The industry talk is dominated by talk of how to push it even further. Make it nastier. Make it, in the terms of one industry observer, 'brutal and real.' That's the way the pornographers and the customers like it: Brutal. Because brutal is real. And real sells. It is real and that's at the heart of the sadness."

Jensen's tears weren't only for the women, but also for himself as a man trapped in a world that offers fewer places to walk and breathe that haven't been colonized and pornographized. Most men who use porn aren't students of the genre or the industry and may figure that a little porn here and there surely doesn't hurt anybody. But Jensen's sights are set on our humanity, a little bit of which he says is surrendered each time a woman is reduced to her sexual parts and a man is coaxed to orgasm by her visual dismemberment. Although porn practitioners and defenders contest that participation in the industry is a matter of choice, Jensen is unmoved by the argument. He prefers to shift the question from why women perform in pornography to why men choose to masturbate to pornography. Speaking at a porn conference in March 2007, Jensen asked the quintessential question: "What does that choice that a man makes to masturbate to pornography mean for women, and what does it mean for the man?"

He makes two arguments: First, when men buy porn, they're contributing to the subordination of women in the sexual exploitation industry and they're robbing themselves of being fully human. Second, though women may choose to be porn stars, their decision may be influenced by factors that make that choice pathetic rather than liberating, says Jensen. If a woman who has been sexually abused acts out that abuse in front of a camera for men's pleasure, then that can't be a choice that any decent person would applaud. It may be true that some women choose porn for other reasons—they find pleasure in exhibitionism, for instance—but consumers have no way of knowing which kind of actress they're watching. Therefore, says Jensen, the consumer "likely is using a woman whose choice to perform was not meaningfully free."

To every "yes, but," Jensen has a logical response. Yes, but: What if men did have access to information about the actresses and knew that the ones they like best are happy porn stars? "So long as the industry is profitable and a large number of women are needed to make such films, it is certain that some number of those women will be choosing under conditions that render the concept of 'free choice' virtually meaningless," Jensen says. His argument continues logically: By buying porn, men are creating greater demand for porn, which leads to a greater demand for women, which leads to a greater statistical probability that some women will be hurt, either psychologically, physically, or both. The question of porn, then, is a moral question—not about sex, but about humanity.

Even casual consumers, when pressed, will admit to some hesitation that all is harmless. Jensen told me he interviewed two young men, both university students, for a documentary about porn and young men. He asked when was the last time they had masturbated to porn. Both said it had been only a couple of days. He asked how long it took for them to reach the finish line. One said six minutes; the other guessed twelve. When one of the students protested to say there's nothing wrong with porn, the other said, "Oh, come on, admit it. Every time we do this, we know there's something f——d up about it. You're turning a woman into an object."

Says Jensen: "When they're finished, they know that something fundamentally inhuman was happening. When I was young and using porn, I was aware of it, too; I just couldn't articulate it. Eventually you realize that when you've turned a woman into an object, you've turned yourself into an object, too."

Walker Percy, the physician/philosopher/author who was right about everything and way ahead of his time, wondered about another aspect of porn: the gradual devaluing that leads inevitably to boredom. In *Lost in the Cosmos: The Last Self-Help Book,* Percy poses the ultimate existential problem. After all the disappointments most people experience with school, work, politics, and social life, what's left to amuse? Sex. But what if sex through overexposure becomes banal and ordinary? Then what?

"Suppose the erotic is the last and best recourse of the stranded self and suppose then that, through the sexual revolution, recreational sex becomes available to all ages and all classes. What if then even the erotic becomes devalued?" Percy asks. ". . . What then? Does the self simply diminish, subside into apathy like laboratory animals deprived of sensory stimulation? Or does the demoniac spirit of the self, frustrated by the failure of Eros, turn in the end to the cold fury of Saturn?"

Percy is the asker, not the answerer, though he does propose a possibility: that when sex becomes disappointing, humankind may turn to violence. And then what? It would seem we are aiming to find out. As adults become desensitized and lower the bar for what is acceptable in the broader culture—and as pornographers seek to push the envelope to become more real and more brutal—children are inevitably in danger. For what comes after the sexualized torture of a woman? Children are the final taboo. As of 2001, some one hundred thousand websites offered child porn, according to the U.S. Customs Service. And it's not just dirty old men watching. In a study of university networks, Palisade Systems found searches for child porn at 230 colleges.

Children are also abused by the porn industry—and by neglectful parents—when they are inadvertently exposed to porn in the home. In 2003, Barna Research Group found that thirty-nine million American homes receive adult channels in scrambled form and estimate that twenty-nine million children are potentially exposed to pornographic images. Sexual imagery is otherwise a mainstay of the American childhood. Focus on the Family reported in 2005 that 83 percent of programming most frequently watched by adolescents contains some sexual content, while the average teenager watches television three to four hours per day.

Little wonder that they're rough and ready by the time puberty hits, if not before.

———

Like most casual visitors to the planet, I am prepared to ignore what adults do in their spare time as long as it hurts no one else. But I'm no longer convinced that porn is harmless, especially as it flows into the homes and into the lives of children at younger and younger ages. It seems inevitable that our ritualized objectification of human beings—and the commodifying of sex independent of meaning—leads incrementally and inevitably to a corrosion of human spirit, characterized not least by a loss of empathy. For empathy is what's missing when we become sexually aroused by watching a woman being brutalized by men.

Ultimately, what our oversexualized, pornified culture reveals is that we think very little of our male family members. The reason the sex industry is seen as liberating to women is that it mocks men. Even prostitution is viewed by some as a way to screw men—without kissing, of course. Men may not care. Everybody's getting what he or she wants. Or are they? A dirty dance of mutual contempt ultimately can't be very satisfying. Undergirding the culture feminism has helped craft, meanwhile, is a presumption that men are without honor and integrity. What we offer men is cheap, dirty, sleazy, manipulative sensation. What we expect from them is boorish, simian behavior that ratifies the anti-male sentiment that runs through the culture.

Surely our boys—and our girls—deserve better.

sex, lies, and bunker blunders

There is an ideological commitment to the notion that any differences occurring between males and females represent a failure of society to create equal and perfect opportunities for everyone so that the sexes will end up the same. This is a mindless concept.

—Lionel Tiger, Charles Darwin Professor of Anthropology, Rutgers University

In Irving Berlin's 1946 musical, *Annie Get Your Gun,* Annie Oakley gives Frank Butler a piece of her mind and a peek at man's future, singing:

> *Anything you can do, I can do better.*
> *I can do anything better than you.*

Men, drop your bayonets and grab your familiars.

I wasn't around when Annie got her gun, but I remember Doris Day's rendition of the song in the sixties. She and Robert Goulet were background music to the American childhood then, and most of us believed the message. While mothers were reeling from Betty

Friedan's revelation that they were miserable in suburbia, daughters were absorbing the idea that they could do anything boys could do. This was largely true—and still is—until puberty. Something happens when estrogen and testosterone make their entrances, and denying that fact will get more men and women killed than all the IEDs in Baghdad.

Nowhere is the assault on manhood and masculinity more explicit—or more dangerous—than in the American military, where the minimizing of men isn't just metaphoric, but potentially deadly. The military is the Maginot Line in the battle of the sexes, the final remaining bastion of institutionalized masculinity and the last place left in the civilized world where characteristically male traits—aggression, risk taking, courage, and strength—are respected and valued.

They still *are* valued in combat but are otherwise viewed as obstacles to some feminists bent on military advancement. Since women can't be more like men—bigger, stronger, fiercer, and roiling with testosterone—the radical feminist approach has been to minimize the importance of the defining characteristics of masculinity, while whittling away at the historical and cultural understanding that war is principally a man's endeavor, notwithstanding the Amazon myth so beloved by aspiring Xena warriors.

What has been presented as a matter of women's rights, meanwhile, distorts the purpose of the military. What we are sacrificing in the push to satisfy civilian goals of absolute equality is the reality of what it takes to prevail against real enemies in war and to save real lives. We have allowed ourselves to enter a pretend world where what is false is true—and we have turned a blind eye to the consequences in the name of equality.

The fundamental falsehood that increasingly drives military policy and that begs urgent correction is that women and men are interchangeable and equally qualified in all areas of military service. We know this isn't true as a matter of observation and common sense, but it has become easier to pretend otherwise—or simply to avert our gaze from the hippopotamus in the powder room. To suggest that women don't belong in combat these days is to risk being labeled a misogynist throwback and invite assault from the PC police. But there are objective reasons to keep women off the front lines and the sexes apart in basic training and other areas. The first reason is physical, and the rest have to do with male traits and behavioral differences that are rooted in our genetic makeup.

This is not to say that women have no place in the military. They clearly do. But the focus in recent years has been to remove all barriers to full equality—even if it's only pretend equality—and put women in direct combat, not to be confused with "in harm's way." Everyone in the armed forces is in harm's way to varying degrees, but direct combat has a specific meaning. Direct-combat ground troops are trained to engage—and attack—the enemy with deliberate offensive action and with a high probability of face-to-face contact. Although women already serve in combat aviation and aboard warships, thanks to the Clinton administration, they are still prohibited from serving in direct ground combat. But recently, efforts to remove that final barrier have gained traction as women have served honorably alongside men in Iraq and Afghanistan. Because there are no clear combat boundaries in Iraq—and because women in forward support companies have been collocated with combat battalions (against regulations)—they have faced some of the same dangers as combat soldiers.

One might be tempted to suggest that this is an abuse of women, who, given their documented physical inferiority, do not have an equal opportunity to survive. Now, there's a feminist point of view worth defending. Instead, we're supposed to infer that, given equal exposure, women are equal to men in their ability to fight back. Women may well be equal to men in courage, dedication, patriotism, and all the other values we hope for and admire in a soldier, sailor, or marine. And they may make excellent pilots and sharpshooters, as women have proved in various environments. But none of these qualities and skills makes them equal to men in the abilities required to engage an enemy on the ground.

Nevertheless, the push for women in combat is stronger than ever. In one of the more curious developments in gender history, some radical feminists and opinion writers have stopped just short of celebrating the fact that more American women have been killed, wounded, or captured in Iraq than in any previous war. When Army Specialist Shoshana Johnson, the thirty-year-old single mother of a two-year-old daughter, was held prisoner along with several male comrades, for instance, *The New York Times* wrote an editorial harkening her capture as another chip in the glass ceiling and a "reminder of how the American military had evolved." Through some sleight of mind, women dying has been construed as evidence of women's qualifications for combat. The thinking seems to be that if they're already in combat situations—if they're already dying and being wounded—any argument against their being included in ground troops is just so much rhetoric. By that logic, children may as well be allowed to play in the streets, since so many of them are getting hit by cars anyway.

News stories from the "front lines" consistently quote women soldiers who believe that rules blocking them from combat are outdated by reality. Lieutenant Colonel Cheri Provancha, commander of a Stryker Brigade support battalion in Mosul, for instance, told *The Washington Post* in 2005: "The Army has to understand the regulation that says women can't be placed in direct fire situations is archaic and not attainable. . . . This war has proven that we need to revisit the policy, because they [women] are out there doing it. . . . We are embedded with the enemy."

"We live and work with the infantry," said Major Mary Prophit, forty-two, head of a four-person civil affairs team with a Stryker battalion in Mosul. "Women in combat is no longer an argument. There is no rear area."

Provancha's and Prophit's points of view are understandable if being in combat means getting hit, but, again, that's not what it means. We don't so much need to reexamine the policy of women in combat as we need to enforce the policies we have. Men who have been in direct combat, engaging the enemy as opposed to driving past a roadside bomb, know the difference, but increasingly few are comfortable talking openly. More to the point, putting women in and near combat requires a denial of sex differences that could put both men and women at greater risk. Women are at greater risk because they have a diminished capacity for survival, and men because having to fight alongside fellow comrades who aren't equal to the task increases the likelihood that they'll be killed. To insist that men pretend women are their equals, meanwhile, only engenders disrespect and resentment. One's life is too much to risk for civilian social policies that have no place in the military.

Don't Hate the Messenger

It is admittedly unsavory to discuss the appropriateness of women in combat when they are currently engaged and at risk. It is also nearly impossible to get anyone to talk honestly on the record. Challenging the feminist orthodoxy is a career-ender if you're in the military and free speech is effectively a prisoner of war. Off the record, men (and many women) mince no words in saying that women in combat-related functions of the armed services have damaged military effectiveness. At the same time, they often express admiration for women's courage and tenacity.

Even if some women are exceptional warriors—and some are— the only relevant question should be: Does having women in combat improve our national security and defense? This question was answered definitively in the negative in the 1992 report from the Presidential Commission on the Assignment of Women in the Armed Forces, which convened to investigate the legal, military, and societal

implications of putting women in combat. Following months of research, fact-finding trips, hearings, and interviews with scores of people knowledgeable in history, war, physiology, psychology, family,
and culture, commissioners voted to keep the combat exemption in
place for close ground combat, combat aviation, amphibious ships,
and submarines.

But irony has a knack for timing. The very day that the commission voted on its report, Bill Clinton was elected president. That, as
they say, was that. Shortly thereafter, Secretary of Defense Les Aspin
ordered the services to allow women to compete for assignments in
combat aircraft, and the navy developed a proposal to repeal the combat exclusion law and allow women on combat ships. Next the army
opened combat military occupation specialties that previously had
been available only to men. You can see where things were going and
who was holding the rudder. Assistant Secretary of the Navy Barbara
Pope summed it up: "We are in the process of weeding out the white
male norm. We are about changing the culture."

Well, at least we've defined our terms. Getting rid of the white
male norm is more important to a certain strain of feminist, both
male and female, than are the findings of a presidential commission,
not to mention centuries of accrued wisdom. Equality over sanity
seems to be the operative mandate these days, and we've seen the consequences. Her name is Jessica Lynch.

Just a Country Girl

Lynch, the lithe nineteen-year-old from Palestine, West Virginia,
who wound up in an Iraqi hospital, battered and broken, was never
the hero the American media wanted her to be but was instead a victim of a politically correct system that betrays women and endangers
men. Through no fault of her own, Lynch was born into a culture
saturated with fictionalized superwomen, and the story that girls
were heroes, too. Sheroes, they call them.

Although her story is generally known, a close inspection of the details reveals how minimizing males is crucial to creating the illusion of gender equality. And while I have no wish to criticize Lynch—she deserves our respect and gratitude—her story is instructive and provides a window into our cultural and military attitudes as they have evolved during the past thirty years or so. Even though real male heroes emerged the day of Lynch's ordeal, they were largely ignored so that the girl from Palestine could be elevated and the image of woman-warrior burnished. Faster than Dan Rather could say "courage," Lynch was transformed from a petite gal who wanted to be a kindergarten teacher and loved the cute baby contest at the Wirt County Fair back home into an icon of feminist lore.

The truth was something else. First, Lynch was never supposed to be exposed to combat. She was part of the 507th Maintenance Company, a convoy of thirty-three vehicles filled with cooks, clerks, and mechanics, including her boyfriend, Ruben, who promised to take care of her. On the fourth day of the war, Lynch's company was traveling from Kuwait to Baghdad when about a dozen trucks fell behind and inexplicably got off course. Suddenly, Lynch and her convoy were smack-dab in the middle of a hostile city where Iraqi militia opened fire with AK-47s and rocket launchers. Piece by piece, they picked off the convoy. Driving trucks that couldn't move faster than forty miles per hour—or that bogged or broke down in the sand—the soldiers were sitting ducks. When Lynch tried to "lock and load" her weapon on command, it jammed. "Chaos," was the way she described it later.

"They were killing us," she said.

Indeed.

The Humvee in which Lynch rode was driven by her best friend, Private First Class Lori Ann Piestewa, a twenty-three-year-old Hopi mother of two young children. While the men in the vehicle returned fire, Lynch sat with her arms wrapped around her shoulders, her head lowered to her knees, eyes closed, according to her own account.

Though Piestewa drove like a demon, she couldn't get them to safety before a rocket-propelled grenade caused her to veer into a jack-knifed American tractor-trailer. Lynch and Piestewa were apparently knocked unconscious; the three men in the Humvee were killed.

What reality doesn't render, fantasy provides. Thus, early reports ricocheting around the globe told the story of a heroic young woman— "Girl Rambo"—alone in the sand, firing into the enemy until she ran out of ammo, taking shrapnel and bullets in a last stand of machisma. One version even had her pulling a knife. The image was irresistible, confirming everything we wanted to believe about can-do girls. We just *knew* it was true. Our girl Jessica could do anything a man could do, and apparently, she could do it even better.

Except it wasn't so.

There *was* a lone blond soldier who made a courageous last stand. Army Sergeant Donald Walters was caught fifteen miles behind enemy lines in Nasiriyah and resisted for as long as he could before being captured and later murdered, according to military author Richard S. Lowry in his book *Marines in the Garden of Eden*. Lowry surmises that Walters was the subject of an intercepted Iraqi radio report that described a blond soldier fighting alone against a relentless enemy.

Another hero that day, who probably helped save Lynch's life, was Private First Class Patrick Miller. You may not have caught his name because a guy hero doesn't have the crowd appeal of a shero, though Miller did get to tell his story to Mike Wallace on *60 Minutes* after the story of Lynch's ordeal had been clarified. Miller, twenty-three at the time of his unexpected call to heroism, was in the last truck of the convoy behind Lynch's and arrived on the scene shortly after the crash. He and his two companions— Sergeant James Riley and Private Brandon Sloan—began taking bullets, one of which fatally wounded Sloan in the forehead. When another bullet knocked out the transmission, Miller and Riley made a run for it.

Meanwhile, taking refuge behind the tractor-trailer were Army Specialists Shoshana Johnson and Edgar Hernandez. Johnson yelled for Miller to take cover, but he had another idea. Since all their vehicles were useless, he thought he might steal an Iraqi dump truck parked nearby. Did he think the keys would be inside? Wallace asked. Nah, Miller said, but he figured he could hot-wire it.

"Where did you learn to hot-wire?" Wallace asked.

"I'd have learned really fast," Miller deadpanned.

As he approached the truck, however, Miller found a surprise—a nest of Iraqis preparing to fire mortars at the Americans. Miller took a dive behind a sand berm twenty-five yards away and counted the enemy. Seven to one were not good odds—and Miller hadn't fired a rifle in seven months. He wasn't even a very good marksman. A mechanic, he had failed the army's marksmanship test. But human beings are often surprised by what they can do when seven enemy combatants are trying desperately to kill them, and Miller rose to the occasion.

When an Iraqi stood up to load a mortar, the firing of which likely would have caused a massive explosion upon contact with the tractor-trailer's fuel tanks, Miller aimed and fired. To his great surprise and relief, the Iraqi "fell over." Then Miller's weapon jammed. After each shot, he had to clear the jammed cartridge and pound the forward assist on his rifle to fire the next round. He developed a rhythm between shots by counting approximately how long it took the next Iraqi to stand up and begin reloading the mortar. At each count, Miller would clear the malfunction and pound the forward assist on his weapon, rise, aim, and fire. Each time he did it, another Iraqi fell. Finally, he counted, stood, and aimed—and no one was there.

The "lousy" marksman from Kansas had single-handedly wiped out seven enemy combatants. Then more Iraqis appeared, and all of them—he, Riley, Johnson, and Hernandez—were taken prisoner. Not until their release twenty-one days later did Miller and the others learn that Lynch was alive and had become a worldwide phenomenon. Miller, belatedly, was recognized for his heroism and awarded a Silver Star for valor. He did not, however, receive a million-dollar book deal, as Lynch did.

The girl-warrior version of events, as it turned out, was based on rumor, incomplete information, and, possibly, wishful thinking. It was just the sort of script the media, military, and feminists craved, validating everything they kinda-sorta believed about girls doing everything boys can do better. Besides, a man blazing away until death is hardly news in wartime. But a skinny little girl from West Virginia, now that's showtime! It's a 90-point headline, a made-for-TV movie, the stuff of hometown parades, book contracts, and poster girldom: *Girls rule, dude!*

Except they didn't.

Piestewa and Lynch barely survived the crash, and only Lynch survived the war. Piestewa, the first female soldier killed in Iraq, perished and was found buried in a shallow grave near the hospital where Lynch was taken for treatment of multiple injuries, including several shattered bones that may have been caused by her captors. Medical reports show that she also had been anally raped, probably during a three-to-four-hour period between the crash and Lynch's delivery to a civilian hospital.

When she woke, Lynch's first words were an unmanly "Don't hurt me." Her first feelings were of desolation and loneliness, as she later described the experience to writer Rick Bragg. She said she cried. Nobody blames Lynch for crying. Real men cry, too. Besides, what sane person wouldn't weep upon finding herself broken and alone in Saddam Hussein General Hospital? Why not just have a flat tire at the Bates Motel? She was a long way from West Virginia, her baby sister, and her mama's lap. I'd cry, too. But the moral of the story is that this girl had no business being anywhere near a war in the first place. That our military depends on young women as ill-equipped for war as a Jessica Lynch—lovely, decent, and well-intentioned though she may have been—is a mockery of national defense and an insult to men like Miller and Walters, who have to pretend that female soldiers are their equals in battle.

Such intentional self-deception should be considered an act of criminal negligence. Instead, we praise Lynch as a hero and pretend that Irving Berlin was a sociological seer rather than a comedic composer. But for the horror of it all, sending a nineteen-year-old girl into a desert populated by enemy militia would be a comedy.

Obviously, not all female troops are like Lynch. Women certainly have distinguished themselves in extreme circumstances and been awarded medals for valor and heroism. Women like Major L. Tammy Duckworth, who lost both legs after a rocket-propelled grenade hit the Black Hawk helicopter she was co-piloting—and who subsequently was appointed director of the Illinois Department of Veterans Affairs—make all Americans proud. On the other hand, if anyone daresay it, does the fact that Duckworth can be injured as badly as any man justify putting women in situations that might result in their being at the mercy of other men? What if Duckworth had also been captured, raped, and tortured? Men suffer these same horrors, to be sure, but the insult is of another order when a woman is being brutalized by men. Rape, either of a man or a woman, is horrible on multiple levels, but there *is* a difference. Throughout history, men have used the rape of women as a weapon of mass destruction and as a form of genocide. Recent history provides a case study in the rape camps of Sarajevo, Bosnia-Herzegovina, of the 1990s, where Muslim women were systematically raped. History doesn't provide comparable examples of the rape of men, probably because sodomy doesn't hold the same appeal nor produce the same practical result from the genocidal perspective. While a man raping another man may be exercising power to produce pain and the ultimate humiliation, a man raping a woman potentially establishes new genetic territory, while also confiscating and commandeering the life-giving power of the victim. On the most primitive level, it also emasculates the men who would be the husbands of these women and the fathers of their children. The trickle-down effect of women's rape is significant and enduring. Bosnian "rape babies," those conceived during rape and abandoned by their families, are now reaching adolescence in state-run orphanages. Those women who sought abortion were only partially relieved of the burden of violation. Dilation and curettage may terminate the product of conception, but it can't remove a woman's sense (or her mate's) that a sacred part of her being has been contaminated, not to mention the sheer physical damage to a woman's reproductive organs that can result from such brutality. Mirella, a thirty-three-year-old rape victim interviewed in 2005 by *The Independent*, was raped for more than a year by Serbian soldiers. Even though she had an abortion, she suffers severe gynecological problems, has been diagnosed with depression, and, at the time of her interview, had attempted suicide three times.

The truth is that as a culture and as individuals, we view the capture of women differently from that of men, as was the case with Lynch and Johnson. The world was riveted not because they were held hostage, but because they were *women* held hostage.

Curiously, it was the false story of Lynch's heroism that prompted proud calls for an end to the combat exclusion for women. I hasten to repeat that none of this was Lynch's fault. She didn't ask to be a heroine and humbly said so several times. She was a class act when she came home, ruing adoration but politely playing along to the minimum extent necessary. Who do you know who would decline a million bucks to tell her story? Hats off, besides, to the girl who, even in the direst conditions, had the presence of mind to convince her Iraqi doctors that they shouldn't amputate one of her legs as they intended. She is strong-willed, but that doesn't make her combat material.

I Saw It in the Movies

The Lynch story, which has reached mythical status and will outlive the girl from Palestine, is more than an anecdote. It is an allegory for the absurdity of executing a gender battle with real people in a real theater of war. But Lynch was also the inevitable offspring in the union of feminist ideology and pop culture. When Jessica Lynch was thirteen, Meg Ryan was kicking Iraqi tush during Operation Desert Storm as a medical evacuation helicopter pilot named Captain Karen Walden in the 1996 film *Courage Under Fire.* Perky Meg, adorable even when she's screaming at the men under her command (talk about a fem fantasy), alas died after her helicopter crashed and before her crew was rescued—but not before she performed a daring rescue of another downed chopper. And not before she heroically held her own crew together as they were falling apart, while holding off a company of Iraqi infantry with an M-16 rifle.

Or did she? In a foreshadowing of what happened with Jessica Lynch, a heroic myth created around Ryan's character begins to un-ravel when Lieutenant Colonel Nathaniel Serling, played by Denzel Washington, investigates the rescue as a prelude to awarding Walden a posthumous Medal of Honor. Through a series of flashbacks, we learn that different folks had different recollections, but no matter. We get the message loud and clear: Women are just as tough as men. Here's Captain Walden after she's been shot in the stomach: "I gave birth to a nine-pound baby, asshole. I think I can handle it." Got that, soldier? You can't even have babies, but women can take lead in the belly and don't need no help from no boy. The film was, alas, just a movie and not much burdened by reality.

Slog forward another year: Jessica Lynch is fourteen years old and Demi Moore is G.I. Jane. *Hoo-yah!* In the movie—which includes a bar scene featuring two gals named Thelma and Louise (get it?) Moore plays Lieutenant Jordan O'Neil, who has hit the glass ceiling in the military because, you guessed it, she's exempt from combat. *No*

agenda there. When crusading senator Lillian DeHaven, chairperson
of the military budget committee, pressures the secretary of the navy
to fully integrate the sexes, he makes an offer he hopes she'll refuse: A
female trainee can try out for the navy SEALs commando force.
O'Neil is given the assignment, in which everyone expects her to fail.
If you're getting bored, that's because G.I. Jane is a cliché before she
does her first one-armed push-up.

Granted, no one looks better bald-headed than Demi Moore, and
she does a sweat-drenched T-shirt fair justice. I don't need to tell you
that she succeeds wildly, exceeding all expectations, while exposing
men as cave dwellers—no offense to the boys at Geico. Here's a sample of the dialogue, for flavor. Note that the male commanding officer is seething with patriarchal resentment, his knuckles practically
bloody and raw from so much dragging on the ground, while O'Neil
is sharp, smart, and snappy. In this exchange, she's complaining to
C.O. Salem about the special training standard that has been set for
her:

> O'NEIL: I mean really, sir, why don't you just issue me a pink pet-
> ticoat to wear around the base?
>
> SALEM: Did you just have a brain fart, Lieutenant?
>
> O'NEIL: Begging your pardon, sir?
>
> SALEM: Did you just waltz in here and bark at your commanding
> officer? Because if you did, I would call that a bona fide brain
> fart, and I resent it when people *fart* inside my office!
>
> O'NEIL: I think you've resented me from the start, sir.
>
> SALEM: What I resent, Lieutenant, is some politician using my
> base as a test tube for her grand social experiment. What I re-
> sent is the sensitivity training that is now mandatory for all of
> my men. The OB-GYN I now have to keep on staff just to
> keep track of your personal Pap smears. But most of all, what
> I resent is your perfume, however subtle, interfering with the
> scent of my fine three-dollar-and-seventy-nine-cent cigar, which

I will put out this instant if the phallic nature of it happens to offend your *goddamn fragile sensibilities*! Does it?

O'NEIL: No, sir.

SALEM: "No, sir, *what*?"

O'NEIL: The shape doesn't bother me. Just the goddamn sweet stench.

Sa-*whish*! That's a wrap and a rim shot in one. America loves the template—from underdog to top dog. And it's so much sweeter when the long-suffering, oppressed sex busts the boys' club. In the most famous scene in the movie, Demi Moore as O'Neil is initiated by an over-the-top head-butting during a simulated POW experience. Her commanding officer rams her head into a post, whereupon O'Neil, hands restrained behind her back, head-butts and kicks the officer. Mighty girl. When O'Neil is knocked to the floor, she gets back up on her feet and, curling the enamel off her clenched teeth, says: "Suck my dick." Hoo. Effing. Rah.

The men (in the movie) love it, of course. The audience applauds. Freud smirks. Later, when O'Neil strolls into a bar, her fellow comrades start chanting: "Suck my dick! Suck my dick! Suck my dick!" Gives you goose bumps, doesn't it?

The same year, *Starship Troopers* hit the big screen, showing a futuristic military where men and women have so successfully shed cultural constraints that they shower together without anyone noticing or reacting to the others' nudity. *Riiiii*ght. This may be science fiction, but it's not far removed from what "progressives" must have hoped for when they installed unisex bathrooms in college dormitories. Once we function as though there are no differences between men and women—not even any need for privacy—then there is no longer any valid argument against interchangeability of the sexes. Perfect equality in a perfectly awful world.

It was into this cultural milieu that Lynch's generation was born. These films were part of the atmosphere, seeping through the vents of the American psyche like an airborne virus. Little girls heard the message everywhere they turned: They could do anything, and in most arenas they could. But not, alas, in the SEAL program, which is still off-limits to women. On the SEALs website is a brief acknowledgment of women's importance to the military, followed by a recommendation that qualified women investigate the diver and explosive ordnance disposal fields in lieu of the navy SEALs.

The SEALs apparently aren't willing to lower their standards and reinvent their elite corps to accommodate women, to fix something that's not broken. Other branches of the military have been more compliant, lowering standards to allow women to fill positions for which they're otherwise not qualified. I realize I may as well tie on a blindfold and smoke my last cigarette, but women are, in fact, not as good as men at war. This is not to diminish Piestewa's or Lynch's bravery, service, or sacrifice, or that of the more than 160,000 women who have served in Iraq and Afghanistan. Women who volunteer for military service deserve every bit as much appreciation and gratitude as men, but that doesn't mean they belong in or near combat. Consent is not capability. Or, as former army chief of staff General Peter Schoomaker was fond of saying when he commanded Delta Force and the Joint Special Operations Command: "Don't confuse enthusiasm with capability."

Patriotism is no substitute for strength, speed, and ferocity. Men are tanked up on testosterone, the hormone that feeds aggression and libido and that spurs men to take risks and compete with one another in ways women rarely do. Men invented war and the hierarchy that makes the military work (and that feminists complain is the architecture of the damnable patriarchy). Physical conflict is in men's DNA in a way it never will be in women's—if we're lucky.

Wrestling with Reality

As a rule, most women are physically weaker than most men—even if Jill Mills can do ten flips of a six-hundred-pound tractor tire and load four kegs on a platform without losing her breath. If Mills's name doesn't ring a bell, you're probably sane. She is a bodybuilder who was training to become the 2002 strongest woman in the world. I found her in an article aimed at ending for all time the notion that men are stronger than women. Even though Mills is certainly a remarkable speciwoman, she is hardly a reasonable marker of the powers of ordinary women or, by extension, how they might perform in the military.

In fact, only 10 percent of women can meet the physical requirements of 75 percent of the jobs in the army. Stephanie Gutmann reported in *The Kinder, Gentler Military* that the average female soldier is about five inches shorter than the male soldier, has half the upper body strength, lower aerobic capacity, and 37 percent less muscle mass. In Iraq, ground combat soldiers carry eighty to one hundred pounds on their backs, yet women have a lighter skeleton, leading to a higher incidence of stress fractures. They also possess the unique ability to become pregnant.

And military women do get pregnant. Between December 1995, when the United States deployed to Bosnia, and July 1996, a woman had to be evacuated for pregnancy about every three days, according to a report in the *Stars and Stripes*. During the Gulf War, the USS *Acadia* and USS *Yellowstone* were referred to as "the love boats" because 31 percent of the sailors on board came home with child. This special circumstance unique to women creates problems beyond the obvious. If equality is our concern, then pregnancy is an unfair advantage to women—either because they can get pregnant to avoid deployment or because they are potentially undeployable, all of which undermines morale and can create resentment. Dr. Anna Simons, an associate professor at the Naval Postgraduate School in Monterey, California, has written what few are brave enough to say:

"No comparable 'disability' renders men non-deployable. Consequently, it becomes virtually impossible to convince men that a woman's gender won't excuse her from duty at some point. . . . All women have to be considered potentially non-deployable for some length of time. The problem this poses is that it flies in the face of why members of a unit intensively train together at all, which is so they grow familiar with one another while perfecting tactics, techniques, and procedures."

This also adds to the conundrum American men face in other areas of modern life. On the one hand, they're told women are equal to them; on the other, they're told women get special privileges because they're women. Well, which is it? Most men are perfectly happy to extend those special privileges to women because pregnancy and other female circumstances create unique challenges for women. But don't try to convince them that those concessions constitute equality.

Physical differences aren't supposed to matter in the gender-neutral world some are so bent on inventing, but they do matter. A soldier who can't pull her weight is a burden to those who can. What else can it mean but that men end up carrying an extra load, taking care of girls they are hardwired to protect, and consequently placing themselves at greater risk of injury—and failure? Never mind the resentment any soldier would feel toward another who can't or won't carry his or her own load. Or who can't pick up a two-hundred-pound wounded man.

Beyond the problems pregnancy presents, military women are also four times more likely to report ill, according to Mackubin Thomas Owens, associate dean of academics and professor of national security affairs at the U.S. Naval War College in Newport, Rhode Island. The percentage of women medically nonavailable at any time is twice that of men. And although a woman may be able to drive a five-ton truck, says Owens, she'll need a man to help change the tire; and though a woman can be assigned to fill an artillery unit, many won't be able to handle the ammunition.

Once again, it's not women's fault that they're smaller and weaker than men. There's no dishonor in that. Nature doesn't hold grudges, but she does discriminate. Apparently, she didn't think women should go mano a mano with men. Let's sue.

Girling Down the Military

The solution to women's physical inferiority was simple enough for feminists intent on integrating the sexes: "gender-norming" standards, which means lowering standards for women so we can pretend that men and women are equal. For example, in the army, men have to be able to toss a grenade thirty-five meters, while women only have to be able to throw one over a concrete wall. Women, unlike men, get a three-minute grace period for the three-mile run, while orientation videos tell female recruits, "It's okay to cry."

It *is?*

Gutmann tells of a young woman in basic training who cries because she's afraid of heights. Her drill sergeant says, "It's okay to be afraid . . . you'll be okay."

"Will you catch me?" she asks before swinging on a rope over a crevice.

"I'm here," he says.

Finally, the drill sergeant, unhappy in his role as nursery school minder, has a meltdown and leaves, saying what we're all thinking: "I'm sick of this." Not all women are weepy and not all men are brave, though I doubt a male recruit would survive a good public cry on the obstacle course. The rationale behind gender norming is that physical strength doesn't really matter, anyway. Technological advances have changed the nature of war such that hand-to-hand combat has been virtually replaced by smart bombs and "information dominance." Patricia Schroeder, the trailblazing feminist congresswoman from Colorado and the first woman to serve on the House Armed Services Committee, once famously said: A woman can push a button just as well as a man.

One word: Fallujah.

In the grisly battle to liberate Fallujah from an insurgent occupation, U.S. Marines and soldiers went house to house, routing out the enemy in hand-to-hand combat. There were thirty-nine thousand buildings in Fallujah. During two weeks of continuous fighting, fifty-one U.S. troops died and another one thousand were wounded. To read accounts of those days is to know that women have no place in combat, even if some women ended up there against policy. There was nothing button pushing about it. Someday we may be able to decimate planets and alien vessels from the sterile comfort of the mother ship's bridge, but for now, we cannot realistically expect to have a military without boots-on-the-ground combat units.

For a taste of what combat is like, one need only read the first five paragraphs of a controversial article Senator James Webb (D-VA) wrote for *Washingtonian* magazine almost thirty years ago. Webb was lamenting the sexual integration of America's service academies and expressing his view that mixing men and women was ruining our nation's combat readiness. He may have tempered his opinions as a Democratic politician, but war hasn't changed. His description of his marine days in Vietnam makes a case that requires no translation:

> We could go for months without bathing, except when we could stand naked among each other next to a village well or in a stream or in the muddy water of a bomb crater. It was nothing to be walking at midnight, laden with packs and weapons and ammunition and supplies, seventy pounds or more of gear, and still be walking when the sun broke over mud-slick paddies that had sucked our boots all night. We carried our own gear and when we took casualties, we carried the weapons of those who had been hit.
>
> When we stopped moving we started digging, furiously throwing out the heavy soil until we had made chest-deep fighting holes. When we needed to make a call of nature we squatted off a trail or straddled a slit trench that had been dug between fighting holes, always by necessity in public view. We became vicious and aggressive and debased and reveled in it, because combat is all of those things and we were surviving.
>
> We killed and bled and suffered and died in a way that Wash-

ington society, which seems to view service in the combat arms as something akin to a commute to the Pentagon, will never comprehend. And our mission, once all the rhetoric was stripped away, was organized mayhem, with emphasis on both words.

None of this is to say that a properly trained woman can't pull a trigger as well as a man or that women aren't as motivated as men to protect their country and their families. If women are threatened on their home turf, their offspring placed at risk, no warrior is more ferocious. When "they" come to our towns and start bombing our Food Lions, killing our children, and burning down our houses, then all hands on deck. War isn't about attitude. It's also not about "sending a message," but about prevailing against the enemy. Here's a message: There's a reason there are no women in the NFL.

Did Not, Did Too!

At the same time we ask men to pretend that women are their soldierly equals, the media have helped construct a myth of equality in terms of service and suffering. For a barometer of how the P.C. winds are blowing any given week, I turn to Dick Wolf, the genius behind the NBC series *Law & Order*. The show is well done, but mainly I'm riveted by the didactic philosopher-cops as they wrestle with the human condition. Each episode is a little morality play through which characters vet current events. In one that caught my attention, a female desk cop has just one arm. When someone glances down at her empty sleeve, she shrugs: "Fallujah."

"Thank you for your service," he replies.

And we do thank her for her service, but the implication was that women were swarming those foul streets right alongside the men. In fact, women were present in Fallujah in a support capacity—and they shouldn't have been. But anyone tuning in to *Law & Order* would surmise that American women and men are equal in combat. Similarly, a 2000 *Detroit News* story about the Vietnam War read in part: "Everyone has their own personal Vietnam. It wasn't just the men and women who traipsed through the Vietnamese jungles, rifles strapped on their shoulders, fear racing through their minds."

No, it wasn't. In the Vietnam War, fifty-eight thousand American men died, compared with eight military women. (Another fifty-nine civilian women were killed, according to the Vietnam Women's Memorial Foundation.) This isn't to diminish the sacrifices of those women, but to read that account, you'd think the rice paddies were swarming with Rambas. In 1998, Peter Jennings reported during a pre–Memorial Day story about the civil war that "more than six hundred thousand men and women died before the war was over." That would be true. But how many of the six hundred thousand were women? About sixty.

Yet you'd think Johnny and Janie were marching off in equal numbers to spill their guts at Gettysburg. Even the film version of C. S. Lewis's *Chronicles of Narnia* was edited so that little girls could see themselves empowered as warrior princesses rather than protected by men. In the original book, *The Lion, the Witch and the Wardrobe,* upon which the movie is based, Lewis was clear in conveying that women have no place in combat. When Father Christmas gives three of the children, Peter, Susan, and Lucy, weapons to fight the White Witch's army, he makes it clear that the girls should not fight. He gives Peter a shield and sword. He gives Susan a bow, a quiver of arrows, and a small ivory horn, saying, "You must use the bow only in great need, for I do not mean you to fight in the battle." To Lucy, he gives a small bottle of healing elixir and a dagger. He tells her, "If you or any of your friends is hurt, a few drops of this will restore them. And the dagger is to defend yourself at great need. For you also are not to be in the battle."

When Lucy wonders why not, she says, "I think—I don't know—but I think I could be brave enough."

To which Father Christmas responds: "That is not the point. . . . Battles are ugly when women fight."

Alas, those words didn't make the cut. What moviegoers heard when they saw the film version of the Lewis classic was: "I hope you don't have to use them, 'cause battles are ugly affairs." Not quite the same sentiment, but more in tune with the times.

This politically correct revisionism obviously betrays Lewis's intent, which was to prefer a world in which women are not forced to participate in the brutality of battle. Not because they are less brave or less committed to cause. Lewis was careful to avoid any such implication. But because women have a higher calling—to give life. They pay a high price and shed blood to give birth, and men throughout history have paid the ultimate price to protect women and children so that there might be another generation. Why we are determined to make a competition out of the best and worst of life is a source of great bafflement.

Soldier Moms

Despite claims to the contrary, we *think* differently about women and men in the military. When fifteen British marines and sailors were taken prisoner and held hostage by Iran in March 2007, the lone woman hostage—Leading Seaman Faye Turney—received special attention from Iranian president Mahmoud Ahmadinejad, who scolded Great Britain for sending the mother of a three-year-old to battle. Just beautiful. A radical Islamist, terror-supporting Holocaust denier whose theocratic state cites women for "bad *hijab*" (not being sufficiently covered up) suddenly casts himself on the world stage as Dr. Phil.

Ahmadinejad turned Turney into his own little propaganda doll. As a woman, Turney was far more useful to Ahmadinejad than the other fourteen sailors and marines in his hold. He wasted no time dressing Turney in a *hijab* and parading her before cameras. At his bidding, she wrote letters of apology, falsely confessing to having trespassed in Iranian waters.

No doubt Turney's willingness to play along was due in part to her fear that her three-year-old would be left motherless. She also risked missing her baby's birthday party. In interviews following her release, Turney admitted that one of her chief concerns when cutting a deal with the Iranians was her daughter. "If I did it [agreed to confess], I feared everyone in Britain would hate me. But I knew it was my one chance of fulfilling a promise to Molly that I'd be home for her birthday on May 8."

Turney's propaganda value is of no small concern in the debate about women in combat. In response to Turney's capture, Major Judith Webb, the first woman to command an all-male field force squadron in the Royal Army, now retired, wrote an article for the *Daily Mail* to voice her opposition to women in combat—a complete turnaround from her own days in service:

"The response of the public to the news that there was a mother of a three-year-old child among the 15 hostages showed that however much we pretend otherwise, we are not capable of viewing a vulnerable female in the same way as her male counterparts. Our reaction to her plight handed the Iranians enormous leverage for pressing home their publicity victory."

The question that popped into Webb's mind was, *What was Turney doing there in the first place?* Turney's own answer in an interview with the *London Telegraph* just before her capture was that though she loved her daughter, she also loved piloting the navy's inflatable speedboats Webb's view from her perspective as a commander, but also as a mother and headmistress of an all-girls school, is that women have no business on the front line.

"It may not be fashionable but it's time that society accepted the simple fact that women are different," she wrote in the *Daily Mail*. "Not, please note, inferior, but different physiologically, mentally and emotionally to men and there are some roles for which we are simply not suited. Yes, we may be capable of incredible mental and physical toughness, but there is no getting away from the fact that we are the more compassionate sex; instinctively more nurturing and lacking the thirst for aggression that drives our male counterparts."

Webb's perspective is a complete shift since her days as a squadron commander. Her change of heart comes from experience. She recalled that while serving in Germany and Cyprus with the First Squadron, Twenty-eighth Signal Regiment, in the 1980s, soldiers were "keen to go to a war zone." The men had joined up to fight and "relished the prospect of a skirmish." The women, by contrast, entertained no such fantasies but merely contended with the possibility that they might be put in danger. She cited a Ministry of Defense report on women in the armed services that found women's "capacity for aggression was generally lower," and they "required more provocation and were more likely to fear consequences of aggressive behavior." All things considered, women sound far saner than men, which invites the question: What kind of person trades sanity for false equality?

Webb also expressed concern for men's behavior around women. Contrary to what some feminists hope for, Webb says that "when a soldier sees a female colleague lying injured, he immediately feels his first duty must be to protect her rather than stick to the military plan."

Man's Best Instincts

We seem not to want to admit that women have a profound effect on most men or that most men might feel inclined to protect women. Women can be charming, and when they are, men also have been known to become recklessly brave in their presence. Even Israel, which briefly put women on the front lines during the 1948 War of Independence, changed its policy thereafter, prohibiting women from combat and most superior military roles. This has begun changing again as feminists pressure for combat roles. As reported anecdotally from the War of Independence, part of the problem with women in combat was that men especially do not want to see their female colleagues tortured or slaughtered. A present-day Israeli soldier, Daniel, corroborated this idea in a recent letter to me: "It's already tough to lose any of your buddies, but to see a girl get killed is just devastating. I don't think morale can survive. I don't think soldiers can continue to function after seeing something like that. We simply like women too much."

Colonel Bob Stewart, a British commander in Bosnia in 1993, says that men put women in a "special" category. When two women died under his command, he was deeply upset and felt "incapable of coherent thought for some time."

Feminists have an answer for that, too. Deprogram the men to not care or think of female soldiers as women. Indeed, the American military has adopted programs aimed at conditioning men to ignore or endure the cries of women being tortured. The U.S. military's SERE (for Survival, Evasion, Resistance, Escape) program involves training to desensitize soldiers to the suffering of their buddies, male and female. Techniques include mock interrogations and simulated torture. One program that included a rape scenario has been discontinued, but female actors still play the "tortured woman in the next room" to help men overcome their caring natures.

Syndicated columnist R. Cort Kirkwood, who served as a staff member on the Presidential Commission on the Assignment of Women in the Armed Forces, perfectly describes what is necessary to make men and women equal in war:

"It will require training men and women to regard the brutalization of women, and a woman's brutalization of others, as normal and acceptable. . . . Successfully integrating women in combat means this: A soldier must ignore the screams of a woman POW being tortured and raped."

Feminists reject such arguments because they smack of honor, chivalry, and patriarchal protectionism. They also argue that rape isn't a concern unique to women, that male prisoners are also brutalized. In theory, that may be so, but it isn't factually true. The 1992 Presidential Commission found no documented cases of male prisoners being sexually abused in Vietnam. Moreover, it's not rational to pretend that men run a risk of being raped equal to women. Kingsley Browne, author of *Co-ed Combat,* poses a question for the sane: "If the enemy held hundreds of thousands of our personnel prisoner, does anyone really believe that female prisoners guarded by men— enemy men at that—are no more likely to be sexually exploited than a group of male prisoners?" If you're having trouble with that one, try this riddle, says Browne: "Imagine a thuggish guard in a POW camp with both male and female sections. He has two options for occupying his spare time. He can beat a male prisoner or rape a female one. Which would he usually choose?"

Even if we were able to accomplish such desensitizing—making women inured to men's brutality and men oblivious to women's suffering—what would we have gained that is worth preserving? What kind of feminism puts women in a position to be brutalized by men?

The issue isn't only women's right to advance militarily through combat, but men's right not to compromise their deepest cultural values. Simply, good men defend women facing physical threat, and good men know it. The contradiction for feminists is obvious, as Kate O'Beirne, also a member of the Presidential Commission, noted in *Women Who Make the World Worse:* "Feminists recognize the vulnerability of women when they are concerned with the plight of women who are victims of domestic abuse. . . . Their position on integrating combat ranks puts them in the position of saying that violence against women is a terrible thing unless it is at the hands of the enemy, in which case it's a welcome tribute to women's equality."

My favorite comment on the subject comes from John Howland, founder of USNA At Large, an Internet discussion group of U.S. Naval Academy alumni, who counters feminist arguments with what he says is a conversation-ending observation: "The day that the social engineers exorcise the last hardwired remnant of protectionist instinct toward women out of the last holdout male on the planet Earth will be the day that human civilization will cease to sexist."

The idea that we can—or should—teach men not to feel special protectiveness toward women is probably a fantasy anyway. The subconscious circuitry that makes men see women differently from other men is not easily undone. The greater curiosity is why we would want to. And if we were successful, what would happen to these men who are oblivious to the suffering of women when they are released back into American society? More horrifying, what happens to society? Elaine Donnelly, president of the Center for Military Readiness, has an answer: "Deliberate exposure of women to combat violence in war is tantamount to acceptance of violence against women in general."

Eros vs. Philia

Now we come to the small problem of jungle fever—or desert fever, as the case may be—and the inevitable complications born of Eros. You simply cannot introduce sex, romance, love, jealousy—and all the other emotions that surface when men and women in their sexual prime are slammed together under extraordinarily stressful circumstances—and reasonably hope for a cohesive military. In fact, if you wanted to sabotage a military unit's prospects for survival, few ideas come to mind that would be more effective than an infusion of fertile young women.

Thanks to Kayla Williams, one needn't theorize on this point. An Iraq war veteran and author of *Love My Rifle More than You,* Williams may have settled for all time the debate about whether men and women belong together in the trenches. A linguist who speaks Arabic, Williams is a spunky writer and a feisty soldier—by her own account. She can roll with the boys, and, again by her own account, she did. A lot. Williams wrote about her time in Iraq not to indict the military, she said, but to show that women in the military aren't all good or all bad, but something in between. She also wanted to make the case that "women are no different from men in their corruptibility. Women are just as competent—and just as incompetent."

That much is surely true. Witness Abu Ghraib, where Lynndie

England demonstrated to the world that America has transcended gender stereotypes. As no one who saw the pictures can forget, she accomplished this by dragging a naked male prisoner on all fours by a leash attached to a collar around his neck and posing jauntily, giving a thumbs-up sign next to a pyramid of naked Iraqi men piled derrieres to the wind to maximize humiliation. If anyone ever doubted that women are as corruptible as men, those doubts have been put to rest. We have film at eleven and YouTube forever. We also can't pretend that women and men together will somehow resist the call of the wild. By Williams's telling, sex was the primary sport in the deserts of Iraq.

If most women aren't equal to men when it comes to the physical challenges of war, many are apparently men's equals in other areas— just as profane, just as raunchy, and just as promiscuous. It is this recognition, perhaps, that prompted Williams to begin her book with one of nonfiction's more memorable leads: "Sometimes, even now, I wake up before dawn and forget I am not a slut."

As Williams reports, a woman in war constantly juggles her roles as both soldier and object of man's desire. Sometimes she wants to be a slut; sometimes she doesn't. And sometimes the guys have a hard time figuring out what the gals want. Imagine that. Remember that just a year or so earlier, many of these guys were in high school, and going through basic training didn't make them any smarter or more sophisticated about women. All they know is, they're at war; they're isolated in the desert; they're lonely and favorably inclined toward sexual release. *And there are women!*

The joke in Iraq went like this: What's the difference between a bitch and a slut? A slut will f—— anyone, a bitch will f—— anyone but you. Roughly translated, says Williams, this means that if you're outgoing and friendly, you're a slut. If you're reserved and professional, you're a bitch. See what I mean? War may be hell, but if you're a woman, it's . . . complicated.

Consequently, women are objectified by their male counterparts, whose eyes are always on "your breasts, your ass—like there is nothing else to watch, no sun, no river, no desert, no mortars at night," writes Williams. Awful, isn't it? Except, no, it's not. The dirty little secret, which Williams tells without shame, is that the women love it. Especially—she said it, not I—the attractiveness-challenged ones. They're called "queens for a year" because even women who never enjoyed male attention in civilian life are viewed admiringly by the lonely, sexually deprived men in their late teens and early twenties who make up much of the military.

This can't be true of all women—and certainly not of officers. But if even some percentage of female recruits feel this way while engaged in a combat zone, it can't be helpful to unit cohesion and military discipline. Williams writes admirably of her own inner struggle as her emotions and intellect duke it out: "Their eyes, their hunger: yes, it's shaming—but they also make you special. I don't like to say it—it cuts you inside—but the attention, the admiration, the *need*: they make you powerful. If you're a woman in the Army, it doesn't matter so much about your looks. What counts is that you are female."

Some women sleep around, Williams tells us: "lots of sex with lots of guys, in sleeping bags, in trucks, in sand, in America, in Iraq. Some women hold themselves back." She has personal knowledge of both, she says. And then, in the bunker buster of sexual politics, she drops the MOAB—mother of all bombs. Despite our best, enlightened designs, human nature prevails.

"And I know about something else," Williams writes. "How these same guys you want to piss on become *your* guys. Another girl enters your tent, and they look at her the way they looked at you, and what drove you crazy with anger suddenly drives you crazy with jealousy. They're yours. F——k, you left your husband to be with them, you walked out on him for them. These guys, they're your husband, they're your father, your brother, your lover—your life."

And not to ruin the movie, but they're also our first-string defense against a ferocious enemy. Whatever Williams's intent, she most succeeds in conveying the clear conclusion that blending the sexes makes for a dangerous brew. Equal corruptibility and equal incompetence are weak arguments to advance her view that our nation is well served by mixing men and women in combat.

Sexually charged environments attract other enemies to the unit—love, jealousy, resentment, recriminations, revenge. These may make for riveting daytime TV, but in the military, they undermine unit cohesion—the bond that men feel toward one another and for which they're willing to risk life and limb. When I asked my brother, who was with the U.S. Marines at Khe Sanh in 1968, what he was fighting for, he said without hesitation: "I was fighting for my fellow marines." When we introduce Eros (romantic love) into an arena based on Philia (brotherly love), we dilute that bond and put everyone at greater risk.

What we don't need as our armed forces march into battle is a brokenhearted gal sobbing into her MRE or a jilted dude ready to turn on a buddy who flirted with his girlfriend. This forced integration of the sexes and its predictable by-product, sexual interaction between male and female soldiers, has led to some draconian steps with the correspondingly absurd result that our military commanders are effectively chaperoning the equivalent of a high school dance. Instead of training warriors, they're forced to contemplate and execute antifraternizing orders to deal with a new set of completely unnecessary problems.

We Hold These Truths to Be Self-Evident

Despite their many contributions, it is clear that women constitute a special class of people when it comes to military matters. Female military careerists who insist combat is necessary for women to reach equity with men in the armed services hierarchy are, perhaps, correct. Commanding combat is the route to the military's highest positions, and women denied combat duty will not be able to compete for those positions in equal numbers. But life is not fair in all arenas and especially not for other enlisted women who do not, in fact, covet combat but whose choices will be eliminated if the combat-hungry few succeed. Once combat is approved for some women, by what standard can other woman decline to serve in combat? Giving women, but not men, a choice would create another level of discrimination and favoritism that would be disastrous to military functioning. Military sociologist Charles Moskos, writing in *The Atlantic Monthly*, points out that all male soldiers can be assigned to combat arms and that "true equality would mean that women soldiers would incur the same liability. . . .

"To allow women but not men the option of entering or not entering the combat arms would—rightly or wrongly—cause immense resentment among male soldiers; in a single stroke it would diminish the status and respect that female soldiers have achieved. To allow both sexes to choose whether or not to go into combat would be the end of an effective military force."

Beware What You Want

Women historically have been excluded from combat for civilized reasons—not because they were deemed unworthy, but because they were deemed *too* worthy to be sacrificed to grisly men from hostile nations. The combat exclusion wasn't an act of sex discrimination, but an act of decency. Civilized nations for centuries have tried to spare women the cruelty of war. Indeed, it was to protect women and children—the precious cargo of mankind's future—that men often went to war.

That we seriously have to debate women's ability to share combat duty with men is an indication of how little sense we have when it comes to the needs and purposes of a military. This is not another golf club that excludes women as members. The military is not a job, and combat is not a workplace. The rules of civil society are N/A—not applicable. Even certain rules of behavior that are protected in the civilian world—free will, free speech, and freedom to consort as you please—are prohibited in the military. Sometime in our century, women may have no recourse but to suit up and fight to the finish. But the goal, meanwhile, should be to avoid that necessity. A civilized

nation does not squander its mothers in foreign fields. Nor does it require its men to pretend that women are their equal in battle and demand that men surrender their best instincts. Not when their lives
depend on it, literally.

Men, who militarily will always be our best defense against other
men, need to be saved from policies that will get more of them killed.
Less tangibly, men need to be saved from becoming the kind of men
such misguided policies inevitably would create. In order to pretend
that women are equal, men first have to deny what they know to be
true. This is the evil of political correctness of which psychiatrist
Theodore Dalrymple speaks. It is evil precisely because it does violence to people's souls by forcing them to say or imply what they do
not believe—communist propaganda writ small. In an online interview with *FrontPage* magazine, Dalrymple explained:

> In my study of communist societies, I came to the conclusion that
> the purpose of communist propaganda was not to persuade or
> convince, nor to inform, but to humiliate; and therefore, the less
> it corresponded to reality the better. When people are forced to
> remain silent when they are being told the most obvious lies, or
> even worse when they are forced to repeat the lies themselves,
> they lose once and for all their sense of probity. To assent to obvi-
> ous lies is to co-operate with evil, and in some small way to be-
> come evil oneself. One's standing to resist anything is thus eroded,
> and even destroyed. A society of emasculated liars is easy to con-
> trol. I think if you examine political correctness, it has the same
> effect and is intended to.

What effect does this intellectual emasculation have on our fighting men? We have perhaps yet to learn. Meanwhile, in order to survive in the midst of less qualified warriors, men also have to repress
or betray every decent intuition governing the behavior of men
toward women that it took centuries to inculcate.

What's more important than perceived fairness, false equality, and the careers of a few women are the metaphysical treasures of humankind, those gifts handed down through generations of toil, sweat, and blood. When women no longer care about children, and men no longer care about women, we will have accomplished what millions of radical jihadists could only dream about: cultural suicide and an unraveling of the civilizing forces that millions of men perished to preserve.

conclusion

Treat people as if they were what they ought to be and you help them to become what they are capable of being.

—Johann Wolfgang von Goethe

This book was harder to write than I had expected for reasons that are probably apparent by now: Everything in it could be restated as an argument for saving females. Given that we are inextricably bound, what is bad for one sex can't defensibly be good for the other.

Even as I sometimes wondered why anyone would want to save males—watching the nightly news makes this a sometimes dubious goal—I was embarrassed by women who are so blinded by ideology that they can't see what is obviously true. Overall, I was happy to highlight the flaws of radical feminism and its damage to both men and women—and especially to children—while recognizing that sensible feminism isn't so much about advancing women as it is about advancing humankind. There's no such thing as a "woman's issue" or a "man's issue." If something is important, it's important to all.

Sensible feminism recognizes that men and women are not the

same, which should go without saying. But then "sensible" is a word that doesn't get much play in the who's up/who's down, either/or world of gender politics. A conservative has to think this way, a liberal the other. We're either pro-life or pro-choice; either pro–traditional family or "progressive." Writer Walker Percy got it right, as usual, when he said we should repent of labels. Once we stake out a position and slap on the bumper sticker, we essentially end the conversation. What is invariably complicated is oversimplified, and rational debate is thwarted.

Women have as much right to their frustration as men have to theirs, but children have a greater right to grow up in a world run by adults. It must be awful to be a teenager in a culture where parents behave as adolescents and there's nothing left to rebel against except oneself. It also can't be much fun growing up in a culture that tells kids nothing matters, that anything goes, that boys are smelly and girls are sluts. Even if some of them sometimes are. Surely there is a way to honor women without dishonoring men. And surely we can restore man's dignity and purpose without submitting to patriarchal rule. Women can respect themselves, recognizing and tempering the power of sexuality without resorting to the *abaya,* burqa, or corset. We can honor the nuclear family—understanding its importance to children and society—without condemning women to domestic hell.

This task won't be easy because we've managed over the past twenty years or so to create a new generation of child-men, perpetual adolescents who see no point in growing up. By indulging every appetite instead of recognizing the importance of self-control and commitment, we've ratified the id. Our society's young men encounter little resistance against continuing to celebrate juvenile pursuits, losing themselves in video games, plotless movies, and mindless, "guy-oriented" TV fare. Men ages 18 to 35 are the largest "gamers," half of whom spend on average two hours and forty-three minutes daily in front of a game console. These developments are in part owing to availability, but also to a culture that demands little and that sees nothing wrong with "whatever." Men are not, after all, priests. Kay S. Hymowitz, a fellow at the Manhattan Institute, writes:

> There's no denying the lesson of today's media marketplace: give young men a choice betweeen serious drama on the one hand, and Victoria's Secret models, battling cyborgs, exploding toilets, and the NFL on the other, and it's the models, cyborgs, toilets, and football by a mile. For whatever reason, adolescence appears to be the young man's default state, proving what anthropologists have discovered in cultures everywhere: it is marriage and children that turn boys into men.

The call to "traditional family values" is, I realize, a reliable buzz killer. Every time I hear it, I'm reminded again of Percy, talking this time about God. Although Percy was a deep Catholic thinker, he was also keenly aware of man's resistance to external conversion. "Every time someone mentions God," he said, "a curtain drops down in my brain." "Traditional family values" has the same effect. Even though I favor the mom 'n' pop model, pious pronouncements from the religious always-Right make me want to pierce my tongue and join a transsexual commune. (Of course, dogmatists on the secular Left who have fashioned new religions from global warming to vegetarianism make me want to drive a Humvee and barbecue a whale.) But traditional values are traditional for a reason. They have survived the passage of time because they work.

That our individual efforts sometimes fall short of perfection is no argument for adjusting society's bar accordingly. Nobody would confuse me with a mathematics wizard, but I've never insisted that math should be made easier so that I can feel better about myself. Although my thesis that men need saving is bolstered in part by arguments that hug the silly side of the human experiment—vagina worship, sperm shopping, and men in skirts—I want to inch out on a short limb here and suggest that these trends are not innocuous. Viewed singly, they may be maddeningly absurd, but cumulatively, they form an anti-male mosaic that says to men and boys: *We don't like you. We don't need you.* The unconvinced need only imagine a comparable culture in which women are demonized as viciously dangerous, while men prescribe ways to eliminate motherhood and construct cultural events around penis worship.

All things considered, American males have been relatively patient, calm, and compliant. Men's willingness to more or less get along may be a function of the complacency that comes with centuries of domination. Or, just maybe, it could be a matter of goodwill born of evolution and cultural decency. What angry feminism seems to forget or ignore is that women's elevated status in American society hasn't only been earned. It hasn't merely been allowed. Women's liberation from cultural restraint has been encouraged, supported, and codified by laws consciously designed primarily by men. By Western men, to be precise.

Women do have enemies in this world, but they are not men of the West. This is a point worth considering as we measure our discontent. Thanks to the events of September 11, 2001, and thereafter, we've been permitted a close-up look at what primitive manhood looks like. Knuckle dragging in our part of the world might mean a cat whistle here and there, a couch potato who doesn't notice the garbage pail spilling over, or a cad who forgets to send flowers on his beloved's birthday. More extreme examples can be found in the domestic violence files, unfortunately. But on the whole, American men and women have accomplished an eviable level of equality under the law by working together. The problems we face require that we gather our senses and regain perspective. I don't mean that we should be beholden to our stateside boys, but we might recognize that we're on the same team. As long as we wage war against each other, we weaken our defenses against other, more serious-minded enemies.

In the larger picture, bringing men and women back together— inviting our sons and daughters to recognize each other as friends and future partners instead of hostile forces to be one-upped and conquered—may save us from self-destruction. Part of our nation's strength has always been a function of its families. Thus, it would seem that restoring the family—not by external means, but through mature recognition and voluntary self-sacrifice—is critical to our survival in these untidy and dangerous times. Toward that end, respecting men and the important contributions they make to children's lives and to society makes more sense than continuously highlighting the strays, deadbeats, dolts, pedophiles, and morons. That there are enough of these to raise concern merely underscores the need for healthy families. My guess is that the bad guys didn't have healthy families, either.

As important as stable families are to the goal of raising well-adjusted children with character, self-discipline, and purpose, families serve another important function: They keep government in its place. This is not a small point, if one we seldom hear about. When we weaken the family unit, we become vulnerable to other forces. Incrementally, government fills the void once occupied by parents. Social services feed, house, and clothe the children of destroyed families, while the Department of Education instructs proper ways of thinking about moral issues. As long as everyone is feeling good, getting their instant gratification at the trough of fast food and free porn, one hardly notices that autonomy is being surrendered to external authorities.

I'm not suggesting that we ignore the needy, only that we not help create more dependent, dysfunctional, emotionally handicapped people by encouraging a culture that devalues and apparently misunderstands the importance of family and family autonomy. In 1920, the English journalist G. K. Chesterton explained why family is, in essence, an anarchist institution against the totalitarian state: "The ideal for which [marriage] stands in the state is liberty. It stands for liberty for the very simple reason ... [that] it is the only ... [institution] that is at once necessary and voluntary. It is the only check on the state that is bound to renew itself as eternally as the state, and more naturally than the state. ... This is the only way in which truth can ever find refuge from public persecution, and the good man survive the bad government."

When you start talking to Americans about family values as a defense against totalitarianism, you risk being dismissed as reactionary. No one seriously worries that Stalin is coming to Schenectady. But the demonizing of men, which has led to the minimizing of fathers, which has contributed to the dissolution of family, is a breathtaking development in modern human history. As it happens, the brand of feminism that insisted equality could be achieved only by women evacuating the home and outsourcing child care found common cause with Communist ideology. Breaking up the family was not incidental but central to that ideology and was one of the main ideas upon which Lenin insisted most strongly. Karl Marx and Friedrich Engels were unsubtle, if also incoherent, when they wrote, "Abolition of the family!" as a central plank of their *Communist Manifesto.*

Between weak families, absent fathers, a culture that sexualizes the innocent, and government bureaucracies that are designed to grow themselves, one doesn't have to be paranoid to envision a time when freedom as we have known it will be compromised beyond recognition. Already free speech has suffered as those who misspeak—who challenge the orthodoxy of the prevailing ism—are silenced. When former Harvard University president Lawrence H. Summers dared suggest that women's lesser accomplishments in math and science might be explained in part by innate differences in the sexes, he was effectively shown the door.

When Dr. Miriam Grossman's book *Unprotected* came out in 2006, she published as "Anonymous" because she feared professional repercussions for reporting that political correctness had so intimidated psychiatric practitioners that their patients—college men and women—were being harmed. Public acclaim gave her the courage she needed to identify herself in the paperback version a year later.

Once free speech goes, all freedoms are in jeopardy. If you can't even suggest without fear of condemnation that women don't belong in battle—or that men aren't defective if they prefer to play golf with guys—then we're on our way to an irrational and uncertain future.

Given the world we've offered the innocent, it shouldn't surprise us when children seek shelter in the clumsy embrace of their fellow inmates or the numbing solace of emotion-blunting drugs. Boys growing up without fathers sometimes turn to gangs in search of the authority and structure they crave. Girls facing a sexually aggressive world without a dad to protect them sometimes turn to man-boys for security and a shoulder. What they get in return is not always the love they seek.

Yet to point out that we've failed children by indulging adult interests at their expense is often to invite the wrath of those women for whom acknowledgment or compromise is tantamount to being locked in a kitchen with Pat Robertson watching *Parent Trap* reruns. Ever lurking in the periphery of the radical feminist subconscious is the specter of an authoritative, abusive father invoking hellfire and brimstone to subjugate his wife and daughters. Rational feminism recognizes that there is a reasonable place where the sexes function together for the benefit of children without requiring women's subservience to men. Most men I know don't have much use for the patriarchy, either, at least not as some power-wielding hierarchical dominion over women and children. They don't want that burden.

As long as men feel marginalized by the women whose favors and approval they seek, as long as they are alienated from their children and treated as criminals by family courts, as long as they are disrespected by a culture that no longer values masculinity tied to honor, and as long as boys are bereft of strong fathers and our young men and women wage sexual war, then we risk cultural suicide.

In the coming years, we will need men who are not confused about their responsibilities to family and country. We need boys who have acquired the virtues of honor, courage, valor, and loyalty. We need women willing to let men be men—and boys be boys. And we need young men and women who will commit and marry and raise children in stable homes. Unprogressive though it sounds, the world in which we live requires no less.

Saving the males—engaging their nobility and recognizing their unique strengths—will ultimately benefit women and children, too. Fewer will live in poverty; fewer boys will fail in schools and wind up in jail; fewer girls will get pregnant or suffer emotional damage from too early sex with uncaring boys. Fewer young men and women will suffer loneliness and loss because they've grown up in a climate of sexual hostility that casts the opposite sex as either villain or victim.

Then again, maybe I'm completely wrong. Maybe males don't need saving and women are never happier or more liberated than when dancing with a stripper pole. Maybe women should man the barricades and men should warm the milk. Maybe boys need to know more about Martha Washington's pickling processes, while girls should spend more time tossing truck tires. Maybe men are not necessary and women can manage just fine without them. Maybe human nature has been nurtured into submission and males and females are completely interchangeable.

But I don't think so.

When women say, "No, honey, you stay in bed. I'll go see what that noise is"—I'll reconsider.

acknowledgments

With deepest gratitude to:

My husband, Woody, who has put up with my not-always-charming temperament during the writing of this book. My father, J. Hal Connor, and my brother, Jack, whose loving instruction included the fine art of not whining. My little sister, Cissy, who always takes my calls. My three sons for all the obvious reasons.

Doug Marlette—dear friend, comrade, and muse—whose conversations largely inspired this book. My agent, Andrew Stuart, for his amazing grasp of ideas and convincing insistence that, absolutely, a seventy-five-page book proposal can be written in a couple of days. All the folks at Random House who understood the need for this book, especially my divine editor Susan Mercandetti, for her clear vision and gentle tugs on the choke collar; Robin Rolewicz, for her superb skill in clearing underbrush and extracting the Ambien from my prose; Abigail Plesser for her affectionate handling of the occasionally dramatic mood swing. The gang at my syndicate, the Washington Post Writers Group: editors Alan Shearer and James Hill, for their patience as I spread myself too thin; Richard Aldacushion, the world's greatest fact-checker; and Karen Greene, for running interference on those special days when not one thing is going right.

All those herein quoted, who allowed me to share their stories or work, especially Christina Hoff Sommers, whose intellectual vigor and courage on the front lines of the gender wars have been an inspiration through the years. Fellow warriors in defense of reason, without whose work mine would have been much harder: Cathy Young, Kate O'Beirne, Elaine Donnelly, Maggie Gallagher, Richard Lowry, Capt. Robert H. Miller.

Ann Corkery, friend and fellow pilgrim, who makes the world a less lonely place. David Thomasson, for words of wisdom and his tackling first drafts. Eve Tushnet and Amanda Carpenter for their gimlet-eyed research. Will Bralick and his brilliant daughters, Shannon Valenzuela and Jenn Bralick, for their compassionate and careful reading. Donna Hull for her humor and exquisite cuisine, both of which nourished me through the Summer of the Broken Leg.

Janis Owens and Ron Rash, old souls and new friends, for reading, talking, and showing the world what great writing looks like. Pat Conroy, artist and writer extraordinaire, for what he knows about the importance of families, fathers, and men. Katharine Walton for listening. And finally, Melinda and Jackson Marlette, wife and son of Kudzu, without whom I wouldn't have known how to begin.

notes

CHAPTER ONE: WOMEN GOOD, MEN BAD

4 **"When girls came into offices"** Heide Seward, "Take Our Daughters to Work Day: Feminism Class for Young Girls?" Concerned Women for America, April 26, 2002.

7 **"As the river of a girl's life"** Carol Gilligan, *Making Connections: The Relational Worlds of Adolescent Girls at Emma Willard School* (Boston: Harvard University Press, 1990).

8 **Christina Hoff Sommers,** resident scholar at the American Enterprise Institute, "Where the Boys Are," AEI Bradley Lecture Series, November 9, 1998.

In her own research, Sommers found that the drowning and disappearing girls of Gilligan's work were creations based on about a hundred interviews of boarding school girls about their feelings as they entered adolescence. Somebody has to say this: Is there a more spoiled, more over-indulged group of individuals than girls at private boarding schools? Not that there's anything wrong with being lucky enough to attend, for example, the Emma Willard School, where Gilligan found her survey subjects. I'm in favor of good genes and good fortune. But is it the least bit possible that being extremely lucky allows one the luxury of wondering why life isn't otherwise perfect in every way? Gilligan herself said in the prologue of her book *Making Connections* that her findings weren't intended to be the "definitive statement" about girls, but that didn't stop the media from inflating her findings into what was widely termed "definitive research."

Definitive research *was* subsequently conducted by Susan Harter at the University of Denver. Harter interviewed about nine hundred male and female students in grades six through twelve, from a variety of economic backgrounds, and concluded: "There is no evidence in our data for a loss of voice among female adolescents." Between a study of one hundred prep school girls and another of nine hundred from a broad spectrum, which do you suppose comes closer to the truth?

9   **A teacher guide**   Merle Froschl, Barbara Sprung, et al., **Quit It!** *A Teacher's Guide on Teasing and Bullying for Use with Students in Grades K–3* (Beltsville, Md.: Gryphon House, Educational Equity Concepts, 1998).

10   **Leonard Sax,** MD, PhD, *Why Gender Matters: What Parents and Teachers Need to Know About the Emerging Science of Sex Differences* (New York: Doubleday, 2005).

11   **Lionel Tiger** author of *The Decline of the Males* (New York: St. Martin's Press, 1999), speaking at the Independent Women's Forum, July 15, 1999.

13   **girls are more successful students**   Peg Tyre, "The Trouble with Boys," *Newsweek,* January 30, 2006.

14   **James Rees** executive director of George Washington's Mount Vernon Estate & Gardens, in an interview, 2005.

15   **Dr. Sandra Stotsky,** *Losing Our Language: How Multicultural Classroom Instruction Is Undermining Our Children's Ability to Read, Write, and Reason* (New York: Simon & Schuster, 1999).

15   **Thirty years ago**   Tyre, "The Trouble with Boys."

Soon after the *Newsweek* story hit newsstands, the gender wars got seriously weird with a new study positing that the alleged boy crisis was trumped up by antifeminists and men's advocates to draw attention to males. The reaction that somehow males might distract attention from females sheds light on how the gender wars are perpetuated. If boys are winning (dollars and attention), then girls are losing. And vice versa. If one is up, the other is necessarily down. Not only does such measuring and comparing defy common sense, it advances a war that no one wins. Reacting to the "boy crisis," researcher Sara Mead of the Education Sector—a relatively new Washington think tank established by Bill and Melinda Gates—analyzed data from the National Assessment of Educational Progress and determined that boys weren't in crisis after all. They were just doing badly compared with girls, who are doing really, really well.

Mead noted that middle- and upper-class white boys were doing mostly fine, while blacks, Hispanics, and the poor (some of whom surely were white) were doing not just badly, but terribly. What we have here, she said, isn't a boy problem, but a class and race problem. Poor minority boys equals a race/class problem. Except that's not exactly true. In separate research, Dr. Judith Kleinfeld, director of the Boys Project and professor of psychology at the University of Alaska at Fairbanks, found that the reading skills even of white boys with college-educated parents were dismally low and that boys within each demographic were doing less well than girls in the same demographic. Using the same report used by Mead, Kleinfeld found that by the end of high school, 23 percent of the white sons of college-educated parents scored "below basic." Among girls from similar backgrounds, the number is 7 percent.

Translated, Kleinfeld says this means that one in four white boys from educated households can't read a newspaper with understanding. Among Hispanic males with college-educated parents, Kleinfeld found that 34 percent scored "below basic"—compared with 19 percent of Hispanic females. That would seem to indicate at least a "boy problem."

Mead's other findings were less than comforting: Only 65 percent of boys who start high school graduate four years later, compared with 72 percent of girls; 42 percent of boys are suspended from school at least once before age seventeen, compared with 24 percent of girls. Elementary school boys are more likely than girls to be held back a year, while high school boys' achievement is declining in most subjects (though it may be improving in math). Those boys doing best are white males, who in greater numbers tend to come from more stable, two-parent homes. Do I hear "Bingo!"?

I realize this is so obvious that you're having to stifle yawns, but it bears mentioning that the poorest families also are those most often without a father present. Given that having no father in the home is the strongest predictor for poverty, isn't it possible that the absence of a father in the home, rather than the absence of wealth, is the reason for the higher incidence of behavioral problems among boys? Don't give yourself a headache over this one. Let's put it this way: Boys who grow up in single-parent homes are twice as likely to commit a crime. If only they had been drugged sooner.

Or *aborted*!

Don't look at me. In their 2005 bestseller, *Freakonomics,* economist Steven D. Levitt and journalist Stephen J. Dubner posited the theory that abortion had caused the crime rate to drop in the United States. They noticed that in the early 1990s, just when the first children born after *Roe v. Wade* were hitting their late teens—when boys hit their criminal prime—the crime rate was beginning to fall. Why? Because all those boys who would have committed crimes were missing. They hadn't been born because they had been aborted. What a cheery thought. Terminate boys before they're born and, voilà, we have fewer crimes and, therefore, a better world.

The authors' thinking went as follows: Because crimes are most often committed by people who have suffered some kind of deprivation, whether social or emotional, then we might also assume that they were not as wanted as other children. Since abortion improves the chances that babies who make the cut are wanted, it stands to reason that crime would go down as abortion rates go up. Wrote the authors:

"The crime rate continued to fall as an entire generation came of age minus the children whose mothers had not wanted to bring a child into the world. Legalized abortion led to less unwantedness; unwantedness leads to high crime; legalized abortion, therefore, led to less crime."

Well, that's one way to neuter a mutt.

Out on the slippery slope, there's only one way to go with the *Freakonomics* argument, and it's not a pretty trip for the boys. Whatever one's predisposition toward males, masculinity, or the Levitt economic theory, we might try to resist getting too comfortable with the idea that life would be *oh, so much* better if only there were fewer baby boys, who inevitably grow up to be men.

16   **Harvey C. Mansfield,** author of *Manliness,* speaking at the Hudson Institute, March 15, 2006.

17   **Wade F. Horn,** "Fatherhood and TV: An Evaluation Report," National Fatherhood Initiative, Gaithersburg, Md., 1999.

20   **Dr. Jim Macnamara,** author of *Media and Male Identity: The Making and Remaking of Men* (New York: Palgrave Macmillan, 2006), quoted in an online interview; University of Western Sydney, November 27, 2006, www.physorg .com/news83863660.html.

20   **Gloria Steinem,** *Revolution from Within: A Book of Self-Esteem* (New York: Little, Brown & Co., 1992).

21   **women reported *instigating* domestic violence**   Todd I. Herrenkohl, Rick

Kosterman, et al., "Youth Violence Trajectories and Proximal Characteristics of Intimate Partner Violence," *Violence and Victims* 22, no. 3 (2007): 259–274(16).

21   **"Abuse Bowl"**   Robert Lipsyte, "Super Bowl XXVII: Violence Translates at Home," *New York Times*, January 31, 1993.

22   **"flooded with more calls from victims"**   Lynda Gorov, "Activists: Abused Women at Risk on Super Sunday," *Boston Globe*, January 29, 1993.

22   **Ken Ringle**   "Debunking the 'Day of Dread' for Women: Data Lacking for Claim of Domestic Violence Surge After Super Bowl," *Washington Post*, January 31, 1993.

23   **"I complied straight away and moved"**   Mark Worsley, quoted by Patrick Goodenough, CNSNEWS.com international editor, "Airline Seating Policy 'Demonizes' Men," CNSNEWS.com, November 29, 2005.

23   **women abuse and kill children**   Child Maltreatment 1999, Children's Bureau, Administration for Children, Youth and Families; Administration for Children and Families; U.S. Department of Health and Human Services; see www.csulb.edu/~mfiebertassault.htm.

25   **domestic violence literature**   For a bibliography of research on domestic violence, go to www.csulb.edu/~mfiebertassault.htm, which examines 209 scholarly investigations, 161 empirical studies, and 48 reviews and/or analyses indicating that women are as physically aggressive as men. The aggregate sample size in the reviewed studies exceeds seventy-seven thousand.

25   **domestic violence restraining orders**   Jeffery Leving and Glenn Sacks, "The Law Against Men," *Albuquerque Tribune*, January 17, 2006.

29   **"sexual intercourse in marriage"**   Andrea Dworkin interview with Michael Moorcock, "Fighting Talk," *New Statesman & Society*, April 21, 1995. See www.nostatusquo.com/ACLU/dworkin/MoorcockInterview.html.

30   **"distinction between intercourse (normal) and rape (abnormal)**   Catharine A. MacKinnon, quoted by Christina Hoff Sommers, "Hard-Line Feminists Guilty of Ms.-Representation," *Wall Street Journal*, November 7, 1991.

30   **"rape exists any time sexual intercourse occurs"**   Robin Morgan, "Theory and Practice: Pornography and Rape," *Going Too Far: The Personal Chronicle of a Feminist* (New York: Random House, 1977).

30   **one in four college women is raped**   Only 25 percent of the women counted by researchers as having been raped considered themselves to be rape victims. Survey data revealed that four in ten of the "rape victims" and one in three of the "attempted rape victims" voluntarily had sex with their partners, other-

wise known as "attackers." In her book *Who Stole Feminism?* Christina Hoff Sommers posed a question the researchers didn't ask: "Since most women the survey counted as victims didn't think they had been raped, and since so many went back to their partners, isn't it reasonable to conclude that many had not been raped to begin with?"

Once the data were adjusted for bias— and the women who didn't consider themselves raped were removed—the numbers changed significantly. Not one in four, but between 3 and 5 percent of the women surveyed had been raped. This isn't a number to celebrate, but it's significantly less than 25 percent.

CHAPTER TWO: HONK IF YOU LOVE DADDY

37 **America leads the Western world** David Popenoe, The National Marriage Project report, *The State of Our Unions: The Social Health of Marriage in America, 2007*. Essay: "The Future of Marriage in America." See marriage .rutgers.edu/Publications/soou/soou2007.pdf.

37 **The National Fatherhood Initiative,** www.fatherhood.org.

38 **staggering array of statistics** Father Facts Fifth Edition, National Fatherhood Initiative, 2007.

38 **National Marriage Project** Barbara Dafoe Whitehead and David Popenoe, "Who Wants to Marry a Soul Mate?" *The State of Our Unions: The Social Health of Marriage in America,* National Marriage Project, 2001, marriage .rutgers.edu/Publications/SOOU/TEXTSOOU2001.htm.

40 **Stephen Baskerville,** *Taken into Custody: The War Against Fathers, Marriage, and the Family* (Nashville: Cumberland House Publishing, 2007).

44 **girls without a biological father** Bruce J. Ellis, Steven McFadyen-Ketchum, et al., "Personality Processes and Individual Differences—Quality of Early Family Relationships and Individual Differences in the Timing of Pubertal Maturation in Girls: A Longitudinal Test of an Evolutionary Model," *Journal of Personality and Social Psychology* 77, no. 2 (1999): 387.

45 **60 percent of rapists** Nicholas Davidson, "Life Without Father," *Policy Review* (Winter 1990).

49 **those dastardly deadbeats** Child Support Enforcement FY 2002 Preliminary Data Report, figures 1 and 2. Available at www.acf.hhs.gov/programs/ cse/pubs/2003/reports/prelim_datareport.

50 **child support debt** Leslie Kaufman, "When Child Support Is Due, Even the Poor Find Little Mercy," *New York Times,* February 19, 2005.

51 **"Americans accused of nothing"** Robert O'Harrow Jr., "Uncle Sam Has All Your Numbers," *Washington Post,* June 27, 1999.

53 **Baskerville,** *Taken into Custody.*

56 **Ross Parke and Armin Brott,** *Throwaway Dads: The Myths and Barriers That Keep Men from Being the Fathers They Want to Be* (Boston: Houghton Mifflin Company, 1999).

57 Testimony posted on Priests for Life website: www.priestsforlife.org/post abortion/.

58 **the effects of abortion on men** Don Kruse, interviewer, *M.E.N.* magazine, January 1993.

58 **Arthur Shostak** and Gary McLouth with Lynn Seng, *Men and Abortion: Lessons, Losses and Love* (New York: Praeger Publishers, 1984).

66 **where fatherlessness leads** Popenoe, *The State of Our Unions.*

67 **black families headed by two parents** Jelani Mandara and Carolyn B. Murray, "Effects of Parental Marital Status, Income and Family Functioning on African American Adolescent Self-Esteem," *Journal of Family Psychology* 14 (2000).

67 **they would like to get married** Scott J. South, "Racial and Ethnic Differences in the Desire to Marry," *Journal of Marriage and the Family* 55, no. 2 (1993).

67 **Maryann Reid,** *Marry Your Baby Daddy* (New York: St. Martin's Press, 2005).

67 **When men were treated respectfully** Maryann Reid, "First Comes Baby, Then Comes Marriage?" *Christian Science Monitor,* April 24, 2006.

68 **"paternal waywardness"** David Blankenhorn, *Fatherless America: Confronting Our Most Urgent Social Problem* (New York: BasicBooks, 1995).

69 **Anyone can be a father** Louise B. Silverstein, and Carl F. Auerbach, PhD, "Deconstructing the Essential Father," *American Psychologist* 54, no. 6 (June 1999).

CHAPTER THREE: FAUX PA AND THE YADDA-YADDA SISTERHOOD

72 **Bergen became a cover girl** Barbara Dafoe Whitehead, "Dan Quayle Was Right," *The Atlantic Monthly,* April 1993.

73 **Midge Decter,** speaking at the Heritage Foundation, April 8, 1993.

74 **tracts of self-justification** Mel Krantzler, *Creative Divorce: A New Opportunity for Personal Growth* (New York: M. Evans & Co., 1973).

74 **happier after divorce** Whitehead, "Dan Quayle Was Right."

75   **children born to married couples** William Feigelman, "Adopted Adults:
      Comparisons with Persons Raised in Conventional Families," *Marriage and
      Family Review,* 25, 1997.

76   **babies born to unmarried mothers**   Jennifer Egan, "Wanted: A Few Good
      Sperm," *New York Times,* March 19, 2006.

76   **Jane Mattes,** *Single Mothers by Choice: A Guidebook for Single Women Who Are
      Considering or Have Chosen Motherhood* (New York: Times Books, 1994).

78   **In women over forty**   Southern California Center for Reproductive Medi-
      cine, http://www.socalfertility.com/age-and-fertility.html.

79   **" 'Don't get too educated' "**   Nancy Gibbs, "Making Time for a Baby,"
      Time, April 15, 2002.

80   **Theodore Dalrymple,** *In Praise of Prejudice* (New York: Encounter Books,
      2007).

80   **"paternal anxieties"**   Robin Silbergleid, " 'Oh Baby!': Representations of
      Single Mothers in American Popular Culture," *Americana: The Journal of
      American Popular Culture* 1, no. 2 (Fall 2002).

80   **Philip Greenspun**   Philip.Greenspun.com.

81   **pregnant surrogates live in group housing**   Sam Dolnick, "In India,
      'Wombs for Rent': Outsourcing Pregnancies Raises Complex Questions,"
      Associated Press, *State* (Columbia, S.C.) January 5, 2008.

82   **Rosanna Hertz**   *Single by Chance, Mothers by Choice: How Women Are
      Choosing Parenthood Without Marriage and Creating the New American Family*
      (New York: Oxford University Press, 2006).

85   **Jennifer Egan,** "Wanted: A Few Good Sperm."

88   **Dear Abby**   Quoted by Elizabeth Marquardt, *The Revolution in Parenthood:
      The Emerging Global Clash Between Adult Rights and Children's Needs,* Insti-
      tute for American Values, Institute for Marriage and Public Policy, An Inter-
      national Appeal from the Commission on Parenthood's Future, 2006.

CHAPTER FOUR: GELDING THE AMERICAN MALE

98   **"trophy husband"**   Betsy Morris, "The New Trophy Husband," *Fortune,*
      October 14, 2002.

102   **"traditional sex-role ideology"**   Steven E. Rhoads and Christopher Rhoads,
      "Gender Roles and Infant/Toddler Care: The Special Case of Tenure Track
      Faculty," August 12, 2004.

103   **E. O. Wilson,** *In Search of Nature* (Washington, D.C.: Island Press, 1996).

104 *He's choosy, too!* William J. McGee, "Mothers, Mothers Everywhere— and Nary a Plug for Dad," *Washington Post,* May 8, 2005.

105 FRENCH MEN YEARN FOR PREGNANCY "Papa's Got the Baby Blues: French Men Yearn for Pregnancy," *AFP,* June 2005, findarticles.com/p/articles/mi _kmafp/is_200506/ai_.

109 Harvey Mansfield, *Manliness.*

111 "undisputed manliness of the Bush White House" Ruth Marcus, "Man Overboard," *Washington Post,* March 21, 2006.

112 Robin Givhan, "Primping for President: A Little Dab'll Do Ya," *The Washington Post,* April 20, 2007.

112 "Do I dare to eat a peach?" Maureen Dowd, "J.F.K., Marilyn, 'Camelot,' " *New York Times,* March 7, 2004. (Note: Kerry's quote is not as Eliot wrote his poem, which reads, "I shall wear the bottoms of my trousers rolled.")

CHAPTER FIVE: THE VAGINA DIATRIBES AND THE SACRED CLITORATI

115 Eve Ensler, *The Vagina Monologues* (New York: Villard Books, 1998).

116 *Our Bodies, Ourselves: A Book by and for Women,* Boston Women's Health Book Collective (New York: Simon & Schuster, 1973).

118 The vulva workshop Betty Dodson, PhD, "Vagina Dialogues & V-Day," www.bettydodson.com/vaginano.htm.

118 Betty Dodson, *Sex for One: The Joy of Selfloving* (New York: Three Rivers Press, 1996).

120 Robert Swope, "Georgetown Women's Center: Indispensable Asset or Improper Expenditure," *The Hoya,* October 19, 1999.

121 William Peter Blatty Wendy McElroy, "Feminists Who Celebrate Rape," Lewrockwell.com, April 2, 2000.

124 "the phallus-breakers of Harvard Yard" Jonathan H. Esensten, "The Broken Phallus of Harvard Yard," *Harvard Crimson,* February 19, 2003.

125 they found it offensive Amy E. Keel, "Destruction of Ice 'Sculpture' Warranted," Letters to the Editors, *Harvard Crimson,* February 21, 2003.

127 Dan Brown, *The Da Vinci Code* (New York: Doubleday, 2003).

128 an effeminate, "biblical-era metrosexual" John J. Miller, "Code Breakers, 'The Da Vinci Code' and Its Discontents," *Wall Street Journal,* April 23, 2004.

CHAPTER SIX: CELEBRITY SLUTS AND AMERICA'S HO-DOWN

132   **thong underwear**   Kriston Tillotson, "From Women's Lib to 'Girls Gone Wild,'" *Minneapolis Star Tribune,* December 18, 2005.

134   **"Permissiveness happened"**   Justine De Lacy, "Germaine Greer's New Book Stirs a Debate," *New York Times,* March 5, 1984.

135   **" 'have to be a slutty nurse' "**   Katherine Hill, "Figuring Out How to Be Slutty for Halloween," *Yale Herald,* October 31, 2003.

135   **Leora Tanenbaum,** *Slut!: Growing Up Female with a Bad Reputation* (New York: Seven Stories Press, 1999).

135   **Emily White,** *Fast Girls: Teenage Tribes and the Myth of the Slut* (New York: Scribner's, 2002).

135   **Jennifer Baumgardner and Amy Richards,** *Manifesta: Young Women, Feminism, and the Future* (New York: Farrar, Straus & Giroux, 2000).

137   A LIFE AS A LIVE! NUDE! GIRL!   Sarah Kershaw, "A Life as a Live! Nude! Girl! Has a Few Strings Attached," *New York Times,* June 2, 2004.

139   **free porn industry**   Claire Hoffman, "Obscene Losses," *Portfolio,* November 2007.

140   **porn is good for women**   Wendy McElroy, *XXX: A Woman's Right to Pornography* (New York: St. Martin's Press, 1995).

141   **films rented by hotel guests**   Richard Corliss, "That Old Feeling: When Porno Was Chic," *Time,* March 29, 2005.

141   **sex really does sell**   TechCrunch, a website that profiles and reviews new Internet products and companies: www.techcrunch.com/2007/05/12/internet-pornography-stats. See also Jerry Ropelato, "Internet Pornography Statistics," *TopTenReviews,* www.internet-filter-review.toptenreviews.com/internet-pornography-statistics.html.

142   **faking their ages**   Amanda Lenhart, Lee Rainie, and Oliver Lewis, "Teenage Life Online: The Rise of the Instant-Message Generation and the Internet's Impact on Friendships and Family Relationships," *Pew Internet & American Life Project,* June 20, 2001.

142   **Christopher Lasch,** *The Culture of Narcissism: American Life in an Age of Diminishing Expectations* (New York: W. W. Norton & Co., 1979).

142   **Joseph Heller,** *Something Happened* (New York: Simon & Schuster, 1974).

143   **sexual dysfunction and performance problems**   Steven Reinberg, *HealthDay News,* April 29, 2006, MentalHelp.net. Researchers from Children's Memorial

Hospital and Northwestern University's Feinberg School of Medicine, both in Chicago, studied 234 sexually active men ages eighteen to twenty-five.

143 **ED complaints** Laura Sessions Stepp, "Cupid's Broken Arrow: Performance Anxiety and Substance Abuse Figure into the Increase in Reports of Impotence on Campus," *Washington Post,* May 7, 2006.

144 **Mary Anne Layden,** PhD, "If Pornography Made Us Healthy, We Would Be Healthy by Now," Statement for *Morality in Media,* April 1999.

144 **women as sex-crazy creatures** Pamela Paul, *Pornified: How Pornography Is Transforming Our Lives, Our Relationships, and Our Families* (New York: Henry Holt & Co., 2005).

146 **Theodore Dalrymple,** "All Sex, All the Time," *City Journal,* Summer, 2000.

147 **"only man makes love"** Theodore Dalrymple, *Our Culture, What's Left of It* (Chicago: Ivan R. Dee, 2005).

147 **Laura Sessions Stepp,** *Unhooked* (New York: Riverhead Hardcover, 2007).

148 **"I got what I came for"** Laura Sessions Stepp, speaking at the Ethics and Public Policy Center in Washington, D.C., November 13, 2007.

148 **"family life" is "extremely important"** Popenoe, *The State of Our Unions.*

149 **Carol Platt Liebau,** *Prude: How the Sex-Obsessed Culture Damages Girls (and America, Too!)* (New York: Center Street, 2007).

151 **Robert Jensen,** *Getting Off: Pornography and the End of Masculinity* (Cambridge, Mass.: South End Press, 2007).

152 **"The pornographers have won"** Robert Jensen, in a talk delivered to the Sexual Assault Network of Delaware annual conference, Woodside, Delaware, April 5, 2005.

152 **the quintessential question** Robert Jensen, National Feminist Anti-Pornography Conference, Wheelock College, Boston, Massachusetts, March 2007.

154 **Walker Percy,** *Lost in the Cosmos: The Last Self-Help Book* (New York: Farrar, Straus & Giroux, 1983).

155 **not just dirty old men watching** Staci Hupp, "Child Porn Viewed at Colleges," *Des Moines Register,* April 1, 2003.

CHAPTER SEVEN: SEX, LIES, AND BUNKER BLUNDERS

160 **more American women have been killed** Editorial, "The Pinking of the Armed Forces," *New York Times,* March 24, 2003.

160 **"We are embedded with the enemy"** Ann Scott Tyson, "For Female GIs,

Combat Is a Fact: Many Duties in Iraq Put Women at Risk Despite Restrictive Policy," *Washington Post,* May 13, 2005.

162   **"weeding out the white male norm"** Stephanie Gutmann, "Sex and the Soldier," *New Republic,* February 24, 1997.

164   **last stand of machisma** Susan Schmidt and Vernon Loeb, " 'She Was Fighting to the Death,' " *Washington Post,* April 3, 2003.

164   **Richard S. Lowry,** *Marines in the Garden of Eden* (New York: Berkley Caliber, 2006).

164   **Private First Class Patrick Miller** *60 Minutes* interview with Mike Wallace, November 6, 2003.

166   **Rick Bragg,** *I Am a Soldier, Too: The Jessica Lynch Story* (New York: Alfred A. Knopf, 2003).

168   **Mirella, a thirty-three-year-old** Kate Holt, "Bosnia's Rape Babies: Abandoned byTheir Families, Forgotten by the State," *The Independent,* December 13, 2005.

172   **army chief of staff General Peter J. Schoomaker** Donna Miles, "Guard Leaders Urge Solid Funding to Close Equipment," American Forces Press Service, April 11, 2007.

172   **Jill Mills,** "Should 'Men Are Stronger' Bar Women from Combat Roles?" *Male Matters,* January 15, 1998, www.battlinbog.blog-city.com/move_qualified _female_soldiers_into_ground_combat.htm.

173   **Stephanie Gutmann,** *The Kinder, Gentler Military: Can America's Gender-Neutral Fighting Forces Still Win Wars?* (New York: Scribner, 2000).

173   **evacuated for pregnancy** Gutmann, "Sex and the Soldier."

173   **"No comparable 'disability' "** Anna Simons, "Women in Combat Units: It's Still a Bad Idea," *Parameters* 31, no. 2 (2001). Copyright 2001 U.S. Army War College; copyright 2004 Gale Group.

174   **Beyond the problems pregnancy presents** Mackubin T. Owens, "Mothers in Combat Boots," *Human Life Review* 23, no. 1 (Spring 1997).

176   **months without bathing** James Webb, "Women Can't Fight," *Washingtonian,* November 1979.

178   **rice paddies were swarming** Jerry A. Boggs, "The Mainstream Media Don't Report Fairly on the Sexes' Risk and Sacrifice in War," *Transitions, Journal of Men's Perspectives* 26, no. 4 (July–August 2006).

180   **"fulfilling a promise to Molly"** Robert Stansfield and Chris Hughes, "Hostages: Our Story," *Daily Mirror,* September 4, 2007.

180 **"handed the Iranians enormous leverage"** Major Judith Webb, "Why Women Should Not Be on the Front Line," *Daily Mail,* April 7, 2007.

182 **"incapable of coherent thought"** "Military View on the Captives and Frontline Mums," *Daily Mail,* April 6, 2007.

182 **"ignore the screams of a woman"** R. Cort Kirkwood, "What Kind of Nation Sends Women into Combat?" Lewrockwell.com, April 11, 2003.

183 **Kate O'Beirne,** *Women Who Make the World Worse: And How Their Radical Feminist Assault Is Ruining Our Schools, Families, Military, and Sports* (New York: Sentinel HC, 2005).

184 **"Deliberate exposure of women"** Elaine Donnelly, "Grim Toll of Military Women Killed in War," Center for Military Readiness, May 22, 2007, updated January 4, 2008.

184 **Kayla Williams,** with Michael E. Staub, *Love My Rifle More than You: Young and Female in the U.S. Army* (New York: W. W. Norton & Co., 2005).

188 **"resentment among male soldiers"** Charles Moskos, "Army Women," *Atlantic Monthly,* August 1990.

189 **"To assent to obvious lies"** Theodore Dalrymple interview with Jamie Glazov, *FrontPage,* August 31, 2005.

CONCLUSION

193 **"A curtain drops"** Walker Percy, *Signposts in a Strange Land* (New York: Farrar, Straus & Giroux, 1991).

195 **family is . . . an anarchist institution** G. K. Chesterton, *Collected Works, Volume IV: Family, Society, Politics* (San Francisco: Ignatius Press, 1987).

196 **Karl Marx and Friedrich Engels** Excerpt from *Manifesto of the Communist Party* (1848):

> Abolition of the family! Even the most radical flare up at this infamous proposal of the Communists.
>
> On what foundation is the present family, the bourgeois family, based? On capital, on private gain. In its completely developed form this family exists only among the bourgeoisie. But this state of things finds its complement in the practical absence of the family among the proletarians, and in public prostitution.

The bourgeois family will vanish as a matter of course when its complement vanishes, and both will vanish with the vanishing of capital.

Do you charge us with wanting to stop the exploitation of children by their parents? To this crime we plead guilty.

But, you say, we destroy the most hallowed of relations, when we replace home education by social.

And your education! Is not that also social, and determined by the social conditions under which you educate, by the intervention of society, direct or indirect, by means of schools, etc.? The Communists have not intended the intervention of society in education; they do but seek to alter the character of that intervention, and to rescue education from the influence of the ruling class.

The bourgeois claptrap about the family and education, about the hallowed correlation of parent and child, becomes all the more disgusting, the more, by the action of modern industry, all the family ties among the proletarians are torn asunder, and their children transformed into simple articles of commerce and instruments of labor.

But you Communists would introduce community of women, screams the whole bourgeoisie in chorus.

The bourgeois sees in his wife a mere instrument of production. He hears that the instruments of production are to be exploited in common, and, naturally, can come to no other conclusion than that the lot of being common to all will likewise fall to the women.

He has not even a suspicion that the real point aimed at is to do away with the status of women as mere instruments of production.

For the rest, nothing is more ridiculous than the virtuous indignation of our bourgeois at the community of women which, they pretend, is to be openly and officially established by the Communists. The Communists have no need to introduce community of women; it has existed almost from time immemorial.

Our bourgeois, not content with having the wives and

daughters of their proletarians at their disposal, not to speak of common prostitutes, take the greatest pleasure in seducing each other's wives.

Bourgeois marriage is in reality a system of wives in common and thus, at the most, what the Communists might possibly be reproached with is that they desire to introduce, in substitution for a hypocritically concealed, an openly legalized community of women. For the rest, it is self-evident, that the abolition of the present system of production must bring with it the abolition of the community of women springing from that system, i.e., of prostitution both public and private.

196 **Dr. Lawrence H. Summers**   "Summers' Remarks on Women Draw Fire," *Boston Globe,* January 17, 2005.

KATHLEEN PARKER is the co-host of CNN's *Parker Spitzer*, a nationally syndicated columnist whose twice-weekly opinion column runs in more than four hundred newspapers around the country. She frequently appears on radio talk shows and is a regular guest on *The Chris Matthews Show*.

ABOUT THE TYPE

This book was set in Granjon, a modern recutting of a typeface produced under the direction of George W. Jones, who based Granjon's design upon the letter forms of Claude Garamond (1480–1561). The name was given to the typeface as a tribute to the typographic designer Robert Granjon.